ROUTLEDGE LIBRARY EDITIONS:
ECONOMICS AND SOCIETY

Volume 35

TECHNOLOGICAL GROWTH AND SOCIAL CHANGE

TECHNOLOGICAL GROWTH AND SOCIAL CHANGE

Achieving Modernization

STANLEY A. HETZLER

Routledge
Taylor & Francis Group
LONDON AND NEW YORK

First published in 1969 by Routledge & Kegan Paul Ltd.

This edition first published in 2026
by Routledge
4 Park Square, Milton Park, Abingdon, Oxon OX14 4RN

and by Routledge
605 Third Avenue, New York, NY 10158

Routledge is an imprint of the Taylor & Francis Group, an informa business

British Library Cataloguing in Publication Data
A catalogue record for this book is available from the British Library

ISBN: 978-1-032-97576-4 (Set)
ISBN: 978-1-041-15628-4 (Volume 35) (hbk)
ISBN: 978-1-041-15633-8 (Volume 35) (pbk)
ISBN: 978-1-003-68044-4 (Volume 35) (ebk)

DOI: 10.4324/9781003680444

Publisher's Note
The publisher has gone to great lengths to ensure the quality of this reprint but points out that some imperfections in the original copies may be apparent.

Disclaimer
The publisher has made every effort to trace copyright holders and would welcome correspondence from those they have been unable to trace.

The International Library of Sociology

TECHNOLOGICAL GROWTH AND SOCIAL CHANGE

Founded by KARL MANNHEIM

The International Library of Sociology

THE SOCIOLOGY OF WORK AND ORGANIZATION
In 18 Volumes

TECHNOLOGICAL GROWTH AND SOCIAL CHANGE

Achieving Modernization

by

STANLEY A. HETZLER

ROUTLEDGE
Taylor & Francis Group

First published in 1969 by
Routledge

Reprinted 1998, 2000, 2002
by Routledge
2 Park Square, Milton Park, Abingdon, Oxon, OX14 4RN

Transferred to Digital Printing 2007

Routledge is an imprint of the Taylor & Francis Group

British Library Cataloguing in Publication Data
A CIP catalogue record for this book
is available from the British Library

Technological Growth and Social Change
ISBN 0-415-17692-1
The Sociology of Work and Organization: 18 Volumes
ISBN 0-415-17829-0
The International Library of Sociology: 274 Volumes
ISBN 0-415-17838-X

Publisher's Note

The publisher has gone to great lengths to ensure the quality of this reprint but points out that some imperfections in the original may be apparent

PREFACE

The philosophical foundations of this book began to take form while the author was a member of the faculty of the American University of Beirut. The actual development of the text began in Costa Rica, where he held joint tenure at the Tropical Science Center and the University of Costa Rica, and it was completed at Colorado State University. As may be inferred from its title and general content, it was written for a wide reading audience – for social scientists and engineers, for academicians and laity, for the member of transitional society who has an interest in identifying the factors stimulating technology, and the member of the technologically advanced society who is concerned with controlling these factors. In short, it was written for anyone having an interest in the areas of technological development and social change.

The writer would like to express his appreciation to the many persons who directly or indirectly contributed to the manuscript. He would like to express his gratitude to the entire staff of the Tropical Science Center, to the steadfast administrative support of the Center's director, Dr. Robert J. Hunter, to Dr. Leslie R. Holdridge, and to Professors Charles G. Curtis and George R. Gebhart, of Beloit and Monmouth Colleges respectively, and to Señores Mario Blanco and Fernando Umaña. The painstaking effort and never failing good cheer of the three typists who helped in the early stages of preparing the manuscript were an important part of the endeavor, and in this connection my thanks go to Miss Dorothy Lankester, Señora Irma H. Prestinary de Dorsam and Senorita María Cecilia Rodríguez. I am particularly grateful for the loyal aid later received from Miss Karen Prosser.

The writer would like to thank all his colleagues at the Colorado State University for their aid. Those reading and criticising the manuscript were Drs. Manuel Alters-Montalvo, Samuel Schulman, Glen Dildine, and Professor Donald Crim. Special acknowledgement is made of the many ideas arising out of interchange between the author and Dr. Joseph A. Tosi, Jr., of the Tropical Science Center, and Dr. T. R. Young of Colorado State University. And finally, but most importantly, I am humbly indebted to my wife, Esther, whose many kindnesses and patient understanding made this work a much more pleasant task, and to my sociologist son, Steve Hetzler, for his excellent editorial help and criticism during the preparation of the final manuscript, and to Professor Roger Williams for his invaluable aid in assisting in getting the manuscript published.

Yellow Springs, Ohio
April 1, 1967

STANLEY A. HETZLER

CONTENTS

PART TWO

OLD CONCEPTS

PART THREE

NEW PERSPECTIVES

Part One

PROCESS AND SYMPTOM

I

INTRODUCTION

The many books recently written on the subject of development bear testimony to its importance. The greater number of these treatises, however, although they pass muster as 'scholarly works,' repeat upon minutiae, elaborate upon old and threadbare themes and, to the extent that their ideas have been testable, have not proven capable of setting the mechanisms of development in motion in the underdeveloped society. The failure of traditional concepts to explain a rapidly changing social world calls for a redirection of effort, for the opening of new avenues of inquiry. This book represents such an attempt.

Conventional views on development are held with tenacity and new ones are admitted only when they align with the existing thought-scheme. The Western concept of development is almost beyond dialogue. It has become a crystalline, unbendingly sacrosanct view of the world, which has given rise to its own rationalizing 'sciences' to whose dicta all new ideas must conform. To challenge the Western approach to development, which rests unalterably upon classical economics, is to call into question the entire economic order which is commonly presumed to have grown out of that philosophy.

U.S. academicians who specialize in development make their livelihoods – through teaching, writing and consulting – in propagating the existing order. Theirs is a relatively closed universe of discourse in which they communicate mainly with one another and in a dialect of steadily diminishing interest to the outside world of developing nations. Indeed, if the academician-developer is to prosper professionally he has no choice but to stay sensitive to the views and wishes of government aid-granting agencies and the private foundations upon which he depends for employment and research funds. The publishing houses, along with the reviewers and others who live by their largesse, form the final shielding integument against penetration of the new. Taken altogether, the domains of U.S. academia, government and publication comprise one of the world's largest and most monolithic authorities on matters of development, and ironically, as they proffer their advisory services abroad, the home society, showing alarming developmental imbalances by race, ethnic group, social class, and by geographic region, slips into an ever-deepening slough of despondency. Nowhere is the impotence of current U.S. development theory more vividly illustrated than that society's own bailiwick. While the historical growth of U.S. production facilities has been striking, the uncertainty of our knowledge of the factors accounting for this growth has been equally obvious. The society is in the predicament of not understanding its most distinguishing feature, technological movement, and failing to understand it is unable to describe it, predict its course, control it, or to distribute its benefits more evenly. For this reason, of the many tracts that have been written on the subject of development, few are likely to survive the establishment through which they have been borne and nurtured.

The U.S. establishment is undergoing rapid transformation, for change it must. The type and degree of change that it will experience will be, ultimately, more radical than that envisioned by communism and, certainly, more momentous. The technology, the crucible within which most of this change is being created, is a set of social relationships between man and machine; but it is a relationship in which, as the technology evolves, man plays a role of dwindling importance and the machine increasingly establishes the ground rules. It is the exploration of this relationship that constitutes the main area of interest in this writing.

The basic approach used in this writing is termed 'socio-technics' a study of the total range of relationships between man and machine. Whatever the seeming mode of interaction between the two, whether it appears on the surface to be physical or social, it is substantively social and in its consequences it is unequivocally social. And con-contained within this interaction are sets of dynamics governing technological growth and creating predictable types of social change. Study of this interplay can provide a base for the formulation of a body of principle which is applicable to technology in general, as it functions in the emerging society and as it operates in the materially advancing nations of the West.

Man is, throughout his being, a social animal. He cannot interact on a purely physical plane with either other human beings or the material facets of his environment. He lives in a world of objects which he animates and with which he behaviorally interfuses in ways and to an extent beyond his awareness; and because of this imputive tendency in man, his world reflexively reacts upon him. This approach abandons the old theocratically inspired notion of man as a controller who structures the environment to suit his own tastes and places him in a broader, more inclusive setting in which he is both innovator and interdependently reciprocating part.

Historically, there have been abrupt and significant changes in the man-machine relationship which have changed radically the dimensions of the society within which the technology operates. New types of controls, increased power and speeds have culminated in vast technological movements which have been essentially social movements, movements in which there has been a redistribution of human populations, a continuing redefinition of concepts of time, quantity, work, living standards, etc. And lying behind these movements have been more general ones in which the machines of production slowly retreat to an 'automation-induced' seclusion while other, and new types of machines, well up increasingly to pervade and enliven the social domain.

In conclusion, it should be pointed out that this is not a meticulously documented work, nor was it intended to be. The author seems to 'jump overboard' in some of the assumptions made, and what begin as tentative hypotheses sometimes seem to move on, in subsequent pages, to an arrogation of certainty. These faults are recognized and freely admitted. This book is meant to be, above all, provocative of new thought. It does not claim to final answers but, instead, aims at the stimulation of theoretical inquiry on a front much broader than that of today and, perhaps at best, it may provide some insight as to how new hypotheses may be arrived at through a multidisciplinary approach. Indeed, many of the crude hypotheses presented within this writing will be answered, if they are worth further investigation, only after protracted study. Our present state of knowledge in development is too rudimentary to allow us pretense to sophistication, and the field too important to indulge complacency. Thus the book is, in many passages, free-soaring and deliberately lacerating. And while it appears to 'play fast and loose' in substituting new for old terms – e.g. 'technological advancement' for 'economic development' – this, too, is done with reason. If one questions the basic validity of many of today's development concepts, it would seem rather contradictory to employ them in the text.

The next two chapters are devoted to a review of the social problems found in the transitional and the technologically advanced types of society. Chapters 4 and 5 present a critical evaluation of current development hypotheses; and the remainder of the book deals with the exploration of new hypotheses and ways in which they might be applied to produce technological advancement.

2

THE DILEMMA OF THE TECHNO-LOGICALLY ADVANCED SOCIETY

A theory for technological development must encompass the development problem over its total range, as it exists in two distinctly different settings – in the technologically advanced, and in the transitional society. A discussion of one without attention to the processes ongoing in the other will not lead to an understanding of either because, although their problems differ greatly in type, they are intimately interactive. Decisions that are made in the transitional society, such as which of the advanced societies to look to for leadership and for finance in development, excite economic and political rivalry among the advanced nations. Problems in the advanced society, such as finding means for insuring a steady inflow of raw materials at the least cost, transmit themselves to the backward societies in the form of inflexible governments, imbalanced economies, and depressed labor markets.

First, it should be noted that the term 'development' is a relative one. All except the most primitive of societies are in some state of technological development. Secondly, the concept of development goes beyond the attainment of mere physical comfort. There are some societies which enjoy an abundance of the necessities of life but they are, nonetheless, ranked low on the scale of development. This scale is a product of the Western value system, which prizes not just the 'abundant life,' but the possession of a diversity of durable, negotiable goods which are classified in Western society as 'wealth.' Ironically, it is within the societies which are already most advanced that planning facilities are most in evidence and that the rates of both, planning and production, are highest. Development movement within these societies is surging forward much more rapidly than it is within the emerging nations with which the concept of 'development' is usually associated. This is simply because technological development began with these nations, and since its beginning it has been given heavy emphasis by this bloc. But it is a type of progress that has not come without its costs.

The Dilemma of the Technologically Advanced Society

THE RANGE OF THE PROBLEM

The dilemma of the materially advanced society is the dilemma of the society undergoing rapid and accelerating growth in technology. It is the paradox of a society advancing at such a rate as to leave the domestic scene in confusion, in a conflicting situation where newer and more expedient ways of behaving clash with old habits and beliefs. Most of the present day social problems in the materially advanced nations trace, in one way or another, to the effects of technology.

Uneven Internal Development

From almost any point that one chooses to view it, technological development is proceeding unevenly and spottily. Not only is there great variation between nations, but within nations, rich and poor alike, there are striking regional variations in progress and prosperity; and at a still more fundamental level, throughout most societies there are sharp differences between social class and socio-occupational groups. Most of the richer, free enterprise nations still have a sizable minority of their people barred from full participation in the rewards of the system. This group, the poor, are having increasing difficulty in finding employment. They are so effectively segregated from the other urban social classes that they seldom have contact with them except through highly formalized channels. Social class differences are clearly related to socio-occupational differences. Even in a country as prosperous as the United States, agricultural wage earners can be generally classified as an impoverished group, and in terms of standard of living may be ranked alongside the struggling masses of the more backward societies. Hence, in none of the free enterprise societies does technology produce a monolithic prosperity. Even the richest nations usually have their 'blighted' areas and must contend with internal development problems.

Individual Isolation

The problems arising out of technological change are both psychological and social. Technology impinges upon the individual in his relationships to his work and to other persons, and it disturbs all his social institutions, keeping them in a continuous state of ferment. The psychological perturbations created by technological growth are many and, except for convenience in discussion, it is difficult to separate them from the more general social problems growing out of conflict within, and between institutions. Everyone is aware of the gradual psychological disengagement of the individual from the work arena. Mass production methods are based upon the minute segmentation of tasks and upon a corresponding specialization of human functions. The worker, under this condition, takes on no more significance than the mechanism which could be built to replace him. He is said to be robbed of the satisfactions of whole authorship, of creative pride. Whether he is a white collar worker drafting a management program, or a blue collar worker operating a machine, it is highly unlikely in any large organization that he will guide the entire process on which he works from its inception to its end. The management program will pass on to other hands, it will encounter bureaucratic delay, it will sometimes undergo radial modification, it will require a final endorsement from top management, and before endorsement it will probably be given one last revision by some person in the upper echelon of authority. The machine operator, as the director of a rather delimited machine process will never enjoy the satisfaction in overall craftsmanship said to be enjoyed by the earlier artisans. The blue collar worker is forced to work at an uneven pace, he is hired or discharged at the convenience of his employer, and he comes to regard himself as a small piece in a very complex machine whose rationale is beyond his understanding or control.

To the degree that the foregoing contentions are valid, the conditions they depict are, perhaps, an inescapable aspect of the industrial age. However, such effects as there may be upon the individual worker cannot be made grounds for the condemnation of the whole system. It might be rejoined that the productivity of this system releases man for the personal enjoyment of time away from the job, which he otherwise could not have. Further, and somewhat overlooked, are the facts that the medieval artisan worked under the most fatiguing of conditions and the strictest type of regimentation, as did practically all classes of workers of that day. Labor was carried out by the majority of peoples under conditions ranging from near serfdom to outright slavery. Indeed, the working conditions of the medieval period bear a similarity to those existing within the retarded societies of today. The human chain-line passing rubble from hand-to-hand in the construction of a dam, or a gang of farm laborers breaking clods with wooden mallets may be free of some of the symptomologies of industrialization, but they are hardly paragons of human freedom. The fact of the matter is that the majority of the world's workers are preoccupied with the single proposition of securing enough food each day so that they and their families may survive from one sunrise to the next. Such niceties as an adjudgment of the psychological effects of industrialization upon the worker must await a much later state of development, one where the culture can afford to support social scientists and others who concern themselves with problems of this ilk. Harsh as the problem of individual adaptation to industrial society may be there are few cultures whose value system would not prefer it to starvation. Finally, this whole problem area of psychological deprivation may be a passing phase wherein the individual is finally completely emancipated from production drudgery by a complete, or near complete automation.

Another often noted psychological problem of the technologically advanced society is the dehumanization of all classes of people under the steady pressure of competition. Competition for a position, competition for promotion, competition for commercial profits and even the competition between husband and wife for the affection of offspring attest to the importance imputed to the acquisition of material goods. Competition has dressed the stage for inter-individual suspicion and hostility. In the commercial garb of sales promotion and in its typical gambits at public suasion, its unswerving crassitude has engendered a wholesale reaction of public distrust. However, it might be answered that although economic rivalry may hone competition to an unusually keen edge, there is no known method by which a group may structure itself so as to avoid competition altogether. In all groups there is interaction between individuals, and within interaction there is always some element of competition as well as cooperation. The problem is one of keeping the intensity of competition within tolerable bounds through providing other types of motivation, incentives which operate on planes other than raw competitive behavior.

Employment

The foregoing might be classified as individual, or particularized problems. If one were to take the broader social problems, and treat them in order of their magnitude, standing at the forefront would be the massive confusion growing out of an inability within much of Western society to devise means for the distribution of its great, and growing production. In the United States, where the general technology is most advanced, society, without being fully conscious of what it was about, inadvertently struck upon two makeshift, temporary, and somewhat dangerous methods for distributing the annually increasing surpluses growing out of its annually spiralling technology. The lower classes, who are the first to be disemployed by technological encroachment, are being temporarily accommodated by an enlargement of public relief facilities. The upper blue collar class, and especially the occupational elite, are being maintained by progressive expansions of defense industry and military establishment.

With each economic recession occurring since World War II, there has been an added inflation of the public relief roles. At the outset of these economic dips workers typically are released from their jobs, whereupon, new types of automata which were developed during the preceding period of prosperity are moved into the production line. The result has been that at the termination of each recession period fewer workers are rehired, and those that are not rehired are left stranded on public relief. The public tendencies to view the disemployed as charity cases and to attempt to solve the problem by steadily expanding public welfare facilities (a movement which, ironically, is accompanied by steady growth in production volume and commercial profits) is a holdover of the traditional folkway of giving temporary aid to the 'deserving poor.' It is obviously a short-term solution applied to a long-term problem. Automation and the irreversibility of the conditions which feed it presage much worsened conditions to come.

Public relief's psychological costs are high; it is a socially and morally objectionable method for providing subsistence. It produces feelings of lack of individual worth and it grants too little advisory and material aid to make full family rehabilitation possible. It is accompanied by a high rate of school drop out, adult crime, juvenile delinquency, and a general discontentment with social conditions.

The conventional solutions to public welfare urged upon the public ring of either rank cynicism or evasion. Some politicians simply exhort that the encumbents of public relief be forced to go out and find jobs, knowing full well that jobs are not available. At a less cynical level are the promises to create employment opportunity. This is a formidable task and one which, if successful, would be deleterious to machine-sustained types of production. There seems to be general oblivion to the fact that raw employment is not, in itself, an ultimate social end.

Still other objectors to public relief urge that the publicly supported be forced to engage in some type of public work program through which they are made to exchange their labors for publicly contributed cash or commodities. This latter recommendation, if put to trial on a fairly broad scale, and with sincerity, would defeat the very ends which these advocates of free enterprise are championing.

It would lead to the socialistic condition of having local governments serve as the wholesale employers of large numbers of people who would then be in direct competition with free enterprise. It would also extend the federal and state bureaus to encompass these lower socio-economic groups as public employees, although probably under conspicuously discriminatory terms of employment.

Meantime, the marginal aid being given to relief families is nowise sufficient to provide the education and facilities necessary to move the family toward genuine rehabilitation. Instead, public dependency and the conditions and attitudes nurturing it are socially transmitted from one generation to the next.

At the opposite extreme are the elite occupational groups, the engineers and related professionals for whose services, just as in the case of the lower occupational classes, there is an annual decrease in demand. While the lower work classes through historical inadvertency fell upon relief, the elite groups have been buoyed along by the fortuity of a Second World War and the relatively uninterrupted growth of the defense establishment since the time of that conflict. While people on public relief are considered unemployed, those working in the Defense system are, for the most part, pseudo-employed. The two groups share a common malady-moral conflict.

The publicly-supported chafe for an opportunity to escape relief and to express themselves through worthwhile employment. The Defense-supported alternate between 'busy work,' that is, types of work done solely for the sake of activity, and enforced idleness. The defense organization ramifies through a complex structure in which successive echelons of authority must successively endorse every proposal of any magnitude. This forces the greater segment of the work force to engage in the game of 'hurry up and wait.' The objectives of a proposal or program are often lost before its design is completed; or an unexpected organizational change creates entirely new goals. Items of materiel, painstakingly designed, are often obsolete before they emerge from the production line, and in almost all cases, until they are so old as to warrant sale as surplus these goods are nonutilitarian in nature; they benefit no one. The individual in this particular work situation is entrapped in a moral dilemma which has been described under the covering term, 'Protestant Ethic.'

The Protestant Ethic, a concept said to have grown out of the Mid-European revolt against church authority during the sixteenth century, became the psychological working implement of the newly emergent commercial class. It equated individual industry and thrift with virtue and happiness. Poverty was taken as evidence of individual shortcoming if not of downright sinful behavior; and it was believed to be damaging to the needy individual's initiative to give him anything more than temporary aid, and this was given only on the assumption that it would help him 'get back on his feet.' The present day worker trying to busy himself within the structure of the bureaucratic organization is plagued by this culturally implanted conscience which dictates that he earn his way by an honest day's work; but he must work within a system in which it is not possible to return a full day's measure for a full day's wage. The Protestant Ethic conceptually depicts the conflict created within the individual living in a society which unremittingly constricts his individual powers to contribute by increasingly efficient methods, by mechanization, and by the diversion of a growing part of the labor market into areas of pseudo-employment. The overly energetic person who enters into the bureaucratic system often proves to be a troublemaker who must learn how to pace his efforts to the tempo of the organization, or withdraw from it.

The Protestant Ethic, it has been pointed out by several observers, is an oversimplification that is prone to overly simplified interpretation. They say that John Calvin is being forced to carry a heavy burden, indeed, if the Protestant Ethic is imputed to the Japanese, the Israelis and the many non-protestant countries showing sociopsychological symptoms similar to those found in the Protestant West.

Growing Military Control

There undoubtedly has been a great amount of technological progress growing out of the efforts of the approximately five million military personnel and civilian employees who are in the direct pay of the defense department. The cost of attaining this progress has likewise been enormous, amounting to recent annual averages of about fifty billion dollars. One can only speculate as to what the returns would have been if this investment had been used, instead, in adding to the facilities of schools, colleges, and other public institutions both in the United States and abroad.

Coupled with this waste have been other symptoms far more threatening to the long range interests of national and international society. One of these has been a steady subjugation of other institutions to military dominance. This has reached a point where military expediency – and one of these expediencies is finding release for the goods and energies pent up within the defense system – now overrides and replaces statecraft. The claim that the defense department is still under the control of a top echelon of civilians is a meaningless one; in intent and action the department is, in every sense of the word, a military establishment. Its civilian head tends to *serve* the department primarily as a petitioner for funds and a justifier of its activities rather than acting as its true master. The department controls directly through informal and formal censorship of the press, and it controls indirectly in a prodigous expenditure of funds which filter down through primary and subsidiary contractors in a vast, interlocking complex which embraces, in one way or another, virtually every industry in the nation.

Just as it tries to preserve the fiction of merited employment, every effort is also made within the defense system to preserve the myth of competitive free enterprise in defense procurement. Under discussion here are those industries which are recognized as prime defense contractors, whose primary output is some type of hardware or service for military use. Ostensibly, each defense industry enters its own bid for military work, and if a contract is subsequently offered by the government it is awarded strictly upon the merits of the work proposed and its cost to the government. In actuality, the letting of defense contracts operates in a much different manner. First, defense contracts are not just *let;* to a great degree they are apportioned. Often, without regard for the terms of contract great political leverage is brought to bear to have the contract awarded on the basis of its potential economic benefits to a given geopolitical area. The aggressive support of this kind of economic gerrymandering is tacitly considered to be a legitimate duty of publicly elected officials. The greatest pressures usually come from political representatives of those areas hardest hit by unemployment, or by those faced by the threat of discontinuance of a contract whose cancellation would economically cripple the area.

Aside from political porkbarreling practices, contracts still are not likely to be awarded by defense department officials solely on the basis of a proposal's deserts. If a defense contractor is already overloaded with work he probably will not enter a bid for further business. If the contractor is known to be overloaded but, nonetheless, does enter a bid, this is taken into account by the contract granting authority. It is unclear situations of this type that give the defense authority great informal latitude in decision-making, allowing the defense department, itself, to prorate military contracts on the basis of a given geographical areas' economic need and available manpower.

Free enterprise is defeated within the defense industry framework at the very inception of a proposal for contract. Contrary to the risk-taking character of free enterprise, a company submitting a defense contract proposal does not usually do so at its own expense. Rather, it will first seek permission from the government to enter a proposal. Usually, from three to a dozen prospective bidders will be granted the privilege of entering this circle. With admission to this group (and for the big company entry is not difficult to obtain) comes a special emolument – the defense department will reimburse each member company for all funds spent in preparation of the proposal, whether it be successful or unsuccessful. If the project under consideration is a large one, the mere preparation of the proposal may run into hundreds of thousands of dollars. Usually, of course, there can be only one final winner. Other would-be contractors may venture 'unsolicited' bids if they wish, but the high cost of proposal preparation and the risk associated with being in the position of an 'outsider' usually discourage this. Proposal-preparation grants are awarded out of a special fund which has been set up for this purpose within the defense department. Thus, even in the process of preparing a preliminary proposal a private company cannot help but benefit, inasmuch as its costs are all reimbursed and a certain profit is added.

There is every evidence that the military establishment, which in itself is a thoroughgoingly socialized system, while commonly supposed to be the handmaiden of free enterprise is, instead, through the many ways in which it controls labor and production, rapidly pushing the whole society into deepening socialism.

The Family

Technological growth has had a disturbing effect upon, and has forced change in virtually every facet of the basic social institutions. The great family structure appears to have vanished from Western society. The care and nurture of the young, and especially responsibility for maintenance of the aged, have been turned over in great degree to formal institutions. The small, nuclear family which is characteristic of Western society recognizes obligations only between the spouses and offspring of the immediate family group. In fact, out of this *modus vivendi* has wormed the attitude that it is healthy for the newly formed family to hold relationships with the parents of both spouses to a minimum. Children spend more and more time outside the family, receiving instruction and value indoctrination from the school, church, specially constituted fraternal organizations such as the YMCA, etc. Courtship, once the family-controlled entryway into marriage has taken to the open road, finding its realization in roadside cinemas and other public places of amusement. This same feature of added mobility through automobile transportation, which has so radically affected the Western pattern of courtship, also affects the family in connection with its choice of a place of residence, and the frequency with which it changes residences. The ability to commute to work over long distances has caused a resurgence of population from the city or industrial center to the suburban area, and has given rise to the whole phenomenon referred to as 'suburbia.' More extensive technological effects are to be found in the tendency of industrial organization to completely uproot the family and to displace it by relatively great distances, and often at regular intervals. For the junior executive group, this displacement is carried out in accordance with organizational career development plans for periodically subjecting the individual to a variety of work experiences in various subsidiaries of the corporation. The consequences of this complete up-rooting, for society and the family, are fairly obvious.

Technology is creating a situation which will provide the ultimate test of family cohesion. In the past many have speculated as to whether the family is a natural, bio-psychologically integrated unit, or whether it is a cultural product that originally came about primarily in response to economic needs. If its underpinnings are entirely social, under the influence of certain types of social change it may dissolve. On the social side, it has proven itself in the past to be a unit in which the roles of male and female interlocked so as to gain undeniable economic advantage for both. But interdependencies between the sexes are weakening, and present trends, if they should continue, point to the possibility that throughout its past history the family system may have rested largely on an economic base. The divorce rate, since the turn of the century, has mounted greatly in most of the technologically oriented societies. Bringing this about more than anything else has been the increased freedom of women to work, because with this employment has come increased status and independence of action. Altogether, the foregoing currents may have the effects of changing the family so radically that the basic form which it has had in the historical past, and which it presently has throughout most of the world, will be lost. It might be predicted that its more pleasurable aspects, such as cohabitation, will persist longest while the features thrust upon it by necessity, for example, child care, will shift in increasing measure to other institutions.

Increased employment opportunity for women has been made possible by technological revolution within the home. For the upper and upper middle classes, appliances have largely replaced the domestic staff. Since they are also within the financial reach of the less affluent but more populous classes, appliances and the marked reduction in household tasks that they bring, have enabled large numbers of women to function as both, housekeeper and outside employee. The household revolution has carried over to food preparation, to the placing of foods on the markets which are partially, or sometimes completely, ready for the table. Increasing emancipation from the home and from one another's company is already having its effects upon the behavior of husband and wife. As more effective contraceptives are found it is predictable that both will take increased sexual license outside marriage, and the home will provide a less-and-less stable base for the family. This is a dilemma which is eyed by some of the emerging societies with great misgiving.

Changed work habits have carried over into the training of the child, and to the child's attitudes and orientation toward work. In past generations, a certain amount of work or 'choring' was held indispensable to the moral upbringing of the young. It is no longer possible to assign chores, for the simple reason that significant ones no longer exist. The increased freedom of time on the part of the child goes either into added school work, organized group activities, or into the pursuit of individual enjoyment.

Uncontrolled Urban Growth

Technology has created a giant set of problems in connection with the spatial redistribution of human populations. The early factory system, in its need for a nearby labor supply gave birth to the great urban area. In the process, it concomitantly gave rise to slums, to residential areas in which there was an unprecedented concentration of wealth, and it possibly brought about for the first time the phenomena of uncontrolled population expansion and recurring famine. There is some evidence that so long as people live under aboriginal conditions, these two, particularly population expansion, are controlled by natural mechanisms.

The informal social controls that function so effectively in tribal society and in the rural type of neighbourhood are greatly weakened in the formal social organization of the city. The easy achievement of anonymity in the vast, faceless, secondary society has created new modes of behavior. Freed from informal censorship the sex-ways have become more liberalized. There has been a great increase in the number and type of individual inter-associations which transcend the neighborhood and recruit membership on a basis of common interest, and from relatively distant points. Urbanization has brought about new and intensified forms of juvenile delinquency and adult criminality. The urban area has mothered a distinctive type of malfeasance referred to as 'white collar' crime which bleeds the public through swindle, embezzlement, and fraud, and which, through its connectedness to the stock market and other forms of business activity, is related to the technological development peculiar to Western society. The monetary cost to society of this type of criminality is many times over that occurring through the conventional, so-called 'blue collar' crime.

Class and Race Relations

Technology forms the root system of the whole complex known as *Western civilization.* It created the concepts, 'material progress' and 'backward areas,' and it germinated the ideology of applying science and engineering to the remedy of almost all of the social maladies. By its conucopian issue, which is plainly evident to all, it has caused a massive stirring between the social classes to attain equality. It has promoted the open society and given added drive to the notion of democracy by its endless demands for special talent and by the many channels for upward mobility that it forces open in order to educe this talent. While it has helped to espouse the democratic tradition, the licensing of inter-individual competition has taken enormous toll of the individual ego, and it has, at once, triggered and offered a means for assuaging rivalry between the social classes and the races.

Technology, in its early out-trustings of the compass, which provided a surer means for maritime navigation, and the firearm, which became an implement for subjugation, directly promoted the vast wave of European resettlement referred to by historians as the 'European Expansion,' a movement that began during the fifteenth century. Thus, technology created the tools for its own expansion and, in turn, was carried by its early practitioners to practically all quarters of the world. Technology, through the ties of colonial commerce, first created the race problem and has since then brought it into bold relief. In like manner, it has provided, in one sense, a step toward the solution of race problems. That is to say that technological capabilities, formerly believed by the Caucasian and others to require special inventive genius and a degree of general intelligence not possessed by the other races, created a special prestige arena which was subsequently upset by several historical happenings. The military victory of an oriental nation over a major European power at the turn of the century (the Russo-Japanese war), the later excellent technological account given by the Japanese through the course of World War II, and an increasing evident mastery of technology by other non-caucasian powers has dispelled the old notion of the inviolability of the Western monopoly on technology, and may be expected to increasingly alter the international prestige scheme. The rate of progress in the solution of the race problem has intimate relationship to the retarded nations' rate of adaptation to technology. Material success and power usually awaken, if not love, at least respect.

Education

The commonly agreed upon method in the West for obtaining benevolent change is through the education of the individual. According to the Victorian viewpoint the cultivation of the mentality not only benefits the individual directly, but it motivates him to insist upon a betterment of social conditions in the wider world in which he lives. Until recently it has been held that educated societies, gifted with classroom acquired benevolence and enlightenment will, in time, sweep the world clean of poverty, pestilence and war. The emerging societies are placing prime reliance upon technical education as a means of initiating progress, and the more materially advanced societies depend upon technical education in sustaining progress. Yet all these terms – education, progress, enlightenment, etc. – are shot through with value judgments. All are open to differing interpretation, and argument as to ways and means of acquiring them.

Like education, the word 'progress' has conflicting meanings. What some conceive as progress others regard as a chrome-wrapped infantilism which only further dehumanizes in the frenetic search to secure ever more. Certain it is, that the more affluent, technologically 'progressive,' and better educated nations manifest little ability to control their own more important affairs. It is they who most hold the world in jeopardy, and in their relationships with the technologically backward areas there is detectable more than a modicum of desire to perpetuate their present undue economic advantage. And if the long awaited education-borne benevolence in class, race and international relations fails to germinate, this cannot be laid entirely at the door of a lopsided, technically oriented training. Several race relations studies indicate that relationships between differing groups are more responsive to improvement through appeal to the emotions than through rational examination. If so, this bodes ill for the hopes of the many who view intergroup harmony as achievable by reasoning, and who would depend upon education to reach this end.

The goals which education should seek, and the methods by which they should be approached, are both widely disputed. Within the institutions of higher learning, educators look askance at the growing emphasis on technical training, especially since it usually comes at the expense of liberal education which, in the minds of these same people, is the only form of training having long-range benefits for the society and its citizens. But even as regards the more technical areas, although the scientific and engineering accomplishments of the university and the private laboratory are everywhere evident, there is no method for assaying the degree to which education has contributed to these. The long-standing argument between proponents of liberal education and those of technical education cannot be resolved by test. The dollar value the different occupational groups command on the labor market reflects little more than demand versus supply and, most of all, the dictate of custom. If a given occupational group has been traditionally low paid, even a radical shortage of these people will not likely greatly alter their pay scale. Thus, the salary offered to a group does not establish its contributary value, nor can this value be estimated on an individual basis. What, for example, will be the future contribution made by a newly graduated physicist? Discovery is as often the result of plodding, painstaking labor as it is of a sudden burst of genius. With increasing emphasis upon team research, the value of perseverence becomes ever more pronounced. Education, in its essence is an attempt at 'thought control.' Even in the supposedly socially sterile halls of the institute of technology there are implicit moralities underlying the application of technical skills; both elementary arithmetic and projective geometry are couched in social nostrums, and engineers are taught to revere the social system that nurtures them, without question. Education is a clumsy, expensive process which consumes as much as one-third of the entire lifetime of the individual in its inculcation, and then is of uncertain effect. It is, perhaps, this uncertainty, this lack of clarity in the relationships between teaching and learning that is its saving grace. Otherwise, if indoctrination (education) could be made fully effective, regardless of how humane the goals it aspired to it would be a process of *complete* thought control.

However difficult it may be to assess the intrinsic value of education, its general acceptance as a means for societal and individual advancement have given it great stature in the West. It is obvious that technology has triggered a change in education as to both the type and quality of training to be sought. Technology's growing complexity has made it virtually impossible for the uneducated to find respectable and financially adequate employment. Technology has established an international race in the field of education between the nations in the vanguard of development. These societies tend to reckon progress in technological 'breakthroughs' in space exploration, and in the raw numbers of scientists and engineers annually graduated from their universities. The adulation of technical achievement and, even more, of a few particular types of technical achievement, subverts education from the long cherished view of its being an end in itself.

There are many practical problems connected with an equitable administering of education. Often slighted is the importance of the close relationships between the cultivation of the individual's abilities, the social characteristics of the group to which he belongs, and the opportunities left open to this group. At a time when schooling has become more important to earning a livelihood than ever before, elementary and high school drop-out rates, though showing recent signs of slackening, are severe in the lower classes and particularly in the lower status race and ethnic groups. There is a certain number within the society who are incapable of acquiring adequate education because of limited mental ability, but this incapacitation is exaggerated socially by a starvation of motivation and a restriction of opportunity for members of the less privileged social groups. These conditions, along with the dilution of quality in education caused by the rapid expansion of facilities to accomodate annually increasing numbers of students, exacts from education much less than could be ideally realized.

Statecraft

One of the most severe of the dilemmas facing the Western nations is the schism between their internal and external political philosophies. This conflict is most apparent in the most technically advanced of the Western societies, the United States, and it amounts to near schizophrenia. Internally, U.S. government is still viable and reasonably able to deal with social exigencies if given enough time. As is openly observed by practically all, since the turn of the century there has been a steady domestic movement in the directions of increased socialization and central control; and it is agreed that this trend is not likely to abate in the foreseeable future. Although the ultimate consequences of this movement are hotly debated by differing interest groups, there is a general consensus as to its necessity, if not its desirability.

On the other hand, in viewing the international relationships of the materially advanced nations it is quite apparent that the tolerant spirit displayed toward their own domestic administration does not hold toward the installation of liberal political systems in other countries. To the confusion, and sometimes outright consternation of emerging societies who have long lived under governments repellently repressive by Western standards, and who, for the first time are striking out to achieve equitability in goods distribution and improved production administration, they discover that the United States usually faces these reform measures with open hostility. The reason is not long in the seeking; it usually is inherent in some type of commercial stake held by the U.S. in the emerging society, and in keeping this stake safe from possible jeopardy by strictly preserving the *status quo*. Every movement smacking of nationalism in the emerging nation with whom there are close trade ties will likely be greeted with the same chilliness as if it were a movement into communism. In fact, it will probably be even labelled 'a leftist-led revolt.' This, then, is the nature of the dilemma: While internally, and with the assent of their peoples almost all Western societies are moving into an ever-deepening socialization, externally, they are putting up rigid resistence to the following of this same course by the emerging societies, and they do not hesitate in intervening with armed force whenever the occasion is 'felt to warrant it.'

International conflict is due to an inability of nations to arrive at an agreement concerning future courses for government service and technological development, as well as to semantic confusion. In all probability, the governmental and socio-technological systems that emerge during the next few decades will be radically different from any of those, whether of the so-called capitalistic or socialistic stripe, existing today.

Even more forbidding than the style of the nation's diplomacy, and to a great degree accounting for its weaknesses in this sphere, are the handicaps under which statesmen must labor. Affairs of state have been brought increasingly under the subjugation of the military, and, as this has occurred, statesmanship has taken on the rigidity characteristic of military systems. Xenophobia, which is the stock-in-trade of the military, power expansionism, and the political 'hard line' provide the general framework within which international diplomacy is carried out. As military thinking came to dominate statecraft it gave spawn to the usual military appurtenances –

gigantic spy networks and secret police activity. The combined mischief caused by these people, in time perverts the relations between states into gangsterism and so poisons the air that it is impossible for men of good will to work together. And however carefully the public may elect its top executives of government, the judgment they are allowed to display in office will be no more mature than that of the men who surround and advise them.

THE FOLKLORE OF THE MATERIALLY ADVANCED SOCIETY

There is within Western society, differing by nation but to some degree permeating its entirety, a body of folklore which, like folklore everywhere, provides the rationalization buttressing prevailing social attitudes and institutions. The fact that some of these lores may be half-truths or falsities does not detract from their value as stabilizers. They are essential to the maintenance of the system, and perhaps, more important than their external validity is their internal consistency and the universality, within the society, with which these beliefs are held. But with time all systems change, and within the society which purports to be self-critical such ideas must be held up to light. There are certain of these folklores that have a negative relationship to the entire process of technological development, at home and abroad, in that they prolong the life of social mechanisms that impede technological change. They are worthy of discussion because the ability of a society to accept change is partially dependent upon its insightfulness into these cultural traits.

The folklores of interest here are of a three-fold classification. The first two of these, economic folklore and commercial folklore, have to do with the internal workings of Western society. Some of the economic folklores purport to find a regularity in the sphere of human enterprise that is predictably recurrent and scientifically useful. The commercial folklores are mechanisms by which enterprise justifies its ways and means, by which it makes them interpretable and acceptable to the public. Economic and commercial folklores are both, primarily, arguments for the *status quo*. The third category, externally directed folklore, is concerned with the viewpoints prevailing within Western society toward international relationships in general and toward the peoples, cultures, and social conditions of the materially retarded societies, in particular.

Economic Folklore

Labor theory This theory presumes that human output norms can be set accurately and that maximum output capability also can be determined with precision. Studies made during the past forty years of the relationship between human productivity and morale indicate that human labor is anything but a fixed quantity. Productivity can be changed radically by manipulating factors within the social environment, such as the physical placing of workers in relation to one another, by the attention displayed toward them by management, or by exterior changes of great moment such as war. Within any work situation, the difference between existing output norms and the maximum output attainable solely through increased human effort represents that situation's latent potential for reduction in the number of workers. Thus far, no one has succeeded in working out valid indices by which this difference between normal and potential maximum output can be measured. This is an important segment of labor theory, and a murky one.

Financial incentive Classical economics has been responsible for a great deal of misunderstanding about the nature of human motivation. If a monetary system is postulated to be a natural and major aspect of all advanced economic systems, it may follow, thetically, that the desire for monetary gain (or for material acquisition) will be the basic driving force within advanced societies. However, under searching examination, even in Western society there is no regularity in the relationships between effort, reward and occupational status. To attempt to go further and apply the financial incentive 'axiom' to all undeveloped societies, many of whom have little or no monetary orientation, is the grandest of follies. It can be demonstrated rather easily that in all societies people work out of motives far transcending sheer desire for material gain.

Consumption The assumption of a regularized ebb and flow relationship between supply and demand economically stereotypes the human as a conveniently inflexible machine for consumption. Actually, he consumes out of widely fluctuating and psychologically tempered appetites. The momentum created by the growing appearance of a new product will, in itself, broaden the market for this product for a time, and it will just as readily eclipse other products which may not be even of related character. With an ever-growing variety of products appearing on the market it is literally impossible to forecast with any confidence what the future desires of the consuming public will be. It is likewise difficult to draw a line between necessity and luxury items because such a demarcation is subject to widely differing individual and cultural definitions.

Production The myth has grown that production alone will assure prosperity. This holds only to the extent that goods produced can be turned out with reasonable economy of effort, that they are equitably distributed throughout the society and that in the act of consumption there is a utility, or value, for the consumer. If everyone were put to work making mink coats, building burial pyramids or manufacturing automobiles, then, despite both heavy production and full employment there would be a conspicuous absence of social prosperity.

Employment The employment myth complements the foregoing production myth, and the two together are assumed to create, infallibly, prosperity. Pseudo-employment, which is the carrying out of work that has no utility or that can be done better and cheaper by machine must be placed by sociological definition in a category alongside gambling. Pseudo-employment unjustly demands of a person his time, cheats him of opportunity for genuine expression, and culminates in the rather barren accomplishment of passing from hand-to-hand paper certificates presumably redeemable in a precious metal. The propensity for seeing a social value in 'work for work's sake' is a part of our socially maintained fiction.

Utility The next logical proposition, that of determining the degree of utility inherent in a work product, is also shot through with enigma. Utility is treated as a factor in economics, yet there are few measuring devices, and no good ones, for assaying its exact value. How does one distinguish, for example, between the utilities of a theatrical production and the construction of a theatre building? Sociologists are unequivocal in asserting that any attempt to make such a distinction would fall under the heading of a 'value judgment.'

Management through finance Finance is the kingpin of Western economic theory and planning. It is held that the monetary system, in itself, has powers leading to an optimum balance within the economy, to the most efficient management of industry, and to a natural equilibrium of the entire society. In their recommendations of development procedures to emerging nations, Western economists usually take the tack that development is primarily a matter of manipulating finance. While this procedure has the happy effect of tying foreign development to the Western complex, it must be recognized that an initial preoccupation with means of finance is a carry-over from Western culture and is altogether inapplicable to organizing for production within some of the emerging societies.

Even in those where conventional finance does exist, questions of finance should be made subsidiary to the more important problems of determining what types of enterprise are best suited to the physical and social resources of the area, and to the more fundamental principles governing technological development.

Commercial Folklore

Self-seeking The phrase is often heard in Western society that, 'everybody is trying to get something for nothing.' This is generally true. If it creates an ambivalence, this is an ambivalence inevitably arising out of free enterprise philosophy. As for actual success in getting something for nothing, it is undoubtedly the rich who are most successful. U.S. income tax forms show cognizance of the difference between wages and booty in their listing of two separate types of income, 'earned' and 'unearned.' Under the latter category fall income from interest, dividends, business, rents, gambling gains, capital gains and certain royalties. The hope of obtaining something for nothing is the ambition of young and old, and of every free entrepreneur. The hope of producing something for nothing is the motivating force behind automation and the ideal goal of industry. Short circuiting the more arduous routes to wealth by gambling, inheritance (an undemocratic practice so assiduously defended in democratic society) or making a lucky stock market investment is held to be legitimate procedure in most free enterprise nations. Whether or not it is *immoral* to try to 'get something for nothing' is another question. It can only be replied that in most Western societies to 'shop around,' to try to buy at as low a price as possible (this ranging on down to the 'giveaway' point) is considered defensible practice.

Labor and reward Corollary to the foregoing is the claim that, 'people won't work if you give them something for nothing.' This is a common ground for argument against wage increase, public relief, and foreign aid. Again, this belief imputes an intrinsic value to work, and an especially high status to material acquisition. It overlooks the activities and contributions of the very rich, most of whom are anything but drones although they are under no financial compulsion to work, and it overlooks the contributions made by members of monastic types of religious orders, members of the traditionally under-paid world of academia, and the better part of the world's peoples, who receive little more for their work than subsistence. In those few cultures that have such a natural abundance that work is unnecessary, people are still observed to be normally active. Rather than there being a direct relationship between the amount of work a person does and the financial reward he is given, it is probable that in reality the opposite condition holds. In terms of sheer, routine, day-to-day energy output, it is rather obvious in almost all societies that it is the lower occupational status groups who work hardest. It is they who must man the fields, the foundries, and the mines, and it is they who live closest to the line of economic marginality.

Sacrifice in time and labor There is felt to be a direct relationship between the position a person holds in the occupational hierarchy and the number of hours he spends in work. This might apply, if rephrased to the effect that there is a relationship between occupational status and the *number of hours spent in the place of work.* As one ascends the occupational ranks he finds that work becomes increasingly variegated. It becomes diluted by travel, by frequent conferences, and by indirect social and recreational activities not open to the bench worker. It is a rare manual laborer who enjoys the privilege of carrying out his work while on the golf links.

Sacrifice of health Because of the added weight of responsibilities and the longer work hours presumably shouldered by the upper occupational classes, it is commonly supposed that it is this group that suffers from the greatest incidence of heart disorder and other so-called 'occupation-linked' disease. Some large corporations maintain watering places to which their harassed executives can periodically retreat. Recently, however, there has been an adumbration of statistical evidence refuting the physical vulnerability of the executive class. These few studies indicate that the incidence of heart disease is highest among manual workers and relatively low in the executive group. As one might expect, the latter receive more adequate medical attention, deferential treatment within both the work environment and the larger society, and they better know how to care for themselves. Like an overworked machine, a physically overworked body shows earlier signs of deterioration.

Externally Directed Folklore

Not the least of the barriers to improved international relations and to technological development are the proliferation of folk attitudes held by Western society toward the emerging peoples. Some of these notions are born of prejudices that are class-linked, others of biases that are race-linked, and to a great extent the two overlap. Their raw materials are the pseudo-scientific espousal of scientifically untested doctrine. In the past, social scientists have donated considerable effort to the scientifically unrewarding job of testing common Western assumptions concerning non-Western peoples. These folk beliefs have implied a significant difference in physical characteristics, in personality and in intelligence level between the races; and unvaryingly these implied differences have favored the dominant Western group. The public puncturing of these myths undoubtedly has helped in preparing the ground for intergroup readjustment and improved relations between societies. The nature of discriminatory lore ranges all the way from the once current myth in the United States that, 'a Negro is insensitive to pain if kicked in the skins,' to the less crass but perhaps more damaging claim, 'that people in underdeveloped societies are naturally lazy.' Tests for physiological differences can be made relatively easily, but in some cases the content of socially held beliefs cannot be proven or disproven, they are simply untestable and for this reason should be accorded the same status as idle speculation or, sometimes, pernicious gossip.

The following are some of the cliches applied by Westerners to peoples of most of the undeveloped societies. It should be interjected that many of the social conditions alluded to in these cliches are starkly and indisputably evident. It is not the purpose of this treatise to attempt to wish away these conditions, but rather to point out that where they are found to exist, they are of a social character and are not an unalterable outcropping of the innate biological make-up of individuals or societies.

Innate laziness Many outsiders maintain that the peoples of undeveloped societies will not work. In actuality, the foreign employer in the undeveloped society exacts far more labor per dollar spent than he ever would be able to get in his home economy. The average work-day in most materially retarded societies runs in length well over that worked in the typical Western society. In many retarded areas the entire family, from the youngest infant upward, is impressed from daybreak to dark into the most unrelenting types of work. Some male adults may hold as many as three jobs, from each of which the income is so low as to scarcely incite any particular show of on-the-job enthusiasm. Again, if the appellation 'laziness' is to be applied to these societies with any validity, it must be applied primarily to the elite groups, to most of whom wealth represents an escape from work.

Dishonesty Most of the undeveloped societies are rife with theft and other forms of property abuse. The best evidence, anywhere, of the rate of criminal behavior is the frequency of appearance of locks and high walls, and in most materially retarded societies these two types of security measures proliferate. Widespread theft makes it difficult to establish more efficient merchandizing systems, such as 'self-service' supermarkets, or to indulge the simpler amenities such as placing unguarded newspaper dispensers on the sidewalks. To people living just above the survival line, honesty is a luxury that seldom can be afforded. Theft and other forms of property violation are often reflections of dire need and abnormally tense intergroup relations. Sometimes when an article of property cannot be conveniently removed, it will be defaced or destroyed.

Preoccupation with sex The outsider visiting in most undeveloped areas tends to the view that there is, among the local peoples, an unduly strong interest in sex. This ranges from general permissiveness in the female to widespread prostitution or concubinage (and this often in societies where sexual promiscuity in the unmarried female of respectable family is not tolerated). It is noteworthy that this belief in 'moral laxity' is propagated to a great extent by visiting males from outside societies. It is further relevant, fortunately or unfortunately, depending upon one's point of view, that, as Freud pointed out, preoccupation with sex cuts rather cleanly across race, ethnic, religious, occupational, sex, and most other lines.

Unpredictability and disorderliness It is charged that the members of undeveloped societies are impunctual in their business relationships, that they may absent themselves from work for days on end without prior notice or explanation, and that in the course of their work they are unable to set or hold to a regular schedule without rigid supervision. Work perseverance varies widely by society. In some, circumstances are so harsh as to almost chain the peasantry to their work and to drive them with a machine-like regularity. In others, there is an indifference to time, and a host of interfering social and religious activities.

Lack of technological aptitude The populations of most undeveloped societies lack the technical *skills* necessary to work with machinery. There are exceptions to this rule. A number of the Latin-American societies, in their understanding of mechanics and in their ability to keep a machine in operation many times over its normal lifetime stand in sharp contrast to the mechanically naive Arab tribesman and the

Asian peasant. Japan and Russia provide examples of a rapid acceleration of technologically backward peoples into the machine age. The acquisition of technical skills is attendant upon a society's having, or acquiring, a cultural interest in technology, and in making provisions for technical training facilities. A present lack of these skills does not indicate a lack of aptitude.

Contentment with existing conditions The remark is sometimes heard that a given undeveloped society does not want technical improvement or social change. If this were true there would be much less turbulence in the world, and fewer problems for the advanced nations. Within the emerging societies there is agitation for change. Technological movement is being stimulated by the infusion of foreign ideas and by an increasing number of young people who are assimilating new ideas at home and abroad. The young generation forms a vanguard of progressives who are demanding change. The present test of the durability of the governments of these societies is their ability to actively assist in creating change, or at least their willingness to accommodate change.

Low level of existing technical development It is sometimes claimed that the level of technological development in a given backward society can be pegged at some corresponding stage in Western history. A South American republic may be likened to the United States at the turn of the century. This generalization usually rests on a few particular behaviors such as Sunday morning band concerts in the park, careful chaperonage of the unmarried, large family gatherings, the unhurried social pace, etc. It overlooks the late-model automobiles on the streets, the bulldozers, air terminals and like appurtenances which are found in most of these societies and which are the evidence of positive, though lopsided forces, which are propelling them further into the mainstream of technology. The parallel belief that the rate of technological development within the emerging society is painfully slow is likewise unmindful of the history of innovation. Veblen and others have pointed out that since they are enabled to start from an already established technological base, the societies recently embarking upon programs of technological development are moving at a much faster rate than did the Western juggernaut which had to invent as it went along. In an historical perspective, change is occurring in most of the world's societies at a phenomenal rate. The degree of change now being compressed into decades exceeds that formerly occurring over decamillenia.

The natural order of things for mankind A small body of folklore centers upon the unalterability of some of the more negative aspects of human nature. The notion that war is an inescapable condition which is rooted deep in the biological make-up of mankind is one such belief and, no doubt, one that is an impediment to improved international relations. In a similar vein, the opinion is often expressed that if development comes to the untouched, backward, society, it will have a despoiling effect upon a paradaisical way of life, upon a 'natural' way of living that is splendidly rural in nature and accords with the Christian precept of 'simple living.' Most of the outlanders voicing this feeling have had little or no social contact with the middle or lower classes of the undeveloped society; they are often insensitive to the squalor in which the lower class lives, and are safely barricaded from it for formal etiquettes and residential segregation.

3

THE DILEMMA OF THE TRANSITIONAL SOCIETY

The problems of the transitional societies are of a different order than those found in the industrial West. The leading nations of the West are beset by the social disabilities growing out of technological affluence. Their productive powers have created within them a range of unprecedented socio-technical problems, problems of a type which have not yet cropped up in the under-industrialized emerging nations. Indeed, the primary question within many of the emerging areas is that of how to go about gaining admittance to the select company of the wealthy and affluent societies who need only concern themselves with the more abstruse social issues. Issues, not of disease and hunger, but having to do with such matters as how to distribute more equitably the 'necessities' of life, most of which 'necessities' the backward societies would consider as luxuries. For most of these societies even the Western standard of food consumption would be classified as luxury. Theirs is the problem of blunting the barb of direct physical need.

The foregoing is not to say that the typical transitional society does not have its *social* problems. Indeed, conventional development theory maintains that most of these societies must first contend with massive social problems before they ever will be able to come to grips with the technical problems of development. It is felt that, in most of them, the social structure is so imcompatible with development that the latter cannot proceed until radical social change has taken place. One of the major dilemmas of the undeveloped society is perceived to lie in the disorganization of the social framework within which development must take place; and this seemingly insurmountable barrier thus becomes the dilemma of orthodox development theorists. While the following account does not, by any means, portray social condition in *all* technologically underdeveloped societies, it does present a panoramic view of the problems of many of these societies, particularly those that are joining, in increasing number, the march toward urbanization.

THE UNORGANIZED SOCIAL BASE

The transitional societies are beset by problems that are characteristically alike in both the technological and the social spheres. These countries best can be described as traditionalistic, overpopulated agrarian societies in a slowed state of technical development. Their economies are monolithically agricultural, with from sixty-five per cent of the work force engaged in farming. These countries usually have a surplus of workers in agriculture, a state referred to by economists as 'disguised unemployment,' and one which is by no means confined to the retarded society. Not only in agriculture, but everywhere, there is employment for employment's sake. A clutter of middlemen in marketing, and frequent operational redundancies in distribution obfuscate the market and dilute profits. The desperate search for any type of employment manifests itself in the forms of extensive numbers of people selling lottery tickets, ablebodied males selling newspapers and curios on street corners, and farmers and merchants hawking farm produce from door to door. Entrepreneurships spring up and die spontaneously. An individual who can reach the street with the latest edition of a newspaper only minutes before his competitors will attempt to exploit this monopoly, if only for a few minutes, through a sharply increased price.

Because of the disproportionately large part of the work force which is dependent upon agriculture for a livelihood, and because of agriculture's low state of technical development, food costs are relatively high. Food expenditures consume a disproportionately large part of a budget from which durable goods may be totally excluded. Most of the energies of the society are consumed in the daily struggle for food procurement and in the elaborate steps of its preparation, facts conspicuously documented in the content of cinema drama filmed in some of the undeveloped countries.

Export trade falls along the lines of agriculture and mining. Exports consist largely of primary goods, with finished goods being recycled back from the factories of the advanced nations and sold at prices proportionately much higher than the prices the exporters received for their raw materials. The terms of trade, that is, the prices received for exports as opposed to those paid for imports, have long favored the advanced nations. The trend continues to move steadily against the undeveloped societies and there appears to be little that this group can do to stem the tide, a force which flows from the advanced societies' highly developed technical abilities. These abilities may be used to develop new sources for raw materials, or to develop synthetic substitutes when the price of imported raw materials exceeds a certain level. Advanced techniques recently have been used by Western industrialists to develop new cacao plantations in West Africa, not because the extra production was needed, but because a cheaper supply of labor insured, temporarily at least, a lower price. Consequently, large tracts of productive cacao land in Central America go unharvested because of the impossibility oı meeting foreign competition. The development of synthetic rubber and the substitution of aluminium for tin have had pronounced negative effects upon the area of primary production within the economically retarded nations. Even though the market were to hold steady, the unequal exchange of raw materials for finished goods leaves the poor society under an indirect and exploitive form of colonialism. The retarded society provides a source of cheap labor over which its advanced trade partners exercise vicarious management control, and worse, unlike the case where labor and management are members of the same society, here they are in different universes of discourse; there is no intermediary third party, such as government, which can hear grievances, reconcile differences or erase abuse.

Several writers, Gunnar Myrdal among them, maintain that trade between technologically advanced nations and emerging societies not only fails to help the latter, but is an absolute detriment to them. The free market consistently acts to the disadvantage of the poorer trade partner; the poorer the society the greater the handicaps under which it must trade so that, at an extreme, exporters of primary commodities are victimized by their powerful neighbours.

The degree to which the cumulative impoverishment of the poorer societies is due to internal or to external factors is difficult to specify, but an examination of foreign trade pattern relationships indicates that the emerging society has made no substantive gains through external exchange. To right this situation, the government of the exploited will have to act to deny outside private buyers unrestricted access to the local market. Seldom do emerging societies send sales emissaries to the richer countries; instead the latter send in their own buyers, and transactions are carried out relative to the local trade setting, sometimes under even worse terms than those prevailing domestically. Special concessions are sought by the outsider by a promise to buy in quantity and over a period of time. Since, usually, very little production equipment is needed, if the producer balks, an outside buyer may easily put other entrepreneurs in business who *will* agree to produce for him at lowered prices. The production of agricultural items as coffee or vegetable oils may see whole societies manipulatively arrayed in international competition with one another over already price-depressed items. Hand made metal wares and leather goods bought at a pittance on underdeveloped markets, are resold on Western markets at prices sometimes so princely that only the rich can afford them. A hand-wrought article purchased in the Middle East for fifty dollars may be resold in the West for five hundred. Not just the laboring sector, but the entire population of the undeveloped society bears the brunt of this type of exploitation.

By properly regulating its domestic sales, the developing government would be enabled to skim off directly a part of the otherwise excess profit that would be realized by the buyer, and to flow it back where it was most needed. Until that step is taken, outside traders will continue doing 'business as usual.' Much less than showing concern for promoting fair play in foreign commerce, they conduct international trade schools which have the specific purpose of teaching the techniques which perpetuate this injustice and rationalizing it under the 'free enterprise' doctrine.

Another pathological symptom within the undeveloped countries is the low level of Gross National Product per capita. Measured in dollars, this ranged from a 1965 high of $2800 per capital for the United States, to a low of approximately $100 for Thailand, the Republic of the Congo and North Korea; and in only two Latin American countries (Venezuela and Argentina) did it exceed $500. This, combined with a low level of income, brings consumption close to the bare subsistence level and makes it difficult to accrue capital through savings. Such surplus earnings as there are accrue to the elite and go into hoarded savings, foreign investment, or further land investment, none of which aid in the formation of capital. The very large landholders usually bank in Switzerland or elsewhere outside the nation. When measured by the Loring scale or any similar device there is a striking inequality between income by social class, the buffering middle class being numerically few or absent altogether.

In general, within the undeveloped society: credit facilities are lacking; marketing facilities are crude; mechanical repair facilities are usually inadequate and meagerly stocked; housing is conspicuously substandard; there is extensive use of child labor; nutrition is inadequate; illiteracy is relatively high; fertility rates are high; the status of females is inferior; the number of skilled workers is inadequate; rudimentary technologies are employed; there is social schism comprised by the presence of only two classes, the elite and the peasantry; and there is a cultural schism between urban society and rural society and, occasionally, between the domestic society and powerful foreign enclaves. In brief, the general plight of the majority of the inhabitants of the entire country is similar to that of the very poor minority in the technologically advanced countries.

Although the way of life of a typical undeveloped country may have certain features recommending it, superlatives on the subject usually come from 'well-heeled' tourists or high-salaried working foreigners who are sequestered in their daily work contacts and places of residence from the more representative social sectors of the undeveloped society. The social contacts of outsiders are largely among themselves or, less frequently, with the autochthonous elite, while their relations with servants and tradesmen are highly perfunctory.

The many emerging societies which are undergoing rapid population expansion and urbanization are manifesting symptoms of individual and social disorganization similar to those found in Western urban slums. Crowding, noise, and the various forms of social and physical deprivation undoubtedly take a toll, but one which, as yet, is unmeasured. Excessive crowding in animal experimentation produces a listlessness and a decline in drive which may find its parallel in human overcrowding. The overly generous latitude allowed for self-expression in many backward societies often overflows into personal license and an abuse of others. Dirt from homes and shops is swept out daily onto the sidewalk and left to lie there. Almost everywhere there is the overpowering odor of human and animal refuse that results from unenforced sanitation laws and under-capacity sewage systems. Even in the largest cosmopolitan centers the night sounds of livestock may be heard around the most fashionable hotels as the congested poor struggle to augment their living by every means possible, including animal husbandry. In order to attract attention, the owners of automobiles and two-wheeled motor vehicles often remove the noise mufflers and replace them with noise amplifiers, and they then supplement this din with incessant horn blowing. Loud music and riotness continue through the night until daybreak when the previous night's disorder is evidence on the street the following morning by the appearance of blood, vomit, feces and urine. Many of these societies are conspicuous, above all, in their human and machine-made clamor. The ceaseless noise and confusion perhaps takes high toll in mental illness, but, again, there is no way of statistically reckoning the cost.

These societies are in a state of transition from folk societies, in which human relationships were formerly well-ordered through informal group controls, to secular societies in which formal codes have not yet been fully established. Blue collar crime is ubiquitous, while white collar crime is passively accepted as part of a long-standing way of life. Various forms of tribute are exacted by the struggling poor. Youths offer to guard a parked car in its owner's absence; clearly implied in the offer is the threat of property damage or theft should it be refused. Implied in the broader situation is indifference, or inability to enforce the law, on the part of the police. Interestingly, the private citizen seldom files formal complaint.

The general appearance of the city of transitional society is one of social disorganization the equal of that found in the worst of the slum areas of the Western *metropoli*. Lepers roam the streets scavaging for whatever is there for the gleaning. For lack of institutional facilities the insane walk abroad where they are treated with indifference or are made the butt of good-natured public ridicule. A dearth of hospital facilities leaves the physically ill also without adequate attention. Untreated diseases such as glaucoma, and chronic conditions such as harelip or clubfootedness are common sights. Jails and prisons are filled to the point of overflow. Prisoners stand because filth on the floor and over-crowding leave no place in which to lie; prison behavior, food and sanitation are all at a sub-primitive level.

Most of the transitional societies lack public laws enforcing food and drug purity. A few years ago in one of the North African nations, olive oil merchants, in seeking increased profits by diluting their product with cheaper United States 'surplus' aircraft engine oil, caused permanent blindness in several thousand people. Death by food poisoning is a frequent occurrence in the underdeveloped societies. Dairy cattle are not inoculated against tuberculosis; dairy products are unpasteurized; meats are uninspected; and insect screening in food markets or residences is practically unknown. Ironically, many people of the underdeveloped areas profess indifference to these conditions, boasting that they have a 'natural immunity' to disease. Despite this 'immunity,' funeral processions are a commonplace to be found along any public highway and the life expectancy, although longer than formerly, is still below that of the West of sixty-five years ago.

In some undeveloped societies the spectre of starvation forever lurks in the background, and day-to-day survival is accounted, in itself, a triumph. Desperate stratagems are sometimes employed to gain succor. A woman with babe in arms beseeches alms of a Westerner who is entering a taxi. Upon being ignored she rushes forward and in one last, desperate attempt to draw attention to her plight thrusts one of the infant's arms in the way of the closing steel door. There is a crunch of splintering bone and the Westerner stands transfixed in horrified disbelief. However, he is immediately reassured by the taxi driver, who is familiar with the locality and its people. He is told that the infant has been dead of starvation for several days but that the mother continues carrying the body about and using it as a 'prop' in begging alms. This is the masque of raw need; few middle-class Westerners have ever beheld it first-hand or comprehended it.

Simple matters, simple because in Western society they are regularized by formal code and practice, are attended by all manner of difficulty in the developing society. A heavy crane is delayed on the highway because a high-tension electric line does not have proper clearance above the road surface. After a full day's delay a linesman appears, elevates the wire to allow the crane to pass, and then reanchors it exactly where it was before. A driver punctures a tire on a protruding iron stake which was driven by the side of the road and carelessly left there by a surveyor. He repairs the tire and drives on without making any attempt to remove or neutralize the stake. Most of the cities in these areas, regardless of their size, lack an address or residence numbering system. Because more precise designations cannot be made, the location of a business or dwelling must be painstakingly described in its relation to some landmark which may be, itself, poorly known.

There are almost endless delays in the undeveloped society in even the most trifling type of transaction. A simple business negotiation that could be carried out in the West in a few hours may run into days or weeks. It will often fall into limbo and will have to be resuscitated by some form of aggression, such as threat. Lack of organized bureaucracy in the larger organizations leads to a needlessly redundant rain of individual efforts. Tied to this lack of formalism is a blind adherence to what few standards may exist. Upon being notified of a certain administrative error committed by his office, a clerk may answer, 'Impossible, it could not have happened here because it's against the rules!' The peoples of these societies have great difficulties in their dealings with one another. Fraud, embezzlement, and reneging on indebtedness are commonplace. Cash or credit are usually scarce and difficult to obtain. The statement is often heard from a prospective buyer that, 'I will definitely buy this item on condition that so-and-so repays me the amount which he is indebted to me.' Small tradesmen and peddlers are chronically short on monetary change or, if they have it, make change grudgingly. Almost every detail of business, which in the industrialized society would be concluded by a brief telephone call, must be attended by a personal visit. In most undeveloped societies telephones are few in number and are interconnected by switching systems so inefficient that it is often more convenient to make a personal visit. Moreover, the folkways of some of these societies *require* that business be transacted on a face-to-face basis.

The custom of rendering special services to the elite has spilled over into sometimes rendering these same services to the masses, and where this has happened the whole system becomes hopelessly bogged down in the process. Rather than have air passengers meet at the airline's downtown office for transportation to the airport, a special bus shuttles randomly through the city picking them up at their residences. If a prospective passenger is still in the act of dressing, the bus driver will agree to return for him later. This kind of disorganization is symptomatic of a broader type of social malaise – a difficulty in joining into selfless organization for the sake of critically important endeavours. The kindly, tolerant outside observer who remarks that, 'These folk won't die of heart attack,' overlooks the point that they are already dying of starvation.

The mechanization of industry and agriculture suffers for lack of parts replacement and repair skills. Replacement parts must often be ordered from abroad, and a subsequent waiting period of several weeks is not unusual. Heavy machines must be airlifted into isolated regions and supplied with fuel and oil by air. Accident rates are inordinately high in commerce, industry, and on the road. Industrial machines are often without safeguards. Street and highway intersections are unmarked, poorly marked, or fringed with natural or man-made obstructions to vision. Automobile accidents are frequent and violent. There is sometimes a complete absence of industrial safety laws or of highway traffic law enforcement. The maimed, whose relatives number are manyfold over that found in Western society, are everywhere in evidence; they seldom enjoy the luxury of prosthesis and get by as best they can in the absence of any system for public aid.

Because they were poorly chosen and because the planning that preceded their development may have been faulty, whole industrial sites occasionally must be abandoned. New highways may be poorly surveyed, lead nowhere, and terminate abruptly. In many of the larger cities of the transitional areas, streets are repeatedly torn up and repaved to permit the underground installation of additional utility lines, etc. A lack of underground conduits, coupled with a steady growth of the metropolitan area, leads to patchwork upon patchwork in street paving and to a perennial obstruction of traffic while this work is underway.

An important moral of the foregoing is that *few people in the developing society are happy with the existing situation.* These social perturbations are never accommodated placidly. They are a source of continuing irritation to all. In general, irresponsibility is most noticeable in the elite because it is they who occupy positions from which they are expected to exert leadership for improvement but instead, usually display indifference. Although the elite are relatively few, the poverty of the masses and the nature of the social structure highlight their presence vividly. Undeveloped society appears in blacks and whites and without much subtlety of in-between shadings. The beggered ask alms of those attired in the most properly cut English woolens. The illiterate move among erudites who were educated in the world's most renowned universities. Mud-walled and tin shacks nestle against, and form the very boundaries around the city's estated zones. Thus separated socially and physically from the lower class, and from what middle class may exist, the elite have little raproachment with, or compassion for the masses. It is the practice of the aristocracy in some countries to refer to the general body of the population in the somewhat contemptuous and distant term – 'those people.' Yet it cannot be gainsaid that occasionally one of the more feeling and better informed of the aristocracy may help to act as an instrumentalist in achieving reform.

FOOD PRODUCTION

Of the three basics, food, shelter and clothing, there is little doubt that in the majority of climates the most important of the three to human survival is food. Most of the emerging nations are purportedly working toward a goal of net advancement. In truth, however, their more immediate goal is that of forestalling deepening food deficiencies. In the face of phenomenal population growth, most of these countries are not showing notable success in holding their own in food production. The most densely populated of the developing societies are slipping most conspicuously in maintaining workable food-to-population ratio, and there are many reasons beyond net population growth accounting for this.

Practically all the emerging societies are basically agricultural. A society in which agriculture is the leading sector seems foredoomed to economic instability and, at best, will enjoy only limited periods of prosperity. In these societies there is an excess of labor in agriculture, a surplus of such magnitude that its very physical presence impedes the introduction of improved methods, and syphons off revenues that could otherwise be ploughed back into better land maintenance, and into mechanization.

Related to a surplus of farm labor is a fragmentation of farm holdings into unfeasibly small parcels. Traditional agriculture, with its land splintering effects of inheritance over the generations, has reduced some societies to tallying individual holdings by numbers of production items rather than by the actual land area units held. In some parts of the Middle East, the individual's wealth is calculated in the number of olive trees he owns with little regard to land acreage. Five adjacent trees in an olive grove may belong to as many different individuals, with individual holdings interspersed in what would appear to be, to the uninitiated, a patchwork of confusion. Fragmentation does not lead to more intensive and masterly cultivation, but leads, instead, to significantly lowered yields. Its inhibitory effects on mechanization and crop yields are all too well known to agricultural economists. Although this criterion differs from one region to another, for general farming twenty hectares (2.47 acres per hectare) is considered the minimum land area that can be economically mechanized.

Further adding to the difficulty of mechanisation is a fear of disemployment by the peasantry. In many folk societies labor is sold by the family unit. With an apprehension characteristic of workers everywhere, these folk view any new movement toward mechanization as a direct threat to job-holding. In many phases of backward agriculture, primitive methods are retained solely from a desire by the peasantry to preserve the right to labor. During an olive harvest, for example, the fruits are shaken onto plowed ground where they are laboriously picked up from between the clods by women, children, and old men. More efficient techniques, such as placing a light canvass upon the ground before shaking the olives from the tree have been tried and cast aside.

Beyond inefficiency in the use of land and labor, agriculturally retarded societies are besieged by other types of problems which are universally characteristic of agriculture. One of these problems is the price instability of farm produce. Agriculture is an occupation offering at least, an insurance of family subsistence, and this is one factor making it difficult to eliminate the marginal producer. The marginal producer's omnipresence in the transitional society and his ability to produce quickly for a rising market just as quickly oversaturates the market. The farmer must produce for a marketing date which lies at least six months ahead, and he tends to plan his output upon the present market. Wholesale planning in response to this year's highest commodity prices leads to annually recurrent price oscillations and massive swings in production planning.

If agriculture is to reach a plateau of real efficiency it must employ machinery. Agriculture is not likely to develop an interest in, or a demand for machinery unless society first mechanizes in other sectors. It is historically evident that before there could have been a widespread mechanization in agriculture there first had to be an industrial base large enough to *produce* agricultural machinery. Nowadays, agricultural machinery may be imported, by a developing society, from abroad, but this still leaves the problem of training people in how to use it. It appears that interest, experience, and knowledge in machine use originates in industry and then diffuses to agriculture, so that agriculture is the last sector to be reached by mechanization. It is easier to indoctrinate mechanical skills within the factory setting than on the small farmstead.

One of the most basic of all agricultural problems in the emerging society is the fact that the domestic market does not have enough purchasing power to absorb food at much above what the domestic culture defines as a 'sufficient' level. And that level is usually pegged close to the bare subsistence line. Food consumption, in the quantity in which the West knows it, is a luxury, and in order to buy food in this abundance there must be a surplus of wealth in the society. In brief, however successful an agricultural program may be in raising its production, the domestic market of the undeveloped country will not be capable of absorbing an appreciable part of the increase. The development of such purchasing power depends upon the industrialization of the society.

There is strong evidence suggesting that agriculture, in itself, cannot become an independently healthy, self-sufficient sector but must be buoyed up by price supports and other types of farm enablement measures. The vast finances required for this insurance must be obtained from other sectors, chiefly from industry. The backward society is, therefore, in the dilemma of not being able to assuage its first need, food, until it will have satisfied some of its secondary requirements which are met through industrialization and industrial production.

If so many factors are militating against the growth of domestic agriculture, it would seem rational that foodstuffs should be imported. The obstacles to this course are severalfold. While a limited quantity of farm commodity is available on credit or as outright relief, to acquire, through import, the amount of food stock actually needed would call for a purchasing power far beyond what most of the backward societies have. Finally, even if sufficient quantities of food could be imported, and whether through cash or charity is beside the point, most backward societies would rule this course unacceptable on the grounds that food imports of any magnitude would only further weaken their domestic agricultural system. Because they are predominantly agricultural in character, in most of these societies there have arisen around agriculture, strongly entrenched political interests. And in the planning briefs of these societies agriculture is, at once, the present mainstay and the future hope for social prosperity. The fact that agriculture is failing to meet this expectation seems to be strangely immaterial to many national planners.

INDUSTRIALIZATION

A recurrent problem in the industrialization of the transitional society is a failure to plan properly. Usually, national plans for development place heavy emphasis upon the promotion of existing industries rather than giving thought to the creation of new and altogether different types of industrial enterprises. Again, because early industry, like early agriculture, cannot place much reliance on the weak domestic consumer's market it must do what agriculture cannot do easily, it must go abroad and compete successfully with the technologically advanccd societies on the international market. The small industries predominating in most materially retarded societies are not likely to reach this point in size and efficiency.

In addition to the foregoing difficulties standing in the way of basic planning, there is an initial failure to develop, in proper detail, the plan itself. As international agencies of finance point out, there is a dearth of good plans. Those submitted usually are incomplete, lacking in detail and are not based upon sound engineering data. Most developing nations are remiss in failing to comply with the first preliminary requirements in planning – carrying out a comprehensive survey of their natural, cultural and human resources and integrating these into a meaningful development pattern. Prospective projects usually place excessive stress on labor consumption in an effort to alleviate surpluses on the labor market, or they are overly reliant upon the development of crude industries designed to carry out only the first basic steps in natural resources refinement. There is a general failure to follow the pattern of extended industrial development that has proven so highly successful in the technologically advanced nations of the West.

In most developing societies, industry must compete intensely, and usually at a disadvantage, with agriculture for public interest and financial support. There is an overweening orientation toward landholding and agricultural enterprise, these being perceived as means for attaining psychological security and as an ideal way of life even more literally than is the case in Western society. Excess earnings are promptly plowed back into further land investment. The elite have a particularly strong confidence in land investment, and since it is they who control finance, and therefore the lands, the greater part of the land is owned *in absentia*. Preoccupation with agricultural investment drains off funds that otherwise might find their way as adventure capital into industrial development. Industry must compete for finance with short-term, and immensely profitable loan commerce, with commercial inventory speculation, and with the more secure and alluring investment prospects abroad, particularly in the industries of the advanced nations. However, even though all potential domestic investment funds *were* somehow made available, it is estimated that they would cover only about one-third of the cost of a national program large enough to promote substantive growth. The bulk of industrial finance must come from private sources within the richer foreign nations and, although there is an abundance of investment money within these societies, little of it flows out to the backward areas. In fact, the removal of colonial controls and a lack of confidence in the governments and industries of the emerging areas has constricted the inflow of finance, relatively, to a fraction of its volume at the turn of this century.

Industrial development has a special need for power, and a common source of power in the coal and petroleum-poor countries is electricity. But laying a power base through a general program for electrification is no small undertaking. Most backward societies, thus far, have not been able to extend electrification much beyond their major population centers. Electrification programs are so large as to usually require that they be undertaken as public utilities. Even then, they are slow in getting started, uncertain in operation, and increasingly costly as their services are extended to the rural areas.

The developing societies generally lack skilled manpower as well as the financial means for obtaining training. There is a shortage of trained personnel at the managerial level and there are even more serious deficits in skilled and semi-skilled labor. The most effective method of training people from transitional societies is by on-the-job placement in the industries of advanced societies, installing them at all possible levels of labor and management. Trainees thus placed have an opportunity to acquire not only job skills, but knowledge of the broader aspects of industry and the industrial society, and, in addition, they are exposed at the same time to a higher material standard of living. One of the few objections to this type of training program is its expense. For this reason the usual solution is to send key personnel abroad for training and to simultaneously import foreign instructors and teaching supervisors for the lower cadres of workmen. If the population has attained a reasonable level of literacy, domestic training can provide a partial base for skills development. However, home training neglects the broader value orientation that can be acquired most expediently by having the individual live and work among industrial workers in an industrial society.

Contrasting with an almost total absence of skills in some societies, there is an overly rigid specialization of skills in others. Traditional artisans, jealously guarding the techniques and tools handed down by their ancestors, work within a narrow band of skills to turn out highly specialized products. The broad spectrum of skills required by mass production, and the generally skilled mechanics that it needs, are not available in the underdeveloped setting. However, if the culture is tolerant of change, trained people can be produced from within this vaccuum if aggressive planning measures are employed.

Finally, although the technologically advanced nations may have something of an avuncular interest in the welfare of the undeveloped societies, they also have an interest in preventing changes from occurring within these societies which may infringe upon their own commerce. Since almost any significant development program will likely conflict with Western interests, there inevitably will be Western encouragement of the *status quo* and pressures against integrated and far-ranging programs. This will hold for both, the home production of finished items presently being imported in large quantity from the West, and for the development of domestic industries based upon, and heavily utilizing crude natural resources which the West is importing from these same areas. The big Western producers of finished rubber products would take a dim view of any plan by the latex producing societies for absorbing all their crude output through home-based factories. The developing society can only take this problem into account and deal with it as adroitly as circumstances permit.

There are still other impediments to industrialization that are not at all of a social or technical nature, but are outgrowths of the Western trade system to which many of the emerging societies are being linked increasingly by political alliance and material aid. One such problem area is the ever-present threat of an unduly large foreign trade deficit. When imports, regardless of how desperately they may be needed, exceed exports by such a margin as to make a decisive drain upon a nation's currency, the nation has no choice but curtail its imports if it is to avoid economic disaster. India has been facing just such a problem for several years and, despite her vast need for capital production goods, is prohibited from purchasing them in the quantities in which they are needed.

COMMERCE

Whatever the techniques it may use, commerce is the channel through which industry and agriculture express themselves, and by which they relate to one another. Since commerce is essentially a socio-technological pipeline for the movement of materials and services, its volume will reflect directly the potencies of industry and agriculture. At the beginning of a development program, commerce can flow with a minimum of cost, delay and friction, or it can rear up as a formidable bottleneck. In the latter event, as industry becomes successful it will build up pipeline pressures that will shake the antiquated commerce from its lethargy. Commerce, like the other two sectors, also evolves technologically, and like agriculture it follows in the wake of industry. The pristine methods of trade and traffic abounding in most of the backward areas are altogether unsuited to the promotion, or even accommodation of technological growth, and they may not be expected to change until industry moves forward.

Whereas, in most of the retarded societies industry is conspicuously absent, there is a ubiquitous welter of commercial activity. Commerce, like agriculture, is so heavily fractionized as to give most of these societies an unhealthy, top-heavy, commercial orientation. Small merchants, tumbled in a profusion of stalls lodged in every conceivable type of nook and cranny, carry out an almost endless duplication of sales effort and inventory. Such excessive splintering of commerce leads to an intensive competition which in the end spells submarginal profits for all.

At the very outset of a development program the great fragmentation of underdeveloped commerce will invariably exert an inhibitory effect upon the development of industry and agriculture. There will be an absence of the type of large retail food merchandizing outlets that encourage a large scale agriculture. The present lack of large 'self-service' marts is due in part to a well-founded distrust of the public's honesty, and in part to cultural inertia. Although mass food and durable goods' outlets are beginning to make faint appearance in the elite residential areas of some of the largest cities, by-and-large, commerce is carried out by a host of small businessmen who operate without standardized prices and who know no moral compunctions against excessive profiteering. They view the system as one in which an article somehow originates, and then passes through however many hands the public will tolerate on its way to the final buyer. Redundancy in trade is aptly mirrored in a superficiality of transportation modes. In passing from one distribution point to another a commodity may be reshuttled physically over the same route several times because there is no credit or invoicing system by which paper transaction might be substituted for actual handling. When such administrative mechanisms *are* worked out, the process of working them out usually highlights the repetitiveness in the whole chain of negotiation.

Rampant commercialism smothers the impulse to create. The ethic of industry is one of origination and creativity, and this stands in sharp contrast to a concept of progress through idle profiteering. To catch hold in the soil of these cultures, the philosophies of science, invention, and technological development must be systematically implanted and diligently cultivated.

Perishable commodities are lost at a high rate because of a lack of techniques for preservation. Shipping losses are further aggravated by improper packaging. An absence of food preserving facilities makes itself felt all along the line of transaction, from the grower to the consumer. The producer must harvest his produce in small quantities, get it to market with dispatch, and as it nears the spoilage stage he must sell it for whatever he can get. Correspondingly, the homemaker must carry out grocery shopping on a daily basis because there are no preserving facilities in the home. Altogether, this suppresses larger scale production and harasses seller and buyer alike.

One would expect commerce, because of its enterprising nature and head start, to take the lead in development, but brief examination discloses that it has not fulfilled this role even at the fundamental level of providing essential public utilities. Neither agriculture nor industry can develop far without some corresponding initial forward movement in the tripodal base of transportation, communication and electrification. Agriculture cannot move its produce, nor can industry secure its materials or dispense its finished goods without at least some supporting transportation. An advanced industry and agriculture depend upon prompt communications and upon a broadly available power base for illumination and motive force. Transportation, communications and electricity would appear to be the basic responsibilities of commerce, if not its natural progeny. Therefore, where commerce flourishes one would expect to find the three major public utilities in a relative state of advancement. In reality, not only does commerce fail to supply these three basics on its own, but it seems to have little influence in evoking them. A highly fractionized commerce will likely support little more than its own weight, while an effective new system of commerce will come about only as an aftermath of a beginning industrial growth.

A destitution of bureaucratization is apparent throughout the commerce of the undeveloped societies. A dearth of formally encoded regulations, and the frequent making of exceptions to the few that do exist leads to extensive graft. Public and private funds are usurped in so many different ways that the label 'white collar crime' is simply not applicable in many of these societies. Police, customs officials, and public servants, in general, are, in many countries dependent upon graft as a necessary supplement to their meagre salaries. In essence, the system is tantamount to a labyrinth of informally levied and collected surcharges in substitution of formal taxation and accounting.

In elaboration upon the foregoing, most of the technically retarded societies lack a rational tax policy. Tax systems are inequitable, the brunt of excise falling upon consumer goods rather than being based upon ability to pay. Income tax is nominal or, sometimes, non-existent, and frequently has its top bracket set below the ten per cent level of total earnings. And even this modest obligation is evaded for the most part. Annual property taxes are often levied upon the possession of radios, television sets, or electric ranges. In all, the tax revenues collected are too meagre to maintain the needed public services much less to finance technological development. Roads are usually pot-holed or in a stage of complete deterioration, schools somehow struggle along with few facilities and poorly trained teachers, and such luxuries as libraries, public parks, and universities go abegging. Taxation is a show of public responsibility which most of the backward nations are not, as yet, willing to assume.

Another taxation practice, and one worth mentioning because of its near universality, is the levy of heavy import duties on automobiles, household appliances, and similar types of goods which, in these societies are classified as luxuries. In principle, this duty would seem to fall upon those who can best afford to pay, and it would appear to fulfill a second objective of protecting domestic labor. Both assumptions are questionable. A strong case can be made for motor vehicles being essential to technological expansion, and therefore, for their being made generally available throughout the society. As for labor protection, it has become commonplace for the Western manufacturers of complex items to set up assembly plants on the importer's home soil. Parts are shipped in, and assembly is carried out by the labor of that society. In one current case, a nation of less than one and a half million in population has nine different 'automobile assembly plants.' This maneuver, which receives official encouragement, avoids the import duty and employs local labor.

But a detailed cost analysis reveals, not surprisingly, that the packaging and shipping of individual parts, and having them assembled by relatively inexperienced labor working within an inefficient setting adds at least thirty per cent to what would have been the final cost of the preassembled item before import duty was levied. This excess cost falls directly upon the public, for such usage is nothing more than a raw public subsidy of labor. Were this labor able to add to the value of the product it would be a different matter, but such is not the case.

Another trouble besetting the commerce of backward nations is an inflexible pricing of all types of commodities. The retail price is often established *not* upon the cost of production, but upon the local price of similar types of *imported* goods, or it may be pegged at some entirely arbitrary, but usually high point. Pricing at a minimum in an effort to induce volume sales is practically unheard of in some emerging societies.

In addition, there is usually a lack of a fluid credit system. Bank loans, because of short finances and frequent difficulty in collection, are usually difficult to obtain. Even the relatively simple matter of negotiating payment by check is not yet in wide vogue. Most of the peoples of undeveloped societies are unfamiliar with, and skeptical of checks, whether the check is of personal or corporate issue. Because their employees demand payment in cash, much time is spent by private concerns and public agencies in drawing and meting out cash to satisfy the weekly payroll.

Finally, the markets of most backward societies tend to emphasize the sale of luxury goods at the expense of the more utilitarian consumers' commodities and production goods. This is a symptom of elite control, a reflection of elite interests. There is often more mercantile preoccupation with the sale of foreign sports cars than with clothes washers and the other less romantic equipments for doing work. This is not to say that the latter categories are not marketed, but that the market is imbalanced relative to that found in the technologically advanced nations.

To reiterate, commerce, like agriculture, apparently is dependent upon a forerunning industrial development and cannot flourish until the society reaches a certain plateau in basic industrial productivity. Once this stage is reached, production pipeline pressures and new industry-invented methodologies will force rapid change in commerce. The discount house of the West is a direct manifestation of this condition. Thus, in most of the technically retarded societies a new and more efficient commerce must await the development of an industrial base.

EDUCATION

Although the undeveloped societies are primarily exporters of raw materials, some of them are almost altogether lacking in natural resources. When this is true, the only ready alternative is to substitute human resources, as the Swiss and Japanese have done, for natural ones. This is more easily said than done in most backward societies because training and education are so limited as to provide very little springboard from which to jump. But despite this handicap, the society that is devoid of natural resources has no choice save to jump off from 'scratch' and move forward in the cultivation of its skills as rapidly as possible.

Those societies that do have resources and a corroboratory potential for industrial development, face the somewhat different proposition of deciding priorities. Since the social objective should be to obtain the highest rate of productivity within the shortest possible time period, the equation often becomes one of balancing the cost and difficulty of training the human against the cost of installing a maximum of automata. Some experts have concluded that first priority should be given to those industries adaptable to intensive automation, that a high production goal should be given priority over education and other immediate social objectives. In fact, these people maintain that only by first creating extensive automated production will a society be enabled to build up the resources needed *for* general education. This is especially true, they contend, for those societies having a massive population, a low literacy level, and an immediate need for material alleviation. The planners who attempt to make the decision as to which should come first, material wealth or education, will run headlong into conflicting social issues.

Every society has its system of education or it would not be able to perpetuate its culture and so retain its identity. Under discussion here is education of a socio-technical type, that training most expeditious to the society's adaptation to technological change. Although some planners would minimize the importance of education to technical development, the argument usually depends upon how broadly education is defined. The ability to follow instructions in operating a simple machine, the interpretation of a blueprint, or the reading of a road map take literally years of education. Chief Sequoia of the Cherokees perceived written expression to be the real bastion of European strength and upon the basis of this conclusion he set to work to develop, successfully, an alphabet and a literature for his people's tongue. Unfortunately, in many of the transitional societies technical education must begin at about the same rudimentary level. Some languages have no means for written expression and even if graphics for them were developed, some of these languages would be ill-fitted for expressing technical ideas. The linguistic vehicles for technology have been, thus far, fairly much confined to the West, and for this reason the developing society often finds it advantageous to carry out education in a European language. However, this objective is not easily attainable because of the strong predilection in all societies for the mother tongue and its perpetuation, and the society's members do not yield easily on this point. The most basic problem of all, perhaps, lies in the facts that in most developing societies, if a major accent is to be placed on it, adult education must begin at a quite elementary level and continue for years.

Views on education grow out of culturally shaped attitudes and, therefore, may be expected to differ between, and within, societies. For example, inside Western society the Amish, in an effort to preserve in-group solidarity, have placed an astringent limit on the amount of education permitted their children. Needless to say, this is hampering their agricultural technology and degrading their ability to keep abreast with outside competition. Many emerging preliterate societies have a similar problem, and one originating at an even more basic level. Tribal elders debate whether education has even a *nominal* worth as they observe among foreigners and some of their own young what they interpret as an educationally inspired corruption of the family, religion and other institutions. Small wonder that the education-conscious West shows more concern about education in the backward society than do the society's own people.

There are conflicts in systems of education. Societies without a body of literature have a long tradition of rote learning. This is an almost impossible mode for disseminating technical information and it is a method of teaching and learning that is directly contrary to the free-roving, inventive mentality that lies at the base of technological advancement. In most backward societies, rigidly disciplined instruction and rote learning permeate the higher, as well as the lower institutions of learning. Within their colleges there is a pronounced preference for philosophical subjects over technical areas. This is a reversal of the situation in the West and is attributable to an historical preoccupation with religion and a cultural preference for dialectics over positivism.

For those students in backward society who do elect a technical education, there are the additional problems of availability of technical training facilities at both the trade school and college levels. It is almost essential that higher technical education be acquired abroad in one of the advanced societies. Such technical institutes as there are at home must teach technology in a near total industrial vacuum. Cooperative engineering training, or any other type of opportunity to gain firsthand experience with an ongoing technology, is out of the question because sufficiently extensive modern technology does not exist in the transitional society. Instruction takes on a rhetorical aspect and folk taboos against working with the hands stay in full force, thus interfering with the invaluable 'shirt-sleeve' method of practical engineering training. But in neither academic milieu, at home or abroad, will the engineering student be able to avail himself of the more generalized, liberally rounded, socio-technical education that he will later need. If he is to remain in the engineering profession in his own society, in all probability he will have to found, personally, his own industry and this will demand knowledge of marketing, finance, personnel management and training, as well as of technical management. Lacking this training and a motivation to strike out on his own, the student trained abroad returns to his society and usually, disillusioned, turns to a non-engineering type of work.

There is also the problem in many transitional societies of education's serving as a status device. Where the educated are in a tiny minority (and they usually are in these areas) education serves as a means for monopolizing social power. Because of its cost it is mainly available only to, and is associated most exclusively with, those of wealth; and it thus remains in the hands of the elite. The tendency for the elite to monopolize education sets up a resistance within this group toward disseminating higher education to the masses. They may have little quarrel with the 'practical' training proferred by trade schools, but there is a general feeling among the elite that college and university training are 'still a long way off' for the majority of the society.

UNCONTROLLED POPULATION GROWTH

Most of the world's technologically retarded areas are gaining in net population at a phenomenal rate, some as high as four per cent annually. Life expectancy, which has been estimated to have been about eighteen years during the early bronze and iron age, has almost quadrupled in the better cared for sections of the modern world so as to reach an approximate seventy years. During the past 300 years, world population has increased about sixfold. Interestingly, the great population expansion has taken place chiefly during the past three centuries and is most pronounced in those societies which, during that period, showed strong tendency toward urban aggregation.

Population pressure is a prime force agitating for technological development in the emerging areas. Somehow, and quickly, these societies must provide means for feeding, clothing, and sheltering increasing numbers of peoples. But ironically, uncontrolled population growth is also one of the chief impediments to net gains in productivity. The net production increases emanating from each year's programming are more than swallowed up by the relatively greater population increases that have occurred during the same period. The causes of population growth are but dimly understood, and attempts at control measures must contend with cultural resistence and the costs and other practical problems connected with placing contraceptive knowledge and devices within public reach.

The malnutrition that accompanies overpopulation sets up certain inertias of its own against improvement. The clamoring need to save the lower economic fringe of the society from outright starvation consumes resources that could otherwise be invested in development. Crowding and malnutrition cause a general lassitude, making it difficult to interest the population in supporting programs for technological development or to generate significant enthusiasm for any type of social change. Despair at ever achieving anything better in this life heightens the tendency to seek deeper refuge in religion, and to defer the whole issue of practical action.

There is a conflict in many traditional societies between control of family size and family values. Most of the undeveloped societies are agricultural, and agriculture has a history of encouraging family size, especially as regards male offspring. And an eventual excess of agricultural labor will not necessarily stem this philosophy and the population tide. In time, the large family becomes a value in itself, a mark of prestige and high social *status*.

There will likely be a conflict in traditional society between the birth control measures and religious values. The rationale for religious opposition will differ from one society to another and between religions. The Catholic clergy take the grimly businesslike attitude that sexual intercourse should be solely for purposes of procreation. Progeny are regarded as an expression of divine will and the process is not to be tampered with except under a few highly qualified conditions. Among the Hindus, birth control is opposed for a different reason. Religious ritual and admission to the next higher step in reincarnation demand that the father's funeral rites be presided over by a son. Under life conditions so uncertain as those under which this society lives, the best guarantee that there will be at least one son surviving the father is to allow the family to distend to maximum size. Obviously, in neither of the foregoing cases will aversion to birth control be easily overcome. These predisposing attitudes will be changed only to the extent that new value systems can be surrogated for the old. Embodied in the new framework there must be an outlook that birth control is not only permissable, but morally obligatory; and practical means for its accomplishment must be made quickly realizable.

Some students have speculated that population size among preliterate tribal peoples is regulated by natural mechanisms. There seems to be some evidence shoring up this point, and even better evidence that population did not begin to grow apace until the advent of an industrially created urbanization. Subsequent to this happening another trend set in, in which the rate of population growth began leveling roughly in coincidence with the society's state of industrial development. This is not to say that industrialization itself somehow curtails population growth, but rather that some of its concomitants, such as a higher standard of living and a raised plateau of education, begin competing with offspring. Further, education acts as a vehicle in disseminating contraceptive knowledge and techniques.

To the extent that the foregoing are valid observations, they pose still another conumdrum for the undeveloped society. The society will succeed in controlling population growth only as it progresses industrially, and it is prevented from growing industrially by uncontrolled population growth. The best that can be done is to develop the simplest, most effective, and least expensive contraceptive possible, and where permissable, place it before the public as a test of its general receptivity to grappling with this problem. Even though there is much resistance to such a program at present, there are many straws in the wind betokening a softening of attitude.

CONCLUSIONS

This, and the preceding chapter were intended to portray, generally, conditions in the technologically advanced and the transitional society but, more importantly, they were meant to dramatize the proportions to which the development problem may balloon when the observer makes the mistake of dealing with *symptom* rather than cause. An examination of the problems of these two types of societies on the usual, superficial, social and economic planes (and as they were described here) seems always to provoke in the observer the same feelings of hopelessness, and tends to produce a massively impractical patchwork of nostrums wherein each problem that is perceived is accorded its own individual solution. These 'myriad' problems appear to grow out of 'anomie,' or conflicting social conditions for whose resolution there is no agreed upon standard of ethics or guiding scientific principle. Hence, a spate of homilies to the effects that: although men and societies may behave badly, given a deeper understanding of the issue they will change their ways and act as men of good will; that increased liberal education is the key to improved understanding between men and nations; that democracy must be implanted in all the emerging nations (despite the antagonism shown toward this procedure by some of the world's leading democracies); that the democratic creed, if not the street to improved inter-group relations, will at least arrest deteriorating group relations short of the point of fratricide; that the world is inevitably headed toward an ecumenical amalgamation of political and economic systems in which there will be an ultimate surrender of the trappings of nationalism (including its obsolete power politics and supporting military anachronism), toward a union in which there is uniform fiscal policy, free trade, unrestricted migration, and eventually, world-wide prosperity. Some of these utopianisms may very well be assuming the form of future realities, but if they are, they are not drawing their substance from the familiar cliches and exhortations. They are not consciously directed movements but are mass responses to fundamental conditions which can be scientifically isolated and studied.

Development must be, and can be, carried out as a concise program with achievable goals; it can be directed by a coherent set of hypotheses. Chapters 6, 7, and 8 attempt to delineate such hypotheses and describe specific modes for applying them to development.

Part Two

OLD CONCEPTS

E

4

ECONOMIC HYPOTHESES ON DEVELOPMENT

The promotion of technological development and production in the materially retarded society raises a number of fundamental questions. What types of stimuli are most effective, and where, and how, within the structure of the developing society can they be applied? In asking these questions one is, in effect, interrogating several disciplines which have been steadily compiling data and developing theory relevant to the functioning of the economic institution in Western society. One must first ask how validly the principles propounded by these disciplines hold within their own native Western setting and, more poignantly, with what confidence may they be applied to culturally *dissimilar* societies. The two fields which dominate development planning are economics and, to a much lesser extent, the behavioral sciences.

The factors underlying development are usually sought in well defined domains. Those that have been explored most exhaustively are economics, psychology, and sociology and, to lesser degrees, history and political science. Economists seek for the seminal factors of growth in the processes of saving and spending. Psychologists supplement the work of economists by trying to get at why a particular group saves and why it invests as it does at a particular time in the overall society's history. Some psychologists purport to have found the entire key to development within the innovative personality and the processes of its formation. Sociologists look to the cultural milieu and interpret change in terms of changing relationships between groups and between institutions. A sudden social catastrophe, a general depression of status, or the slow succession of dominance of one institution over others are viewed as major interpretative factors. Historians look for broad patterns which may reveal interaction between all these individual disciplines. Political scientists, who are more lately adding their voices to those of the longer established development theorists are, of course, preoccupied with what happens with certain changes in the political climate and what predisposing factors may lead to desired political changes.

Old Concepts

CONVENTIONAL ECONOMIC VIEWPOINTS

The classical school of economics, which is generally agreed to have had its start with the treatises of Adam Smith during the latter half of the 1700s, represented the first stringent attempt to develop a set of principles which would put the study of society's economic institution on a scientific footing. The attentions of these pioneers settled upon the interplay between land, labor, and capital, and upon the market which provided the medium for their interplay. Interestingly, early classical economics was production oriented, and it adopted the thesis that maximum production was attainable through allowing land, labor, and capital to settle into a natural balance, a balance which would give long-term equilibrium to the society. This pivotal point was described by Say, a nineteenth century French economist and late contemporary of Adam Smith, as being the economic waterline at which demand for funds in the form of investment, equals the supply of funds in the form of savings. At this level, the rate of earnings from each source would be exactly the same, and society would be afloat on a long-term period of 'equilibrium' which would sustain full production and employment.[1] It was not until the Keynesian period of the present century that the counter-proposition was accepted that the relative quantities and values of investment and savings funds might stabilize at some point where they are quite *disconsonant* with one another, and might remain at this point of static disequilibrium for a long period of time. If the perspective is broadened to include underdeveloped society, the classical ratio is seldom if ever, found to exist, and for several reasons. First, there may be little conventional saving: earnings may be immediately reinvested in land, loaned at usurious interest rates or hoarded. Secondly, in many of these societies production is governed more by social custom than by economic principles. The society may be able to maintain all the production it *desires* through its established crafts and with the capital it already has on hand. Many of the early economic philosophers recognized that there were factors beyond land, labor, and capital, which played dominant roles in shaping economic behaviour. They realized that there would not be a substantive investment in production unless the society was production oriented and unless it had people with certain skills. Both of these are usually absent in the underdeveloped society. The majority of underdeveloped societies are not production oriented. Their basic interest is in trade. Their technologies have been static over the

[1] Jean Baptiste Say, *Les Finances de la France sous la Troisieme Republique* (1898–1901).

centuries and their peoples lack the skills required by modern industry and agriculture.

Modern day economic viewpoints range over an extreme from the theorists whose works are still shot through with classical overtones, to the empiricists who proceed by manipulating certain variables and then follow up with a statistical study of the effects. Adherents to the first school still accept the market as the locomotive of the economy and the businessman as its energetic but unconsciously acting driver. At the heart of the market is the concept of 'scarcity.' Scarcity exists whenever there is less than a fully satisfying supply of goods and services available. The condition of scarcity is self-perpetuating because of man's well-nigh limitless appetite for more and more. In reacting to this 'natural' scheme of things, the businessman is more of an agent *through* whom the market works than a conscious director of the market. Indeed, many of the earlier classicists held that the less thinkingly and the more reflexively the businessman acted, the more lucidly the economic system would respond. Charity, state controls, and so forth, it was believed, could only impair the natural functioning of the system.

The modern day conservative viewpoint is explained by Gitlow, in a book on economic principles, as follows:

> *Spending decisions are at the heart of the price-profit system. In aggregate, they determine the level of spending and consequently, the level of production and economic activity. In particular, they determine the specific mix of goods and services which are to be produced, the allocation of resources, and the distribution of output.*
>
> *Where does the businessman fit into this picture. He is coordinator of production. He brings together (hires) the ingredients of production and organizes them into producing units (business firms). He does this in order to get profits so that he and his household will have as much money income as he can gain with which to satisfy their wants. To win profit he takes great risk, for he hires productive agents, organizes them, and produces in anticipation of demand. If he 'guesstimates' the wants of the consumers correctly, they buy from him and thereby vote for his continuance in business. By providing the businessmen with income, the consumers expand production. If the consumers do not favor the businessman with sufficient patronage, he is driven out of production. Profits become the clue to consumer preferences.*[1]

There are several patent weaknesses in this general approach,

[1] Abraham L. Gitlow, *Economics* (Oxford University Press, 1962), pp. 10–11.

some of which were mentioned earlier. Its methodologies are slipshod because they must rest on such uncertainties as 'guesstimating consumer desires.' In an underdeveloped society many new habits of consumption will have to be learned before there will be a demand for the type of goods which Westerners consider as evidence of advancement. The economic approach described by Gitlow invests the businessman with a social responsibility that has never come up to public expectations when he has been left to operate without restraints. Indeed, unless there are some controls, free enterprise eventually becomes either anarchy or oligopoly and self interests are more likely to collide with social interests than to serve them. It is difficult to find scientific principle in a set of propositions which are dedicated to the infallibility of human shrewdness.

The empirical approach is a prime example of the modern liberal viewpoint. This approach uses the statistical method for gathering and analyzing data, and it examines these data for the presence of uniformities which may lead to certain generalizations and rules of procedure. There is much available data, for example, on the functional relationships between credits, prices, and employment. When one of these factors is changed, we have statistical knowledge of how it affects the others. The difficulty, of course, is in the identification and quantitification of the numerous variables which may be at work. While this methodology is superior to proceeding upon blind doctrine, economics still remains a body of data in search of theory. Moreover, in every economic approach, however liberal it may pretend to be, there is a lingering and inseverable dependency upon the concepts of scarcity and monetary controls. These are the lifelines without which economics loses its academic identity; and the verity of these two concepts is increasingly open to question.

FREE ENTERPRISE APPROACHES TO DEVELOPMENT

Because it was observed by eighteenth century philosophers that all societies seemed to have some method of creating, transferring, and holding goods, it was inferred by these early students that underlying these behaviours there must be economic 'laws.' So preoccupied had become early economists with these so-called laws that soon after the time of Adam Smith attention came to focus almost exclusively on the processes of distribution and consumption, with little attention going to the basic process by which goods are produced. Until recently, economics has been more of an academic exercise in the interpretation of past economic events than a program of leadership in forward-looking planning. It has been only recently that economists have been asked to point the way, to design concise and coherent development policy for the emerging nations; and it is at this point that economics has been clearly revealed as a 'shoe-box' approach. Factors which economists have singled out as being primal to development – wage rates, savings, investment, cost of operation, etc. – turn out after study to be only derivatives. They are the ever-changing by-products of deeper lying processes which themselves must be better understood before development can be intelligently directed.

Economists have been charged with making recommendations which, for many of the emerging societies for which they are intended, are unrealistic, and this has been explained by their apologists on the grounds that economic theory is peculiar to the growth and development of Western civilization and is applicable only to the problems of this group of societies. It is doubtful that it is even applicable to the West, a fact that seems to be tacitly recognized in its general omission from the planning of these same societies. Economists have occasionally, in the role of public officials, been in control of planning but there has never been an attempt at a thoroughgoing, disciplined type of economic planning. Top government policy-makers almost always have their economic advisors but because the recommendations coming from these individuals are usually conflicting and fragmentary, they are utilized or rejected at the common-sense discretion of the policy-maker. Some strike out more boldly as recently did one special adviser to a U.S. president, who bolted the musty halls of academia to lend his genius to devising strategy for the war in Vietnam. Policy-makers who themselves at one time may have been professional economists, as in the case of a late German chancellor, may be hailed for their sagacity as economists so long as they ride the crest of an unblemished prosperity, but when the tide changes or they are found wanting in ability to deal with simple social issues they may fall quickly from favor. The doctrines which have been foisted off under the name of 'economic theory' have even had something of a pernicious influence upon the world. Adam Smith, in his construct of capitalistic society and Karl Marx, in the formulation of the communist doctrine, have created conflicting dogmas which have been used to rationalize both change and maintenance of the *status quo*, and in the most militant of terms. Both dogmas are pictured as 'natural systems,' the one as an evolving ideal, blueprint for the future and the other as an immutable way of life which can be altered only with the direst of consequences to the experimenters. Both concepts were formulated within the narrow confines of economic theory and both have blinded rational analysis where such analysis has been badly and widely needed. The one aspect of economic endeavor that might be said to be benign, and even quite helpful, is the type of statistics-gathering carried out by people like Simon Kuznets. These data have been generally useful to all the social sciences.

Capital Formation

Early economists, in examining the Western industrial pattern were content that the three factors, land, labor, and capital, were all-inclusive of the economic environment. Land referred to the sum total of natural resources. Labor was the human factor which was to be defined later by Marx as the total human resource of the community and as hard-and-fast commodity bought and sold on the market. Capital was a stock concept, the goods in existence at a particular moment. Of the income accruing to a society during a given period, a certain portion may be plowed back into future production (investment) while other goods and services may be utilized within a short time after their production (consumption).

Having developed the three-fold construct of land, labor, and capital, economists next took the position that a precise value could be set for each of these relative to the other two. The stage was thus dressed and the rationalization provided for an abiding conflict between labor and capital. This scheme also became the tool for economic analysis. Its weaknesses, when it is applied to development are evident. Many of the undeveloped societies have natural resources, but they go unexploited; and most of them have an abundance of labor, but it is inefficiently utilized. The element which is missing in most undeveloped societies is production stock.

Since capital is formed out of income, it may be increased by steps which curtail consumption, or by bringing into play additional factors not presently, or at least not *properly* utilized within the society.[1] There are two general means for encouraging capital formation *without* making a reduction in consumption – the importation of capital and the employment of underutilized resources. Capital imports become of importance when the society is not able to produce capital goods in the quantity needed because of a lack of natural resources or technological abilities. In this latter case, arrangements may be made to import technical training along with the capital goods. Capital imports may be used in support of projects of a socially important nature. Using them in the construction

[1] Henry J. Burton, *Principles of Development Economics* (Englewood Cliffs, N. J.: Prentice-Hall, Inc., 1965), Chapters 9 and 10.

of dams or highways or in the development of especially promising private industries are cases in point. Imported in critical areas, capital from abroad may serve as a stimulus in opening up new types of domestic enterprise and in drawing forth domestic investment that otherwise would not be made.

The drawbacks to importing capital are formidable. First, it is extremely difficult to attract funds, loans, or equipment in any appreciable quantity from foreign sources. Secondly, out-of-pocket purchases for capital imports soon create, within most of the developing countries, a balance of payment strain.

Because most of the developing countries have a conspicuous oversupply of labor, attempts are frequently made to utilize this resource in capital formation. Since the oversupply of labor is most abundant in the rural areas, these sections lend themselves particularly well to grand-scale projects. Laborers can be marshalled on a national scale and paid through allowing them to substitute work for the annual payment of taxes. Roadways, and water control projects, such as canals, can be carried out at relatively low costs since the laborers will ordinarily work within commuting distance of their regular places of residence. In way of a generally *more effective* utilization of capital stock, improved work procedures and the addition of one or more additional work shifts will aid in more fully exploiting the capital which the society already has on hand.

As economists view the proposition, the surest route for forcing growth in saving, investment, and consequently, capital formation is through a reduction in consumption. Inasmuch as most of the developing nations are already living submarginally, this is a harsh prescription, indeed. The surest method of saving is through taxation, but taxes are difficult to raise in the backward areas and the policy mechanisms of these governments are usually irrational and distrusted by the population. Attempts may be made to encourage private saving and investment by persuasion but this presumes a relatively high literacy level among the population, an ability to appreciate the relationship between investment and national growth, and in general a sophistication and a confidence in government generally not found in the emerging society. Another feature that is felt to contribute substantially to saving is the payment of higher rates of interest.

The foregoing methods of enforcing saving are, in general, non-inflationary. Saving can also be enforced by making inflation a deliberate policy, through steadily raising price levels to force a curtailment of consumption, thus freeing additional resources for capital formation. Inflation, in this situation, means controlled price increases of relatively short duration, and somewhat in excess of two per cent per annum. There are several ways in which to trigger inflation. An inflationary wave may be excited by a governmental action which simply prints more money and places it in government coffers. Another method is to lower the interest rates on investment loans. These new circulating funds now begin competing with consumer goods so as to cause the production of goods to fall behind. As output in the consumer industries falls, a production of capital goods increases; and, as long as wage increases can be made to trail well behind price increases, the process of capital formation will continue.

There are several dangers latent in the deliberate use of inflation to encourage capital formation. One of these is the ever-present possibility that the inflation cannot be controlled. It may continue to spiral and do little more than increase wage rates. The more ambitious the policy attempted through inflation, the greater the danger, since the longer the inflationary period persists the more difficult it becomes to control it. Additionally, maintaining a stable balance of payments is one of the most difficult propositions facing an emerging society, a problem that will invariably be greatly aggravated by any inflationary trend. These negative possibilities, which will usually be magnified by a maladroit fiscal management found in most of these societies, should be cause for serious deliberation before making inflation a deliberate policy instrument.

Whatever the method used for encouraging saving, it is equally important that investment opportunity be *made apparent* to the members of the society and that investment be encouraged in those industries showing the highest potentials for growth and the promotion of general economic health. Thus, new industries that may help spearhead the development of whole new sectors which are of great potential value to the society may be opened up by government aid and programming and may be made more favourable investment areas by various types of announced government subsidies such as tariff exemptions, tax exemptions, etc. Established sectors already showing a rapid growth rate may be similarly singled out and, through government patronage, made more inviting opportunities for investment.

Limitations of Capital Formation Hypotheses

The foregoing are generally agreed upon by seasoned economists as basic procedures for development. But unfortunately, they have done little to promote capital formation, and for several reasons. First, capital growth implies the acquisition of machines and unless the society has a predisposing interest in, and knowledge of machines it is unlikely that this vital element of capital will ever be formed. If it should be formed by importation from sources outside the society, there will be no internal base by which to sustain it and the makeshift system that results will sooner or later collapse.

Economists, however, since they are mainly unconcerned with technology and the production process, tend to point to other and more strictly economic factors as the cause of failure in capital formation in the undeveloped society. Most of these factors are so circularly related in a concatenation of cause and effect as to appear almost irremedial. The failure of capital to form is not viewed as disinterest or reluctance on the part of individuals to invest, but rather as due to a dearth of investment funds. Because wage rates in these societies are depressed there can be no surpluses. Because industries are small production flows at a low ebb, and because of this worker productivity is too low to allow substantial profits for the enterprise which, in turn, must reward its labor at a low wage rate. Low income and low productivity recycle into one another to perpetuate a poverty condition. Still another negative factor is introduced into the analysis, and that is the feebleness of the domestic market, its inability to absorb the output of domestic production when such output appears in any appreciable, mass-produced quantity.

There is little doubt that these factors are cyclically related, although the situation is not as extreme as economists usually represent it to be. Even the poorest societies apparently accrue a surplus, an excess which is invested in land, let out as short-term, high-interest loan, etc., but almost never allowed to find its way into production facilities. The elite of undeveloped society are unquestionably profit makers. It is estimated that as an average, about five per cent of a society accrues approximately forty per cent of its annual income. Although it is maintained that this group has a tendency to indulge in profligate living in imitation of the standards of the rich of the Western industrial societies, the extent to which they dissipate funds in this way is highly debatable. It *is* well established that this same group does tend to bank abroad, to invest in the stocks of Western industry, and to otherwise display rather conservative behaviours. The question of why some of the elite will aid in the formation of capital abroad but refuse to aid the development of their own societies is a poignant one. Moreover, savings are not confined entirely to the rich. Even the poorer classes of the emerging society are known to accrue annual surpluses. There is some evidence that the rate of saving of one class relative to another is approximately the same regardless of the absolute wealth of the society.[1]

Another impediment to development which is often cited by economists is the lack of 'social overhead capital' in the emerging society. By social overhead capital is meant those basic facilities which serve all industries as well as agriculture and which are presumed by many to be essential pre-conditions for general growth on all fronts. General communications, transportation facilities, hydroelectric power, and such related features as water management are considered by some to be prerequisites for any meaningful development program.

A general lack of facilities, low productivity, and low flow of income in the emerging societies has created a few champions for the type of development program referred to as the 'big push.' This is a concerted, all-out drive to achieve a totality of development goals which it is felt would never be attained by piecemeal approaches. Advocates of this type of programming believe that this is the only way by which to get all the needed social overhead facilities in place and to instill in the population a confidence in, and a personal dedication to promoting national growth. The 'big push' substitutes action for theory. Unable to formulate a sound approach it attempts to accomplish everything, and probably will achieve little or nothing. This philosophy is unmindful of the fact that for a single developing country of moderate size and population the funds needed for a big push program would exceed the combined total of the world's annual development assistance loans and grants. Its operating costs for one year would be crushing, and if it were to be sustained until it caught hold, that is, until the society developed enough conversancy with technology to sustain forward movement, the big push might have to be maintained at full heat for at least two decades. The big push approach also ignores the moral that Western technological growth took place, not in one fell sweep, but in piecemeal fashion. Obviously, England's social overhead capital was not in existence at the beginning of the industrial revolution, but she somehow managed to move ahead and to build it as she progressed.

There is fairly strong unanimity among economists as to the best methods for forming capital but there is little consistency of opinion concerning the relationship of capital formation to such other non-economic variables as innovation. Furtado insists that a sound theory of development must rest on an explanation of the process of accumulation of capital and that the 'backbone of development lies *not*

[1] James S. Duesenberry, *Income, Saving and the Theory of Consumer Behavior* (Cambridge, Mass.: Harvard University Press, 1949).

in innovation but in capital accumulation.'[1] He points out that innovation is not a pure and simple matter in itself, but that it demands a set of conditions making it economically justifiable. He points out that despite the world's long historical acquaintance with the automatic loom, hand looms are still in widespread use in some economies and the automatic loom will probably not enjoy preference in these groups until *wages* (italics mine) reach a level justifying it. He believes that even machine-design improvements, as an outgrowth of research financed by universities and other institutions, have a hidden social cost that is not always apparent in the market price. The implication is that innovation does not well up spontaneously but must be paid for, and it cannot be attended until the society first has an operating, productive capital. On the other hand, Robert Solow concluded (and his study is supported by at least one other) that from the period 1909 to 1949, between eighty-seven and ninety per cent of the increase in output per man hour in the United States was due to 'technological progress,' with not more than thirteen per cent of this increase being creditable to an expansion of capital.[2]

The Search for Entrepreneurship

The economists following this approach have abandoned the bare bones of economic doctrine in a search for something more akin to a personality cult. However, the vision of leadership typically entertained by these writers is a sterile one and is fairly aptly described in a text by Williamson and Buttrick.[3] These authors developed the theme that labor, capital, and natural resources are necessary to produce an income in any area, but without that catalytic spark provided by the entrepreneur they are not sufficient. They state that 'in bringing into use the techniques which will bring an adequate income from a group of resources, someone has to make the decisions required to institute new methods in place of old.' In the light of this definition, technological progress becomes more a matter of decision-making than invention. Borrowing from Schumpeter, they define *entrepreneurs* as those who substitute 'new combinations' as opposed to those who institute new combinations but bear no responsibility

[1] Celso Furtado, *Development and Underdevelopment* (Berkley and Los Angeles: University of California Press, 1964), p. 51.

[2] Robert M. Solow, 'Technical Change and the Aggregate Production Function' *Review of Economics and Statistics*, Vol. XXXIX (August, 1957), pp. 312–320.

[3] Harold F. Williamson and John A. Buttrick, *Economic Development* (Englewood Cliffs, N. J.: Prentice-Hall, Inc., 1954), pp. 196–241.

for the results. The latter are mere *innovators*. Entrepreneurs may or may not act as managers. Even though they may *not* act in a managerial capacity, the fact that they represent final authority in the selection of managers confers upon them a vital role in their enterprises. In fact, say the authors, 'They may make no other decision except to hire one manager rather than another,' and 'only to the extent that we want change not simply for the sake of change but in order to get a greater yield of wanted ends are entrepreneurs required.' The argument continues that when managers, rather than entrepreneurs, control large enterprises there is a potent competitive check, in that, unless the managers conduct a business profitably, a new entrepreneurial group may obtain control and replace them with a new and more aggressive management. The history of invention strikingly illustrates 'the greater difficulties of bringing an invention to economic fruition than those of overcoming the initial technical problems.'

The preceding is such a hackneyed set of propositions as scarcely to deserve reexamination. Many underdeveloped societies are cursed with a plethora of private entrepreneurs. These are technologically uninventive societies in which there has been little procedural change over hundreds of years and where every action must be kept in careful accord with convention. In modern corporate enterprise the entrepreneurs are many, they are often divided and, almost always, a rather anonymous group. It is, in fact, the engineers and the resident managers who innovate and who make basic decisions and who, as did the top executive of a leading U.S. mail ordering house, occasionally make a radically wrong decision. The small entrepreneur who also doubles as a manager, although he was doubtlessly a potent factor in the earlier development of Western society, is now becoming an increasingly rare and competitively impotent specimen. The small entrepreneur is simply unable to compete with the innovative ingenuity and broad scale plans made and carried out by the corporate management group.

Recent Empirical Trials

The progenitor of the greater number of the world's development programs has been the United States, and nowhere has the U.S. had a greater interest in development than in nearby and politically volatile Latin America. U.S. support has ranged from direct financial involvement to informal patronage, and whether programming has been carried out under the auspices of the United Nations, the

United States, or directly by Latin American governments, it has been of a typical economic type. There are three prominent Latin America development programs, all of which are still in being and are representative of the economic approach. One of these is a program under the aegis of the United Nations' Economic Commission. The other two are the Latin American Free Trade Association and the Alliance for Progress.

The United Nations' Economic Commission for Latin America has been under the direction of economist Raul Prebisch. His first step was to establish a program objective and this was settled upon as the achievement of a 5·6 per cent annual growth in the gross national product. This goal was somewhat arbitrarily taken as the maximum speed at which the Latin countries might be expected to advance. Because Prebisch shared Myrdal's apprehensions of the possible consequences of trade relationships between the emerging societies and the big outside powers, and because the Latin countries did not possess sufficient internal resources for development, he quite logically arrived at the notions of forming a consolidated Latin trade bloc, and utilizing foreign borrowing to the utmost. In Colombia, where the program is claimed to take on its sharpest focus, the basic method settled upon to form capital was to obtain increased investment. However, two factors thwarted this prospect. There simply was not enough saving available in the general population, and the elite, who were in possession of about fifty per cent of the country's income, could not be made to invest by any means short of coersion. Heavy annual U.S. loans were quickly dissipated by being shunted directly to the offices instrumental in promoting public services and in improving the productivity of agriculture; in the end they were discovered to have made no visible contribution to capital addition. The plan was further caught between the crossfires of stimulating technological innovation in agriculture; and moving excess agriculture workers off the land and yet avoiding having them aggregate in the urban areas where they would become displaced persons in the same sense that they were in the agriculture community. It was felt by these programmers that it would be necessary to break the hold of the elite by the expropriation of lands below their market values, with repayment deferred and at low interest. Latin America desperately needs capital goods but can obtain these only through the sale of primary products, the foreign demand for which lags significantly behind their own need for imported capital. Hence the United Nations' program fell back upon the strategies of forming a defensive Latin trade bloc and obtaining a maximum of foreign aid. As it stands, the program is frozen to a null position and there it will probably remain.[1]

The Latin American Free Trade Association was formed originally as a counterpart to the highly successful European Common Market bloc. But it is far easier to form a harmonious trade community when the participant members are in good economic health. For Latin America as a whole, it is estimated that upwards of one-half of the total work force is *not* engaged in real employment and that the capital facilities which they possess are in operation only one-quarter of the time. Each Latin member nation is ambitious for economic self-sufficiency, each is intent upon duplicating in a miniature system the entire range of industries and services found in the large and technologically advanced societies, and each is bent upon giving maximum protection to its own domestic producers. In addition, each of the Latin member countries is beset with inflation and must undergo subsequent currency devaluations, and each operates on a somewhat precarious balance of trade.

The Latin American Free Trade Association is not a concise development program but a catch-all which was conceived to maintain domestic prices and to obtain a more favorable inter-regional ecological balance. Although it is undoubtedly a step in the direction of both these objectives, its individual members will not develop strength without a more concise and workable development program, and until this state is realized the association will be a case of the halt leading the blind.

The alliance for Progress is primarily a U.S. spending program in Latin American countries. It is comprised of a patchwork of ill-defined objectives and vague suggestions to the recipient countries that they carry out internal reform. The guiding philosophy of the Alliance is that while aiding funds will come from the United States, the real effort to secure improvement must come from within the member country. This 'hands-off' attitude on the part of the United States is partially prompted by a fear that more positive measures would stir cries of 'intervention.' Although many of the U.S. proponents concede that it is a program that lacks defined objectives, it is nonetheless, felt that its funds will filter through to augment Latin capital and to enhance agriculture and the social services of the member nations.

Strangely, economist-planners seem to have no other critics save other economists, who usually urge some minor variation upon the same old tired formulae. The more aggressive administrators within the aid-granting nations win the argument from their less certain

[1] *The Economic Development of Latin America and Its Principal Problems*, Economic Commission for Latin America, Lake Success, N.Y., 1950.

colleagues that greater attention should be given to raising the state of technology in underdeveloped agriculture, to mobilizing labor resources more effectively and, thus, making fuller utilization of capital. The general economic approach seems to be a three-step one of, first, instituting mild central controls to provide the social overhead services needed, with, secondly, an anticipation of small individual gains from a welter of privately competing small entrepreneurs, and finally, a hoped-for governmental system which by taxation and social legislation will make some mild redistribution of national income.

THE CENTRALLY CONTROLLED APPROACH TO DEVELOPMENT

It was inevitable that classical economics in its moralization of the impersonal process of profit-making should be challenged eventually by a counter-doctrine which moralized the highly personal attributes of human labor. Thus, the cold economy of Adam Smith's market place, which was 'thing' centered, amoral, uncontrollable, and immutable, was to find its adversary a century later in Marxian ideology, which was 'person' centered, moralistic, and which maintained that the economic system was controllable and governed by laws of social change. It was as though Marx had begun his work by deliberately reversing the tenants of the capitalistic model, as though he had methodically listed each of its key features and then had placed in juxtaposition to each of them a polar opposite, drawing many of these antitheses and their counter-rationalizations from the theory of classical economics. Marx's theory of 'economics' was a peculiar blend of ethics, social reform and classical thought, but, because he chose to wage the better part of his battle within the teapot of economic theory, Marx's works are most properly classified as economics.

The forcefulness of Marx's observations lay in the original use that he made of the historical method of economic analysis. A series of deductions was shortly to lead him to the basic proposition which was to become the hub of most of his later work, that economic production is a *social* fact which gives form to the relationships between the various factors of production and that these relationships become altered relative to one another as the production system grows. While the classical economists viewed the capitalist system as an end-point in economic evolution, Marx looked upon it as a transitory stage which would be driven by its inner contradictions to an eventual form of state control under which the hold of the bourgeoisie would be eliminated and the worker would become master of his own destiny. As a supporting conceptual tool, Marx seized upon classical labor theory, bending it to support the hypothesis of surplus value. By defining labor as the entire labor fund existing within a community and by giving it the status of a commodity that is bought and sold on the market, he was able to make labor an all-inclusive production factor. Labor treated in this way became the sole creator of value, thus the extent by which the net worth of product exceeds the wages necessary for its creation may be considered a surplus value. Under capitalism this surplus does not return to the work community but is diverted by the entrepreneur who may use it in securing further production. Since these investment funds have been expropriated from the worker, saving and investment must be considered a 'sacrifice' made by the work community rather than by the capitalist.[1] This argument inferentially blocks the notion that capital adds in any way whatsoever to the value of a product. Technological growth enters the picture as a factor augmenting the worker's capabilities and allowing him to greatly increase his output, but the direct value contributed by labor remains the all-important factor. Whatever the increase in productivity, this swell is due solely to the labor input.

With this economic undershoring, Marx next turned his attentions to the development of a doctrine of social class struggle. He saw this struggle as lying in the conflicting interests between those holding a monopoly on the physical facilities of production and those compelled to sell their labor services for a price that could, and would, eventually be driven down to a level of mere subsistence. Conflict of interests was to provide the dynamic force moving the society through the capitalistic stage to a final breakdown and disappearance of the system. The basis for class antagonisms, described briefly, were an increase in the facilities of production, by capitalists, which would lead to steadily lowered wages and unemployment in the worker group. Capital would be accumulated out of the expropriated surplus value diverted from labor, but behind this growth the most potent factor in increased productivity would be technological progress. Marx foresaw in innovation the potential for creating a whole 'industrial reserve army' with which labor would have to compete on steadily lowering wage terms. Meantime, as the worker grew poorer, capitalism would steadily increase its wealth under the stimulus of growingly intensive competition for domestic markets, and, finally, it would fatten still further upon international markets which, incidentally, would not be possessed without an inter-capitalistic struggle. Since intensified competition would

[1] *Capitol*, Vol. I, from the English text prepared by Engels and reprinted in 1954.

appear to lead to declining profits, it was held that in the twilight preceding their eclipse capitalists would resort to a stepped-up accumulation of capital in order to extend the mass profit, that they would exploit more exhaustively domestic labor, and finally they would export capital to the colonies in order to situate in a surrounding offering cheaper labor and natural resources.

Marx looked upon technological growth as the outcome of conflict between the worker and capitalist classes. Marx's belief that it was a natural, inescapable historical foreordainment that these two groups were meant to take form and grapple was no more realistic than his supposition that in time one of the two would prevail and the conflict would be resolved. The labor-management conflict that has threaded through Western technological growth may have been due to the peculiar social setting in which Western technology had its beginnings, and certainly need not have its counterpart in the development of the newly emerging society. Marx's position that any increase in productivity, however great, must be construed as solely due to labor's effort and should be adjudged labor's reward, stands as a strangely barren ethnocentrism in this dawning day of the automatic factory and a disappearing labor force.

LATER SCHOOLS OF ECONOMICS

Late in the nineteenth century, economics gave birth to a new school, the neo-classicists. This group, perceiving that classical economics had armed the socialist movement with its most potent weapon in a wage theory which foresaw man as being gradually displaced by a technological movement which left him no opportunity for self-defense, struck out to repair the breach by the introduction of the notion of growth in the marginal productivity of labor and the thesis that the supply of capital would grow more rapidly than the population. It was reasoned that labor's marginal productivity would expand, and along with it, real wages. The pace of capital increase would be set by the expected profits returned by new capital and the availability and interest rate of savings. The greater the prosperity accruing to the capitalist class, the higher the real income and the greater the welfare enjoyed by labor. But should labor costs bite too deeply into the production process, a stagnant economy would result. If capital is not rewarded there will be no incentive toward investment and no accumulative addition to capital.

The neo-classicists' preoccupation with the investment process as being, in part, an act of spirited citizenship, bridged over to the ascription by Schumpeter and others of a special development role to entrepreneurship. Schumpeter foresaw in innovation a dynamic which would give the economy a momentum forestalling the possibility of stagnation. In this viewpoint there was a universal human penchant for entrepreneurship, and potential profit would supply to the entrepreneur the incentive for innovating.[1] Unfortunately, Schumpeter's definition of innovation as being the creation of a situation which would lead to profits, establishes an excessively broad definition of innovation. Many of the methods leading to increased profits may contribute little to technological growth or may be, in fact, anti-technological.

In a final attempt to rescue labor theory, Keynes, in his turn, also addressed this subject. Throwing the traditional principle of supply and demand aside, Keynes sought for other and more fundamental factors in maintaining a dynamic level of employment.[2] He found the stabilizer in 'effective demand' but he deduced that effective demand in turn rested upon the psychology of saving and investment. Effective demand is that quantity of product that the market can absorb at a given price. Since consumption recycles directly into further production, Keynes was not concerned with the behaviour of this variable but rather with that portion of income that is not consumed or invested, but instead, is placed in idle saving. Thus, Keynes surmised that when the incentives to investment were not sufficient to drain off total savings, unemployment would result. And incentive to invest would be determined by the expected rates of profit and interest. The Keynesian school thus made the full turn of theory and found itself in a position in many respects similar to that of the early classical school of economics. Finding the key to creating savings, forcing these into investment, and inducing the society to respond to the profit motive remain today, as they were with the earlier schools, the major preoccupation of development economists.

CONCLUSIONS

Now and again, one hears among economists the softly whispered heresy, 'Is King Capital dead?' The answer: 'In actuality he never really lived. He was more of a shade, a synthetic conjured up out of Adam Smith's world to briefly strut his day and then to vanish.'

[1] J. A. Schumpeter, *The Theory of Economic Development* (Cambridge, Harvard University Press, 1951).

[2] J. M. Keynes, *The General Theory of Employment, Interest and Money* (London, 1947).

Even fewer make so bold as to ask, 'Is labor a dispensable factor in production?' The answer: 'Labor is a dying commodity. Present day production systems are slowly squeezing it out of existence and the factory of the future will work without it.' One-by-one, each of the three synthetics – capital, labor, and land – will topple, and as it does, domino-fashion it will lead to the collapse of the others. What will be the fate of land, the last of the triumvirate? Land, as a value will probably fall victim to the radical general decline in values that will accompany massive production, but it will probably leave behind debris which will continue to impede production until cleared away by social legislation.

It was only natural that a short time after the onset of the industrial revolution there should be strong interest in explaining this unprecedented new phenomenon. It was a socially precarious movement which brought along with its obvious benefits equally apparent and massive social abuses. Early economists were more successful in rationalizing the system than in explaining it, and the rationalizations that devolved fell upon an eager and affluent audience so that economics quickly became an accepted part of the established academic community. Unfortunately, because they were fated to live with the concepts that were bequeathed them by their founding fathers, or else disappear, economists have held to those earlier day postulates with remarkable tenacity. Adam Smith, in reifying the marketplace as the god-head of his system, gave economics a slant that was to preclude economists from legitimately giving attention to the production processes. Since production was supposed to be regulated automatically by the forces of the marketplace, the interests of economists came to center upon the behaviours of the market, and their energies were consumed in trying to unravel the unknowns of distribution and consumption. This established a theoretical drift which has persisted on through the post-Keynesian period to the present day. It is easy for academicians from other fields to urge that economists give more attention to the place of technology in the growth process, or that they make more intensive analyses of the psychological foundations of consumption, but the fact of the matter is that if economists were to invade these already inhabited fields they would lose their identity as economists.

In the period following World War II economists were called upon for the first time to provide a total and comprehensive approach to development planning. And they have been forced to respond with hypotheses which are not only anachronistic, but inherently impotent. The concept of economic *planning* is self-defeated at its very outset by economics' espousal of the idea that the economic system is a naturally self-generating, internally self-regulating system that operates best under a relatively complete *laissez-faire* condition.

In case after case, economists view the main issue in development as being the formation of capital and, consequently, they see the main problem facing the emerging society as that of stimulating the flow of funds necessary to finance capital expansion. They describe indirect methods by which the society's financial glands may be massaged somehow to obtain development funds but they seem to be unable to provide definite guidelines as to how the resulting funds, if any, should be spent. If successful in tapping off wealth into capital channels, economists assume that this golden flow will axiomatically go into investment, that it will surely initiate and sustain technological growth. As was pointed out earlier, the claim that there are *no* savings in the underdeveloped society is, in part, myth, but that there is little capital investment is painfully true. Historically, many societies have, through conquest, amassed great savings but, as in the case of Spain and Portugal who had held great riches only a short time preceding the initiation of the industrial revolution in England, bare wealth by no means automatically serves as the instrument for capital formation; or if it did would it necessarily create the right kind of capital. That there is a lack of cogency in the capital argument is further evidenced in the wide disagreement between economists as to the respective importance of innovation and capital additions. If one researcher discovers that eighty-seven per cent of the technological growth occuring in a given time interval is due entirely to innovation, while, on the other hand, other mature scholars are equally insistent that production increases are almost entirely attributable to capital additions, then, obviously, concentrated research is warranted in this area and the results should be of considerable significance in shaping planning policy.

In most of the emerging societies, the sources for capital formation are thought to be surpluses occurring in agriculture or industry, or from personally held wealth. In reality, the first two channels usually will be largely dry, and the third one, also inadequate, will be almost impossible to tap for political reasons. And yet, all three must be tapped if there is to be a later possibility for satisfying the economic conventions of making profits through the operation of a healthy market, of garnering wage income for investment purposes, or of paying an acceptable rate of interest to investors. An inability to start the technological process rolling has placed economists in the contradictory position that a society will be able to form capital only *after* it has achieved wealth.

The blind insistence of economists on maintaining a high level of employment in the developing society is a most perplexing thing. The maintenance of full employment, or for that matter the absorption of any sizeable proportion of the work force is a lost cause and, like its foregoing sister concepts, an anachronistic holdover. It promps economic students of the underdeveloped society to suggest a massive redistribution of the agricultural work force in order to obtain a productive relationship between labor and capital facilities. To achieve this probably would require an unbelievably brutal type of social coercion. As it happens, there are already urban migration trends underway in the developing societies which are carrying growing numbers of agricultural workers to metropolitan centers. Here, they simply over-crowd and form the same obstruction to useful production that they did in agriculture. This leads to still other suggestions that they be induced to migrate to village-sized population centers and to engage in hand-craft types of industry which better utilize their potentials. Or that they remain in their former locations but be reassigned to carrying out socially useful tasks such as the building of highways, dams, or other types of social capital. Here again, even the most massive work force cannot compete on acceptable terms with the great construction machines of modern technology. When crude labor is addressed to these types of projects the costs are high, whether they be direct or indirect, the completion of the project is long delayed, and the final product is inferior. Moreover, if any moral may be drawn from the development of the Western societies it should demonstrate clearly that not only is the blue collar work force, in general, dwindling, but for those who remain the per capital output has increased enormously and solely due to technological improvement.

Yet, typical of the economic viewpoint is the reaction of an economist upon viewing a highly mechanized and efficient synthetic fiber plant in a Latin American country. This observer deplored the fact that in the same city he counted in one block no fewer than twenty-one able-bodied men who were employed shining shoes. On the superficial assumption that situation 'A' was the direct cause of condition 'B,' this observer called for a 'changed calibration of the system,' a system which he felt had been distorted in an irrational manner. He drew a distinction between the efficiency of an individual enterprise and the efficiency of the economic system as being things apart. 'The efficiency of the firm is a splendid thing. But infinitely more important in dealing with the economics of developing countries is the efficiency of the economic system in making the best use of available resources – human, natural, and man-made. The profit motive continues to work to the end that in each plant fewer people can produce more goods. What is not working is the mechanism for picking up the released people (and millions more) and putting them to equally useful, remunerative work.'[1] This reasoning is blissfully oblivious to the facts that unneeded labor, whatever the circumstances under which it is employed, is always supported by public subsidy, and that it usurps finance that might be utilized for further production, and wastes its own time.

The deliberate cultivation of labor in this machine age, however backward the setting in which it is attempted, can only result in restriction and increased costs of production. A socially rational solution, such as placing purchasing power directly in the hands of the consumer without first forcing him into the unnecessary relationship of wage earner, evokes a highly irrational reaction from economists, who must now defend their system on bare *moral* grounds. Burton sums up this position very nicely with the baleful observation that, 'If there is literally nothing that can be produced with the available labor because of technological reasons, then there is nothing more to say except advise the population to immigrate or to obtain foreign help.'[2] This reasoning leads to a madness which would recommend for a fully automated society that everyone except the few who owned an interest in the production facilities should resign themselves to sure starvation because, although they lived surrounded by unparalleled plenty, they could not be gainfully employed.

The strongest indictments that can be brought against economic thinking is the basic irrationality of its concepts and an insistence that these ideas inter-relate to form a 'system.' The idea of making profits is itself a social peculiarity, a behavioral pattern existing in only certain parts of the world. If the drive for profits were the universal incentive its advocates claim it to be, it would seem that this great force would have long since revolutionized the backward nations. The viewpoints that profits create wealth, and that wealth is a natural route to social power can be contested by pointing out that in many societies there is a lack of interest in wealth, and that power can be seized by simpler and much more direct means. Even in the advanced society, economic advantage will be readily relinquished when more direct avenues to power are opened. The surrender by corporation executives of high private salary for top

[1] Lauchlin Currie, *Accelerating Development* (New York: McGraw-Hill Company, 1966), p. 56.

[2] Henry J. Burton, *Principles of Development Economics* (Englewood Cliffs, N.J.: Prentice-Hall, Inc., 1965), p. 130.

ranking but relatively low paying government jobs are prime examples. The notion of profit is, even in the Western mind, too intangibly associated with other needs to make it a compelling motivator. Western workers have foresworn the opportunity for greater income in preference for a shorter work-week and increased leisure (personal freedom). If the profit motive applied at the individual level, then it would seem that it would have to apply at the group level. How, then, to explain the squandering of productively investable wealth on types of warfare that cannot conceivably bring commensurate economic returns? If the struggle were solely for markets, why is it that after the conflict ends, trade relations usually revert to relatively free international competition? If the struggle were for a permanent monopoly of markets, and if the contending societies were of nearly equal strength and were 'economically rational,' they would compromise through maximizing their benefits by a peaceful division of markets.

A total economic orientation, if such a state were attainable, would create a rigidity of social structure more repugnant than that depicted in Aldous Huxley's *Brave New World*, which at least allowed its subjects some room for emotional reaction, even though synthetically supplied. If a society were to degrade its mentality to the extent of responding fully and predictably to the profit motive, this would soon create a set of conundrums and a social architecture which would make economists (who are after all social beings with strongly implanted non-economic values) blanch. First, wealth as it is presently defined would largely disappear in a profit-inspired economy. In an effort to maximize profits, the society would logically cut its expenditures for consumers' goods to a bare minimum, plowing its excess income back into production facilities. These facilities are obvious instruments of value in that they can be used to create still further value. Hence the profit-minded society would live in a Spartan simplicity which it could otherwise achieve, by proper planning, with the expenditure of very little time or effort. But, since the society is profit-directed, it will frenetically go about the creation of more and more production capital. At a certain level in productivity, however, it will be forced to change its trade policy. A society can go only so far in producing production equipment and then it must initiate the creation of consumer goods, a point which our developing society has awaited anxiously. It may now release a flood of consumer goods, goods which it has no interest in absorbing and which it will, therefore, release on foreign markets (an eventuality already planned for). The profit-minded society will consolidate its advantage by a refusal to export production capital (a policy hewed to an early industrial England and still guardedly carried on by the West) and by taking raw materials in return for its finished products. In the process, it will buy its raw materials on the underdeveloped market on terms even lower than the usual ones because the costs of processing raw materials are clearly visible to the outside buyer, and local suppliers can be set into intensive competition with one another (also a situation having familiar overtones). In return, since the foreign buyers do not have production facilities and do not know how to develop them, and because the costs of production are not evident they will be forced to pay the maximum for finished goods.

Having attained this situation, the profit-oriented society will be in somewhat the position of a colony of bees who have successfully launched an enterprise for the manufacture of synthetic vinegar. There will be few liquid assets. Rather than be left idle, income will be immediately reinvested to form further production capital. There would be no durable goods except those explicitly aiding in profit-making, such as news media for broadcasting marketing and business information. Private transportation probably would not exist, nor, as city planners recommend, would they be replaced by a more economical public transportation. Instead, individuals would more likely live on a second floor built over the factory in which they worked. Since it is more economical to manage people in larger groups, and because the spirit of economic competition being pervasive as it is will also inflame the female population to strike out for itself, the family will give way to communal living arrangements. Schooling would be completed early so as not to impede the individual's economic life and it would consist altogether of technical and business training. Music and the arts, to the extent that they were cultivated at all, would be services sold abroad because they would be expensive luxury items that had to be sold, not consumed.

However, before the society ever reaches the happy state just described, it will encounter a number of obstacles on the road. First, none of the members of the profit-oriented society would be willing to work for wages. As everyone knows, wage earners never become rich. All would insist on a share of the net profits arising out of the sale of those things they produced. Being rational men, they would accept the fact that individuals differ in their capacity to contribute to the process of wealth making, but because this difference is not really as great as it appears to be to irrational men, and because of the practical difficulties of awarding each his exact due, the society would undoubtedly communize its entire production process. Since the family already will have been communized, this will provide a convenient base for the step to full communism, and the gains in efficiency made by this step to full collectivization would be enormous.

Internal difficulties notwithstanding, the profit-minded and now communized society would, sooner or later, run into problems in its external trade relations. It would discover, to its chagrin, that since the profit motive was universal it was no more confinable to given nationalities or race than it had been to the male sex. Trouble would soon start brewing in the foreign market, for the poorer but rational foreign trade partner, having run the profiteering society into tight trade interdependency, and perceiving its psychological inabilities to consume its own products or to stop production so long as any margin of profit whatever remained, would now begin a ruthless campaign of his own to drive down the cost of imported consumer goods and to raise the price of his primary products. He would maintain this position of advantage so long as his wants remained relatively simple and within his abilities to control them. With this last point in mind, the foregoing trend might be expected to prevail until the profits in finished goods were reduced to a pittance and the emerging society became relatively rich in consumer goods, meantime managing to maintain a respectable distance from the grime and labor of the production complex which it now indirectly controlled. Nor would there be much chance that the producing society could redress this injustice, because it will have no armed force. It would lack a military establishment, not just because soldiery is a morally degrading way of life, but, because a military establishment could not be demonstrated, however extreme the national predicament, to contribute to profits.

The foregoing was not meant to depict what *would* happen within the fully profit oriented society, but what *could* happen. In actuality there never has been such a society although there have been numerous instances of 'barracks' subcultures, usually agricultural, living under conditions fully as austere as those just pictured. The reigning motive, however, usually has been religious, never economic. What *will* happen within a given society is unpredictable outside the contexts of its evolving history and present behavioral systems.

It was perhaps inevitable that Western technology should come about as it did. The system of exploitation setting its background had pre-existed for centuries. It mattered not that the patricians were joined by a newly emerging class of exploiters, the bourgeoises, the pattern itself had already been set in the feudal relations between patrician and serf. Nor was it necessarily true that the industrial revolution worsened the plight of the masses. Under industrialization the peasant moved physically from the land to the urban factory setting, but socially, his position was at least no worse, and probably better, than it had been before. The difference lay in the fact that under the industrial system the nature of his services became altered; they were augmented rapidly by mechanization. Today's worker continues to serve alongside the machine and he will do so until he is eventually displaced by it. The trap he then will find himself in is that of being an unneeded entity in a synthetically (economically) created environment. What is to happen to the masses of people under the conditions created by this mode of technical governance? The inference is that since they no longer can contribute to the production goals of the society they are no longer capable of rendering deserving service, that they be cast outside the economic system and left to fend for themselves or die. This is an inference that may be drawn from economic reasoning, from a total steeping of the population in the philosophy of economics.

While both free enterprise and socialism embody the evils that come from proclaiming themselves absolute systems, of the two, for the present socialism finds itself in the stronger position. Because of its preoccupation with the labor factor, socialism inadvertently has been led to concentrate upon the production process. Working to its future advantage is the fact that as its production burgeons it will not have to reckon with the artificial restraints imposed upon distribution by free enterprise economics. However, the very notion that either of these doctrines, free enterprise or socialist economics, is a hard-and-fast, closed system sets the stage for conflict. The emergence of the Red Guard in China and the Minutemen in the U.S. is evidence that the competition between the two doctrines is not a casual one. The pat hope that since they have 'many features in common' they will eventually find a common ground leading to a new 'mixed' system is probably a fiction. The two are savagely clashing *doctrines* whose edges are continuously rehoned in both camps by special interest groups and by politicians who prefer to make the management of this conflict their nation's main business.

Until such time as its concepts have been tested, economics must be ranged alongside the other social sciences as being in a 'pre-scientific stage.' It owes this status to the mixed forces which gave it origin. First, as mentioned earlier, classical economics provided a welcome, new rationalization of the differences in wealth and privilege between people and between nations. The hereditary right of the aristocracy, under the massive social shifting accompanying the industrial revolution was no longer sufficient rationalization.

Secondly, economics was undoubtedly helped to its early stature by the flowering of the sciences in general, and by a popular desire to make the workings of commerce and industry rational and, thereby, manageable. Thirdly, it is well known that when confronted with a phenomenon of great importance (such as the industrial revolution) a society will insist upon an explanation of this phenomenon and it will tend to accept answers from whatever source they may come, whether from demagoguery, science, or devination. And of all the doxies that have existed through time, few have waxed so feverish as the money cult of the West. Few have stirred greater mass anxieties or presented a more inscrutable visage, and few have produced such a profusion of soothsayers. But it must be remembered that just as early occultism produced astrology, astrology, in time, laid the groundwork for modern astronomy. If economics is to similarly open new pathways, it is probable that it will have to be examined from outside its own body of doctrine, from a *coign of vantage* allowing for different, and broader, perspectives. As for the other and more closely related social sciences, there is more than a modicum of disquieting evidence that they may owe their origins and their present structures, in part, at least, to classical economics.

Development rests upon production, and production is a genie defying constriction within any such static system concept as is now held. Production is an on-going process which calls for changed methods of management as it progresses. If it is to be successfully initiated and later managed successfully, it must be dealt with directly as a force in its own right. It is most improbable that development will ever originate in economic activity. But capital will be formed, in one way or another, just as it was in early industrial England before the age of economists, if the springboard comprised by technical skills and knowledge is present in the culture. If these two factors are not present, no amount of economic inducement will create technological movement. It must be promoted by more basic and direct means than the economic ones. Chapters 6, 7, and 8 describe new methods by which development may be treated as a combined social and technological process.

5

OTHER SOCIAL SCIENCE HYPOTHESES ON DEVELOPMENT

The other social sciences which are mainly interested in development are sociology, anthropology and political science. The development hypotheses propounded by each, along with the subsidiary area of social psychology, are discussed in this chapter. The overlapping of these fields is evident in the frequency of texts which attempt to draw ideas from all four sources together into a common body of theory. And yet, the best ideas that can be gleaned from the social sciences as they stood prior to World War II, and the best that has emerged during the twenty year period following the war, a period of intense interest in development, is a mishmash of trivia. There has been an outpouring of conflicting concepts and superficial hypotheses; and there has been a rising tendency to substitute 'research approaches' for theory. Born of European economic and political philosophies and still leaning toward this same authority, social study seems to be devoted more to the perpetuation of pedantry than to finding a legitimate place in the universe of science. Social scientists have attempted to overwhelm their problem areas by sheer verbal assault. The endeavor to sum up the character of cultures in such broadly meaningless adjectives as 'ideational,' 'idealistic' and 'sensate' and to portray societies as historically drifting from one of these states to another, labored listings of the universal 'wishes,' 'instincts,' 'needs,' or 'ethics' supposed to motivate individual behaviour and to supply drive for the whole society have provided grist for the training of graduate students in the social sciences, but little else. No field invokes the names of its authorities more effusively than do the social sciences and in none are the impotencies of theory more securely masked behind a façade of 'scientific complexity.' Meantime, the everyday community, which supports the social sciences on a surprisingly generous scale, must proceed upon the same tattered old folk wisdoms because its social scientists have failed to bring forward a more substantive type of knowledge.

Other Social Science Hypotheses on Development

SOCIOLOGICAL HYPOTHESES

The General Sociological Viewpoint

An economic system of some sort is found in all societies. Everywhere, there is a network of customs and behavioral patterns governing the ways in which men secure food, clothing, shelter, and above this, whatever other goods and services they desire. These behaviors are heavily encrusted with tradition. Bound together by supporting attitudes and physical facilities, the entire matrix is referred to as the 'economic institution.' The conditions under which men work, the ownership and management of the tools and other facilities with which they work, how, when, and to what degree they are to be rewarded and how the goods produced are to be finally delivered into the hands of the consumers are matters which are dictated by the culture. The individual, however, is not mindful of the degree to which the economic institution varies from one part of the world to another, or of the fact that its various forms seem to work equally well for the particular societies they serve. His attitudes regarding the way in which man makes a living are crystallized. They are drilled into him from that point in his life when the older members of society are first able to establish communication with him and thereby influence his thinking. These thoughtways become so fixed as to allow no inner questioning and, because of this myopia, economic means often become confused with social ends. The attitudes and behaviours buttressing the economic system are acquired at such an early age that the individual is not conscious that they have been learned; they become accepted as 'natural,' unalterable ways of life.

The foregoing is an abbreviated description of the way in which sociologists treat a society's economic institution. They devote much effort to emphasizing the cultural relativity of the economic institution – the fact that each society has its own customs governing production, distribution and ownership. While this is a surprisingly hard-to-acquire insight, it is not the type of positive foundation upon which a science can be built.

Development Concepts

Most of the ideas found in sociology's development literature lack the fullness and stature of hypotheses, but they, nonetheless, occasionally filter into the empirics of development planning. Echoing through writings of development sociologists is the phrase 'establishing preconditions for economic growth.' Since economics much earlier had singled out this process as of vital importance to development it is apparent that the two fields have joined in common cause. Unfortunately, as mentioned earlier the identities of these preconditions are somewhat hazy and their final objective, capital formation, also lacks clear definition. Universal education and the attainment of literacy is deemed a precondition for growth by many social scientists, but the manner in which general education may augment technical progress has never been demonstrated convincingly, and there are those who maintain that it is possible for a technology to move forward under technical training alone if it is judiciously administered.

The modern industrial society would seem to serve as a model by which one could isolate the essential preconditions for development. It would appear offhand that if one could but convert the great family of traditional society into the modern nuclear one, establish the appropriate urban patterns of residence and mobility and instill the habits of thrift and investment in the developing population, the latter might be considered to be well on the road toward material progress. However, several writers, Hoselitz among them, would question this assumption on the grounds that not all the features of traditional society are negative to material progress. Some of them might be used to advantage in expediting material growth.[1] The extended family could help, as it often does in traditional society, in pooling family resources for development and in organizing family labor. If education were biased away from the present practice of expending disproportionate sums on the liberal education of the elite, and directed toward providing technical training for the masses, the social returns would probably be greater and more immediate. Many of the underdeveloped societies already are organized on a semi-modern urban basis but show no promise of moving out of the preindustrial stage. Thus far, the preconditions for growth have not been successfully identified or assigned development priorities, and to attempt to treat them somewhat equally and simultaneously, as it is presently being done, entails an expensive and massively unmanageable program. Moreover, it is quite likely that most of the features found in modern society *did not* provide the framework within which the growth of those societies originally occurred but were the later outcropping of underlying technological forces. The preconditions for economic growth as they are presently prescribed by sociological theory leads to a situation analogous to

[1] Hoselitz, B. F., Tradition and Economic Growth. In R. Braibanti and J. J. Spengler (EDS.), *Tradition, Values and Socioeconomic Development* (Durham, N. C.: Duke University Press, (1961) pp. 83–113.

advising the individual to secure a yule log, decorate a tree, deck the halls, and to hang the stocking just so in the expectation that all these rituals will produce 'Christmas.' To enhance the analogy between the expectant individual and the underdeveloped country let us suppose that the individual is of voting age and, although in poor health, is considered by his neighbours (parents deceased) as being responsible for caring for his own needs.

Running headlong into the proposition of establishing the preconditions for economic growth are the emotion-laden moral judgments which sociologists refer to as 'values.' The term 'value' has a somewhat different meaning for different sociologists, but, in general, it may be said that every society has clear-cut rules of conduct which are referred to as 'norms,' and lying behind these physical behaviors and enforcing their execution are psychological themes or sentiments which, because of their intangibility and generality, are called 'values.' After a society has experienced countless generations of set modes of behavior and of highly formalized procedures, these ways of acting come to be viewed as 'right,' and any attempt to change them will be fended off as socially harmful, or even immoral. The 'value' concept runs directly athwart the rather casual supposition of changing conditions within the society to suit the criteria for development. According to sociologists, the gulf between traditional and modern industrial modes of living is enormous in its physical aspects alone, but when are added to this difference diametrically different ways of thinking and believing, the gulf becomes well nigh unbridgeable.

The value concept took different directions at the hands of two earlier social theorists. Pareto was of the conviction that underlying the thicket of rules and practices within a society were a few recurrent motives or sentiments which exist universally in all societies.[1] If this were demonstrable it might provide an intercultural methodology for social action. Sumner, on the other hand, attached little separate significance to the problem of values. He categorized the norms or patterns of behaviour as 'folkways' or 'mores' and considered the associated sentiments as by-products of the folkways and mores rather than their determinants.[2] Sumner's dichotomy explicitly recognized the different emotional intensities accompanying the folkways and the much more rigidly enforced mores, but in treating these sentiments as secondary to the overt behaviors themselves, he made human behaviour more amenable

[1] Pareto, Vilfredo, *General Treatise on Sociology.* (The Mind and Society) New York: Harcourt, 1935.

[2] Sumner, William Graham, *Folkways.* (Boston: Ginn, 1906), p. 36.

to scientific treatment. It is the opinion of this writer that if the value concept were set aside altogether, and if folkways and mores were unified within an overall concept such as 'technique' (technique being defined as patterns of physical behavior, exclusively), the relationships between society and the dynamics of change would become considerably clearer and more manageable.

The value concept reaches the ultimate in ambiguity when forced to explain two conflicting norms within the same society and, often, within the same social class. This ambiguity crops up repeatedly in connection with explaining sex conduct. Individuals are observed to publicly uphold the sanctity of marriage while secretly engaging in extramarital sexual behavior, and since this occurs on a widespread basis, it is taken as evidence of values in transition, of the presence of two standards of conduct – an ideal norm which preserves the society's stability and a covert norm toward which the society is slowly drifting. The transition is claimed to be very gradual and difficult. Values are said to be persistent, to yield slowly and only over long periods of time and at great psychological pain to the individual. How do we reconcile this with the fact that a gentle, peace-abiding man may be transformed almost over night into a rampaging killer (Peace: Warfare)? After all, the regard of Westerners for human life and the notions of a universal brotherhood of man are not to be explained away as fading concepts. If one inquires of sociology how long it would take to invert almost completely the behaviors of an essentially conservative group, he will be told that such a change borders on the impossible. Could it have ever come about, for example, that a staid group of early nineteenth-century New Englanders could be persuaded to live under a system of near-communism, to submit marriage and the family to polygyny, and to accept a heretical new brand of religion? As far fetched as it may sound, these very things did happen under the religious movement known as the Church of Jesus Christ of Latter-Day Saints (Mormonism), and all within the space of a very few years. Early accounts indicate some reluctance to share physical property and some social discomfort on the part of first-generation Mormon women under the new system of polygyny, but not the disturbance or deep mortification that one might expect. The abruptness and apparent ease with which people have changed behavior in time of war, and the vast transitions that took place under Mormonism are not adequately explained by advancing the obvious truism that the two different situations facing each group contained different normative structures. The work of the early Mormon founders and the new religious institution which resulted from their labors was probably only an enabling factor, and not the basic one instrumenting group change. The sweeping new behaviours delegated by Mormonism to the family changed its functions and composure in matters ranging from religious rites, through family work patterns, to new inheritance laws. These transformations plus the entire groups' being repeatedly uprooted and forced to relocate with little more than the clothing they wore had the accumulative effects of paving the way for thousands of other, and related, institutional changes.

And this brings us to a major thesis. It is the society's great repetoire of techniques that maintains its social momentum. It is the sheer inertia of the individual's habit complex, a part of which is socially inculcated and a part of which is simply individually internalized through repetition, that creates the broader social inertia. Just as in almost every society some men work out of habit, others loaf out of habit. Some save out of habit and others habitually waste. It is not when the individual follows the approved patterns that he has to rationalize his behavior, but rather when he deviates, or appears to deviate from the pattern and when this has been detected by others. And the rationalization advanced by the deviant individual is always treated as secondary to the physical facts surrounding the 'abberation.' If the act should happen to be out-and-out murder no amount of rationalization will suffice, and at its best it will only slightly moderate the punishment. We may speak of feelings or 'values,' but the basic social quantum, the one upon which society acts and reacts, is the physical behavior pattern, the 'technique.' What we refer to as values may be, in reality, great clusters of techniques caged in the gyroscope of habit. The force with which they resist change will be directly proportional to the number of other changes that would be necessitated for the individual by their alteration. Since some patterns of physical behavior are much more ramifying in their interrelationships than others, the intensity of resistance to change will vary quantitatively with the technique in question. This is not to say that resistance to change can be calculated with mathematical certainty, but there is at least an individual, acquired awareness of the probable magnitude of repercussion of a contemplated change, and a roughly corresponding degree of resistance.

Were resistance to change a matter of values only, the outcome would be a great deal different. Even the taboos against murder, if made a matter of conscience alone, would probably give way to a much greater prevalence of homicide. The European cinema has managed to make this point almost a matter of comedy. When the environmental structure undergoes marked change, techniques will also change. Castaways at sea, the inmates of concentration camps, etc., are quickly forced by the peculiarities of their environment into new molds of physical behavior, behaviors ranging from the extremes of self-martyrdom to cannibalism. When there is a massive shift in the infrastructure of techniques, profound institutional changes soon follow. Since, as developers, what we are seeking is a producing environment, we can most easily change the structure of the under-developed society and the antiquated techniques which it presently harbors by the introduction of machines. A new power tool may effect more change in months than would ordinarily occur in centuries.

Two other concepts causing difficulties for development theory are 'equilibrium' and 'stability.' A long succession of writers have depicted society as being held in more or less a state of equilibrium by nearly equal opposing forces. An example of opposing forces might be the strains toward divorce and the counterstrains for group cohesion. Kurt Lewin, among others, maintained that one set of these forces can be intensified and the opposing forces weakened so as to cause the society to move in the direction desired. However, an attempt to enumerate these forces leads to a listing of not just a few which are predominantly influential, but, because their relative importance cannot be determined with any accuracy, hundreds of these variables may work their way into the analysis. Indeed, what one scholar may consider a positive force another might very well place in the negative category. How one would classify divorce or shorter work hours would depend more upon his moral judgment than his powers of objectivity.

Equally unintelligible is the description of a society as being 'in disequilibrium,' but 'in a state of stability.' Since opposing social tensions can never be of exactly equal strength a society always will be in a state of disequilibrium, but, according to this mode of thought, if changes are consistent with one another, and orderly, the society is said to be changing in a 'stable' manner. As for the inner virtues of stability, there seems to be disagreement among sociologists as to which state, the stable or the unstable one, presents the most promising configuration for development. One writer will claim that a society with monolithically stable institutions holds out an excellent opportunity for entree into development through almost any one, or a combination, of these stable and, therefore, influential organs; while another will explain that social change in the conservative society can be induced only by a deliberate distortion of that society's institutional patterns so as to push it into a state of instability. In consonance with this last idea, the modern industrial society is pointed out as a model of instability and one kept in constant disequilibrium by deliberate internal change.

Abutting to the concept of equilibrium – disequilibrium is that of 'tension management.' This is an operational concept that calls for the identification of internal and external points of change having potential dysfunctional consequences for the society, and a rational reduction of these tensions by conducting the society through an orderly process of change. The principal responsibility for tension management falls to the state, which in the impersonal roles of arbitrator and skilled social manager dampens tensions so as to give social change an orderly continuity. The state is supposed not only to manage tension but, in its omniscience, to identify future points of malfunction within the system and smooth out these potential trouble junctures. The practicality of this concept must be judged within the context of the times, against a backdrop such as the situation in the United States, where the cultural lag between generations is claimed to be creating conflict of opinion as to what is wanted of the government, and at a time when the country's political leadership persists in long-outdated, conservative ways of thinking that are hopelessly bogging the system down. The 'tension management' concept makes a number of unsupportable assumptions. It assumes that the specific causes of tension can be identified and their relative potential for causing malfunction can be determined. It goes on to assume that *if* tension points can be isolated the government will be able to act against them. Too often, the early social steps taken in combatting one set of tensions only arouse other tensions that leave the society in a less settled state than it was in before the program was launched. Every action program has a potential for backlash.

Another sociological construct often aired in connection with development is the notion of producing a new type of social class structure in the developing countries. The presently inverted class structure in these countries, with fewer than five per cent comprising a controlling elite, and the remainder of the population falling into one great, occupationally unskilled mass, is felt to pose an impossible obstacle to development. The problem, therefore, becomes one of inducing, as another one of the preconditions for development, a predominating middle class similar to that found in Western society. Here, again, is a possible fallacy. The middle class may be, to a large extent, a consequence of industrialization rather than a necessary antecedent. No such class structure existed in England at the beginning of her industrial revolution and the social class structure of modern-day Japan, though changing, is significantly different from those of the Western countries. Drawing from the early architecture of capitalism it would seem that, with the exception of a relatively small mercantile group, the middle class could be dispensed with, and industry could be manned, almost altogether, by workers and entrepreneurs.

The last mentioned group, the entrepreneurs, is also cited as being necessary for development, and as an ingredient largely missing in the under-developed societies. The so-called 'entrepreneur class' is credited by some economic historians as being a prime agent in development. This group is supposed to draw its driving force from the facts that it, spurred by the prospects of potential reward, supplies the vision that creates enterprise and the guidance that continuously improves its efficiency; and, because it foots the bills and must also face the hard realities of potential losses, it will act with discretion. This subject was discussed in the preceding chapter and need not be dwelt upon here. Suffice it to say that the underdeveloped countries have, if anything, an over-abundance of free enterprising businessmen, and in most of the industrially advanced nations the entrepreneural bloc has receded to the remote position of shareholders who, much less than giving direction to the managers, cast their votes very much as the managers suggest they should.

Hypotheses

Leading to present day hypotheses were a number of earlier social science postulates to the effect that societies evolve naturally through set stages from the primitive to the civilized state; and there were still others that sought the cause of social change in some single natural determinant. Geographic determinism viewed societies as qualitatively linked to climatic conditions of environment. The invigorating aspect of seasonal change, and climatic conditions favorable to agriculture and to life in general, were supposed not only to have provided a rich environment for social progress, but it was believed, by some, that the environment interacted with the inhabitants of these climes in such a way as to produce special racial characteristics – 'inventiveness,' 'personal industry,' etc. These hypotheses were always biased, of course, toward the Central and North European environment. It requires but a brief search of history to demonstrate that the earliest civilizations took root and flourished for long periods in geographical areas, such as the Middle East, which were relatively barren and inhospitable to human habitation.

Other Social Science Hypotheses on Development

Environmental determinism has been laid fairly much to rest, but lingering on are two other types of determinism, psychological and social Darwinian, which still attract a few adherents. The psychological determinists see man's present and future as an immutable outworking of underlying instincts and innate tendencies which guide his hand in the creation of his social environment. And the social Darwinians superimpose the theory of biological evolution upon the social order, pointing out that individual conflict and war are not only inherently unavoidable, but that they are the hardening fires by which the fitter societies are made still fitter and the less competent are eliminated.[1] As sociology became an established social science, explanations for change were sought increasingly in the social and cultural orders. Some of these explanations, too, are deterministic in that they make change dependent upon a single cultural variable. The broader sociological view regards social change as a product of the interaction of a number of institutional factors. The main vehicles for change are believed to lie in the economic, familial, religious, and political institutions.

Foremost among those attempting to relate social change to economic activity was Thorstein Veblen, who lived until the beginning of the great depression of the 1930's. Veblen viewed the economic institution as a matrix of behaviour patterns which gave the life processes of the community force and continuity. Economic behaviour unfolds itself as a struggle for wealth. In Veblen's thinking, the basic attribute for which men competed was social esteem; and wealth, especially of a conspicuous type such as property, was the basis for securing esteem. All effort, therefore, became directed toward the accumulation of wealth.

Emile Durkheim, a French sociologist and a contemporary of Veblen, ranged far beyond the confines of economics to examine social change as a condition associated with the division of labor. He observed the division of labor to progress with time, and in the process to convert traditional values to those characteristic of the industrial community. There is an increase of individuality and individual freedom along with an economic mandate that now, because of increased specialization, there must be full cooperation, this spirit being topped by a corresponding specialization of political functions and an organization of the economy around private property.[2]

[1] Sorokin, Pitirim, *Contemporary Social Theories* (New York: Harper, 1928).

[2] For a synopsis of the philosophies of Veblen, Durkheim and several other scholars whose works are cited here, refer to: Harry Elmer Barnes, Howard Becker and Frances Bennett Becker, EDS., *Contemporary Social Theory*, (New York: Appleton-Century, 1940).

And then there are those, including this author, who have sought an explanation of change in the nature of technology itself. Marx, whom we already have discussed in Chapter 4, saw, in the early development of technology, material forces that were inherent in the relations of the production process itself and which eventually would bring about interclass conflict. From this conflict would evolve a dictatorship of the proletariat which would finally give way to communism, or the dissolution of state powers.

William F. Ogburn has explained social change as a blend of technological and cultural causation. His theory of social change runs to the effect that social change is largely caused by cultural change, and cultural change, in its turn, evolves from invention, accumulation, diffusion and adjustment, with invention being the principal change agent. He pointed out that the rate of cultural change is closely related to the number of cultural items that a given society has in stock. When the cultural base is small the number of inventions is limited; as the cultural base grows the rate of invention progresses alongside it.

Ogburn's social change concept has been greatly overshadowed by an ancilliary idea lying at its base – the cultural lag hypotheses. The cultural lag hypotheses postulates that there are two aspects of the general culture, the 'material' culture and the 'adaptive' culture. In Western society there is a steady stream of material inventions and the society is forced to accommodate these newcomers by making the appropriate social adjustments (also inventions). The automobile, for example, brought on a necessity for traffic regulations and a host of new social improvizations. But these changes in the adaptive culture are not synchronous with changes in the material culture; they lag behind the latter, sometimes by many years. Since the flow of physical inventions is a continuing one, and because the time required for social adaptation may run oftentimes into long periods, social accommodation never fully succeeds in catching up with material change. Consequently, the society is kept in a continuing state of disequilibrium.[1]

Ogburn's polemic seems at first glance to be plausible, but upon closer examination it shows a major flaw. He treats material inventions and their initial acceptance into the society as though these were nothing more than raw physical processes and physical changes. A physical invention may lie idle, a matter of no social interest. But once it is translated into an actual innovation it becomes simultaneously a ***social invention*** and a social dynamic. The acceptance of

[1] William F. Ogburn, *Social Change*, (Gloucester, Mass.: Peter Smith, 1964), pp. 200–213.

a new physical item requires a state of social receptivity, a ready social niche into which it will fit and carry out what are considered to be socially useful functions. If the physical item happens to be a machine, its operation, maintenance and the management of its products, if any, all are social behaviours. The debut of a new physical item is a social act which can set in motion what may become, in time, a whole social movement. If it were *not* true that for its acceptance a physical item is dependent upon antecedent social conditions favouring its appearance, then the mere presentation of Western artifacts to any group of preliterate tribesmen would set them on the road to technological development. If innovation is viewed in the overall as a social process, then Ogburn's hypothesis says little more than that social inventions occur in a sequence. He does not depict the processes of change but merely portrays a narrow spectrum of the process after technological movement sets in. The process which he refers to as 'adaptive culture' this author would consider to be 'technique.' The term, 'material culture,' is a misnomer.

Another framework for viewing technological change, and one in several respects similar to my own, is that constructed by Lewis Mumford. Mumford portrays the first stage of technology (extending from the tenth to the eighteenth century) as resting upon a power base of wind, water, and wood, and as being a period during which the beginnings of industry in textiles and glassmaking were laid. The period closes with the increased utilization of power-machines. Stage 2, which was a coal and iron economy, began in the eighteenth century and, finally, by the last half of the nineteenth century, dominated Stage 1. Stage 3 set in during the latter half of the nineteenth century and has extended to the present. It is based upon electrical power, the use of the lighter metals, a general movement toward automation, and a proliferation of all types of industry. Mumford believed that Stage 4 was now beginning to emerge, that it was making its appearance in a pattern in which society was beginning to move away from the almost purely mechanical complex to apply the biological sciences to the growth of technology, and was at the same time purposefully reorienting its technology to the attainment of cultural values. He did not regard these stages as immutably fixed, but as a succession of technic-ways which had effects radiating out over the entire culture, and which in the course of this process were producing social change.[1]

Mumford's staging is a discriminating system of dating and it

[1] Lewis Mumford, *The Culture of Cities*, (New York: Harcourt, Brace, 1938), pp. 495–496.

reveals technological outcroppings which can be corroborated by historical analysis and by a glance at present day Western society. However, like Ogburn, in explaining social change he tended to treat the mechanics of technology as cause, and cultural change as effect. He overlooked the possibility that technological movement may be, in itself, a social process, that innovations may not be random processes but may fall into tightly related clusters within well defined technologies, and that supporting each technology there may be an explicit social foundation which sponsors it and whose interests it must serve. Finally, Mumford's growth stages do not take into account the central roles played by the machine and its underlying power technology.

Max Weber looked to still another institution, religion, as a prime factor in social change. Partly in refutation of Marxian determinism and partly as a trial of the historical-comparative method of analysis, Weber set out upon an involved study to determine the relationships between religious orientation and social structure. This inquiry was prompted by a particular question that occurred to Weber. Could the way in which men conceive of their universe, particularly as appertained to the way in which they interpreted it in their religion, influence their social relationships and, most particularly, their economic relationships to one another? He concluded that Protestantism was born as a system of rationalization for the support of capitalism. The creed of greater individual independence in commerce and industry, the interpretations of prosperity as evidence of righteous living and poverty as implying sin fitted in nicely with the early needs of central Éuropean secularism; and Protestantism, in general, catered to the desire of the political and commercial leaders of these countries to rid themselves of the oppressive economic yoke of the Catholic church. This, along with its encouragement of individual inquiry, made Protestantism an ideal seed-bed for the capitalistic society and for science. It should be added that Weber did not intend that religion be taken as a total explanation of social development, although he is widely credited with having taken this position. The fact that the Protestant ethic, rigidly interpreted, is not, by any means, the sole determinant of economic behaviour is readily apparent in the rapid technological ascendency of some non-Christian nations such as Israel and Japan, and also in the regional unevenness with which technology has progressed within the most pristinely Protestant of the technologically advanced countries. As Soviet Russia has demonstrated, technology can be made to progress rapidly without the presence of any religion, and technology is found to operate quite fluidly in some of the smaller religious sects which are bound to the most authoritarian of behaviour standards.

The political institution is still another domain in which the causes for technological movement are sought. This subject will be discussed later in this chapter under the rubric, 'political hypotheses.'

Practical Approaches

Overshadowing all other practical social methods for promoting growth is the process referred to as 'community development.' This grass root approach, popular among sociologists and anthropologists, attempts to get at problems at the community level. It is an action program which attempts to formulate its own type of action theory from first-hand observation in the field. It is something of a holdover from the 'missionary approach.' Within the broad context of national development, community development is basically a casework method applied at the community level, and its work probably could be ably carried out by specially trained caseworkers. It proceeds upon the rather safe assumption that if each of a nation's communities is improved, this will have the overall effect of improving the entire society. Community development has been applied to regionally blighted areas within the technologically advanced societies, and in some of the under-developed nations, India in particular, it has been tried on a lavish scale. The prodecure has been variously referred to as 'rediscovering local initiative,' 'promoting human growth,' or sometimes as 'directed cultural change.' As one community developer put it, 'Social improvement does not occur until the people involved believe that improvement is possible.' 'As people are brought to feel a sense of community' they begin acquiring the conviction that they can better their lot.[1]

Its advocates look upon community development as an educational process, educational in that it contributes to human growth, and as providing a small scale laboratory within which to further study human behaviour. The research which it has produced so far has been 'non-quantitative.' The experience of community development, as it is explained by some of its practioneers, has an element of the dramatic that borders on mysticism. The 'director of community dynamics,' as he is sometimes called, begins his work with a carefully calculated initial contact with the community during which its members usually react toward him with attitudes of curiosity, suspicion or, sometimes, outright hostility. Not dismayed by these

[1] William W. Biddle and Loureide J. Biddle, *The Community Development Process*, (New York: Holt, Rinehart and Winston, Inc., 1965), p. VIII.

reactions, which he had been trained to expect anyway, he persists until he has built up enough rapport to begin his work. He works more as a catalyst – bringing community members together and helping them in the selection of their own leadership, and assisting them in determining what projects should be carried out – than as an outright director. The first stages of organization are of gratifying outcome to all participants, in that old barriers and personal rivalries melt away before a common purpose. The first stages of project work, and these are whatever types of work the community is able to agree upon, are usually marred by some 'flare-up' occasioned by some community member, or members, trying to unduly dominate the proceedings; but the disturbance is skillfully soothed over by the outside director. As it is described in its literature, community development appears in many ways to be an emotional experience more richly rewarding to the outside director than to the community participants. Its motif seems to be that some of the outside director's enthusiasm and 'know-how' will rub off onto the community. It is felt, by its champions, that each community project requires a unique interpretation and a special management based upon that community's particular needs and the special problems it faces.

Community development procedures have a number of shortcomings. First, the assumption that every undeveloped society lacks a sense of 'community' is far from true. Most of the folk societies are much more cohesive in organization and stronger in group sentiment than are the great and prosperous sections of the world which they are being groomed, in some small way, to imitate. Secondly, in the view of community developers the cultivation of certain social processes, for example the strengthening of cooperation, is considered all-important, while the matter of introducing the group to new technological *systems* may go entirely unattended. The community method elects the supposedly easy route of attempting change through social reorganization and the introduction of new work techniques. The hypotheses presented in subsequent chapters indicate that these are the most difficult points at which to attempt change, and the paucity of positive results reported from the field by community developers tend to verify this conclusion. Community development assumes that all cultures are preadjusted to, and will proceed best by pooling resources in the common good. This is obviously *not* the case with all preindustrial societies, nor is it the *modus operandi* within many of the highly advanced technological societies which are giving aid to the former. These are free enterprise societies which place special stress on individual enterprise and on encouraging independent individual growth.

However, it is not its philosophical or cultural orientations that provide the most telling criticism of community development. If the procedure worked it would demonstrate, as its practioneers originally had hoped, that determined empirical effort might well succeed where theory was unable to point the way. But the crux of the matter is that community development, as conceived and carried out by Western planners, cannot be demonstrated to have aided materially in achieving overall progress in any of the nations where it has been tried. India has had a massive program of community development underway for more than ten years with the expectation that model agricultural communities could be purposively implanted and that, once established, they would radiate their effects outward to blanket the entire nation. The program is now under heavy fire, charged with being a purely ornamental and expensive luxury that has contributed little to agricultural expansion.[1] Its home critics are leveling their criticism at precisely the point where community development claims to be most effective, in agriculture. They maintain that the program is *not* getting the farmers to adopt new or improved techniques. Community development programming is likewise failing in the nations of Southeastern Asia.

On the other hand, when one examines the *kabutz* of Israel there is impressive evidence of progress, but it is a progress attained under a distinctly different type of community development. The *kabutz* draws agriculture into the urban complex, relating agriculture and agriculturalists to the mainstream of industrial and commercial life. Orthodox community development, on the other hand, to the extent that it may succeed in making the community self-sufficient, thus isolates it further from the urban complex and may be performing, thereby, an eventual disservice to its technological progress. In all, the general idea of community development closely relates to the Ghandian ideals of cottage-craft industry and crude, self-sufficient agriculture. It should be rescrutinized very carefully for suitability as a development tool. If it can provide emergency field services, carry out meaningful services in support of a regional or national program, and, if it can be shown to do these things at a reasonable cost it might still be made an auxiliary service to national programming.

So widely voiced that it seems to be almost an approach in itself is the incessant exhortation, by those sophisticated in these matters, for better role-playing integration by the visiting outsider with the

[1] On P. Tangri, India's Community Development Program: Critique and Suggestions. In *Dynamics of Development*, Grove Hambidge (Ed.) (New York: Frederick A. Praeger, Publishers, 1964), pp. 306–311.

members of the developing community. This might be called the 'Horatio Alger approach.' Before leaving the hustings for the 'big city' Alger's young heroes (and the many rural youth who perused his books for the practical information they contained) were carefully counselled in the manner of living that would be encountered there, and they were advised as a practical matter of achieving success to fit themselves punctiliously into the ways of the city dwellers. A similar advice is reiterated endlessly to members of the technologically advanced societies who are living in, or are preparing to go abroad to an undeveloped country. They are cautioned not to sequester themselves in ghettos, not to engage in conspicuous types of consumption or to live in the manner of the local elite. They are urged to learn the prevailing folkways and how to differentiate between those behaviors showing social respect and those that might inadvertently reflect insult; and most importantly, they are urged to learn the local language. If drawn upon discriminatingly there is undoubtedly much value in this counsel, but the approach of unreservedly 'selling oneself' is overly suggestive of the belief that technology, and the virtues of the West in particular, must be sold and that there is a special personality magic involved in the selling process. It also imputes to the developing peoples a certain naivete, or low mentality. Underneath the outer plumages of all cultures, individual sincerity is unmistakable, and while there is much to be said for expediting communications through learning the language of the undeveloped, all too often integrative role-playing is intended as a cover, or ruse. It fails to discriminate between educative and propagandistic behaviors and goals. It neglects the more important question of, 'integrative role-playing for what?' Anthropologists integrate into the cultures which they are studying in order to acquire the understanding that comes with more penetrating insight into the culture. In this role they are students, not teachers or exemplars. While developers may also benefit from cultural insight, not to be overlooked is another possibility and one that has been documented voluminously, that social change takes place more rapidly under the influence of external interference (e.g. conquest) and under conditions of role disconsonance than within a setting of relative harmony. Integrated role-playing may succeed in doing little more than perpetuating the old ways, while disconsonant role-playing, with the outsider holding fast in this case to certain of his own cultural characteristics, may, by setting new examples, provoke new ideas and cause the desired departure from established folkways. Selectively exhibited disconsonant role-playing may heighten group instability and pave the way for more rapid technological change.

At any rate, the approach of fetishistically identifying with the technologically undeveloped culture, like most of our development concepts, is in need of a careful re-evaluation.

Sociological research, in the absence of any more trustworthy system of theory, likewise has come to be used as a 'practical approach' to development. Those adhering to the research approach insist that a development plan cannot be drafted intelligently until research has been carried out on the community or area being contemplated for development. Each community is regarded as 'a unique development problem' and the research which is subsequently applied to it is usually of an unstructured, open-end type without guiding hypotheses. The results are, more or less, what any junior scientist would expect. Loosely guided research may be condoned, to a degree, when the study situation is unique, but to attempt to carry out development research without even a semblance of development theory is analogous to the behavior of a research chemist who begins a search for a new type of material without any guidance whatever from the theory of chemistry. In reality, this does not happen in chemistry. The researcher *does* have some idea as to what he is looking for and what general procedures he must follow in order to find it. Sociological researchers, on the other hand, proceed either intuitively or by attacking those microcosmic problems with which they are familiar and at the conclusion of their work have little to report that can be tied in substantively with later programming. More often than not, their final reports are limited to quibbling about whether this, or that, of the so-called research procedures is preferable, lamenting the shortage of properly trained indigenous sociologists for continuing the work they have started, and making recommendations as to what types of research would be most appropriate for the future. Much time and effort has been expended on this niggling type of 'research,' with results which, understandably, almost never find their way into national planning documents.

SOCIO-PSYCHOLOGICAL HYPOTHESES

Mass Transformation of Personality

There recently has been a reawakened interest in innovation as a personality attribute, as a product of the way in which the individual relates to his environment. The apparently rigid social structure of traditional society *vis-à-vis* the flexibility of modern urban society has lent plausibility to this notion. It is held that the nature of traditional society – its demand for obedience to parental and other types of social authority, its outright ascription of status, and its provincial isolation – supresses the appearance of the innovative personality. On the other hand, modern urban society, having values lying at almost the opposite pole and offering a rate of physical and social mobility making it possible for the individual to evade traditional authority, provides a medium encouraging innovation and making for rapid economic growth. The movement of people from traditional rural society to the urban area and their resettlement in these latter areas creates a social fluidity, a standardization of communications, and a feeling of national purpose which will entrain economic movement. The problem is that of determining exactly how these movements and the new individual relationships that they bring about contribute to the formation of the innovative personality. In the literature on the subject, one sees frequent reference made to such factors as 'need dominance,' 'need aggression,' 'need for achievement,' 'achievement motivation,' 'the entrepreneural personality,' etc. Reference also is made occasionally to a point in a society's history 'when the society chooses to modernize,' almost as though this were a simple issue to be resolved by public poll. Nowhere is the teleological explanation given freer rein than in the socio-psychological hypotheses of development.

Two particular literary works jointly epitomize the socio-psychological approach to explaining development. The first of these, *The Achieving Society*, by David C. McClelland, points out the prevalence of a 'need for achievement' and how this felt need is a prerequisite to entrepreneurship and economic growth.[1] Very briefly put, McClelland is of the persuasion that wherever there is a high need for achievement, in all probability economic growth will follow.

The best known of the recent 'personality' explanations for technological growth is that of Everett E. Hagen, an economist who, dissatisfied with economic explanations, turned for an answer to the cultural and psychological variables. His was an inquiry into the causes of disruption of traditional society and its conversion to modernization. In the slow historical change of cultural values and the eventual emergence of the creative personality, Hagen identified an historical sequence of *Authoritarianism*, *Withdrawal of Status*, *Retreatism*, and *Creativity*.[2] The critical stage in the formation of the creative personality is withdrawal of status, to which the individual

[1] David C. McClelland, *The Achieving Society*, (Princeton, N.J.: Van Nostrand Co., 1961).

[2] Everett E. Hagen, *On the Theory of Social Change*, Homewood, Ill.: The Dorsey Press, Inc., 1962), p. 217.

reacts by a deviance from group norms in an effort to secure the social approval that his father failed to achieve and greatly regrets not having won.

Hagen's thesis is another one of those tediously rehashed analyses of intrafamilial relationships which, presumedly, over a period of many generations gradually become restructured so that the individual comes to hold new and radical values. Hagen's book helps to lay the ghost of economic mythology, but resurrects nothing in its place. In actual practice, the innovative individual will find his outlets for gratification channeled by the culture in which he lives. In the West this need *may* be gratified by entrepreneurship, although this is, by no means, necessarily true as some people do become bus drivers, scientists, government workers, and other types of non-entrepreneural figures.

When one ventures outside Western society Hagen's thesis becomes even less tenable. Genghis Kahn was indisputably an innovator but he did not build a factory or open a dry goods store to indulge his frustrations. He built an army. And in the process he brought a wide scattering of independent and often inter-warring tribes into a tightness of intercommunication and overall unity which, according to some social science development hypotheses, surely should have paved the way for Mongolian economic development. But in time the Mongolian empire relapsed into a congeries of tribal societies, a rise and dissolution similar to that of the Egyptian dynasties, the Roman Empire, and countless other societies in each of which there had developed a high degree of social organization, but in none of which was there a strain toward sustained technological growth.

Hagen conveniently looked for the elements of personality change in the histories of those societies which were definitely on the road to, and were destined to reach industrial greatness. He neglected the many societies whose peoples, for example the Eskimo bone carvers, innovate, but not in ways conducive to technological growth. One of the more common fallacies is the belief that only members of the technologically advanced societies invent. If modern industrial society is to serve as an example of the home of the deviant, innovating personality, then it must be conceded that its prime innovators, the engineers, are anything but social deviants or a class of people 'who hold radically new value systems.' In actuality, it seems that it is they who create most of the changes and it is the social scientists who provide the better examples of deviancy.

Because the behavioral transformation he describes is purported to occur over the centuries, Hagen's thesis is not practically testable.

If it were, and if it proved to be valid this still would not answer the questions of how one might go about the gargantuan task of instituting mass transformation in personality and how the process might be telescoped to a reasonable time period. If Hagen's objective was to analyze the relationships between tendency to invent and accompanying transformations in personality, it would appear that his work might have been carried out by nearer-at-hand subject matter and, perhaps, more valid methods. The migration of individuals from technologically backward societies or regions to areas of high development offer current instances in which entire groups have been coerced into change within relatively few years. Cases like these would present opportunities for viewing personality change as it may relate to invention or innovation within the lifetime of a single individual. Depending upon their age and other factors, incoming peoples from backward areas sometimes undergo a rapid and marked change in style of living, and they may develop a surprisingly quick grasp of a technology with which they were previously unfamiliar. Hogbin described the Makah Indians of the northwestern part of the United States as an illustration of deliberately engineered social transformation.[1] An enforced change by the U.S. Government has brought about a modification in the culture of these Indians which at present amounts to an almost complete assimilation into U.S. society. The question that is here of interest to developers is, 'What are the major variables involved in this stepped-up type of change?'

The foregoing is not intended to refute the rather undeniable fact that evolving technologies do undergo change, but rather it is meant to point out that the creative personality, like most of the 'preconditions for growth,' is more likely to be a concomitant or a consequence of technological development than a cause.

I would like to emphasize the importance of distinguishing technological development *from* economic growth. Technological development increases the general rate of production activity and the general level of wealth but, it should be added, not necessarily the general prosperity. However, in time, general prosperity probably will follow. Technological development is the process of a society's adaptation to a machine culture and, although it seems impossible to designate the exact historical point at which this adaptation will occur, one can, with reasonable accuracy, describe its subsequent growth processes after it does set in. The technological growth process is largely inescapable for the machine-tendering society. The members of this type of society are literally lifted into the dimensions

[1] Ian Hogbin, *Social Change*, Watts, 1958, pp. 41–48.

of the machine world and they innovate, in great part, in response to conditions which are established by machines. This viewpoint is elaborated upon in Chapter 7.

As for a definition of 'economic growth,' I have not, to date, seen one that was generally accepted as satisfactory, nor would I care to venture one. Economists, who write so prolixly on this subject, hardly ever bother to define it. One suspects that this is less a matter of oversight than an inability to encompass, by reasonable definition, a growth process that is implied to include just about every conceivable type of material expansion. There is reason to believe that if economists could define more clearly what they mean by 'economic growth,' the suggestions which they make to accomplish this objective would also take on greater clarity.

Another postulate of growth, and one which lies near the heart of personality cultism is the 'great man hypothesis.' This postulate holds simply that historical events are shaped by the personalities and driving forces of a relatively few great men. This viewpoint is exemplified in a recent book entitled *The Vital Few*, by Jonathan Hughes. Hughes declares that change does not come automatically from the 'masses.' 'There are no "masses." There are only individuals. There are no "forces of history," only human action and the human beings involved are individuals as well as parts of society. Men make economic change. The American economy, even including government, is the sum product of the acts of individuals.'[1]

Hughes protests that the great men who have imposed their stamp upon politics and war have been given their due of public attention but too little has been said of the men who have initiated economic change. While, in the history of US society, the personalities who have contributed significantly to economic growth run into tens of thousands, relative to the total population they have comprised a small number, 'the vital few.' Hughes took as his hypothesis the idea that Western economic development moved through what seemed to be five simultaneous 'conceptual categories': idealism; invention; innovation; organization; and stagnation and decline. He was concerned primarily with the first four of these categories because they represented growth processes, and in illustration of each of the four he selected two men who had exercised a vital influence on development. For example, he chose Eli Whitney and Thomas A. Edison to depict how great men have shaped history in the category of 'invention,' and E. H. Harriman and J. Pierpont Morgan as two outstanding forces in 'organization.'

[1] Jonathan Hughes, *The Vital Few*, Boston, Mass.: Houghton-Mifflin Co., 1966, pp. 2–7.

Men live in a web of culture, and the directions which their energies will take will be to a great extent determined by that same culture. While, admittedly, there will always be some degree of personal deviance, its extent tends to be exaggerated in the mind of the casual onlooker and it almost always will occur within what are already well-defined areas of social interest. There is abundant evidence that particular types of personalities are called forth by the times, by predisposing social events; and there is equally convincing evidence that those flying too radically in the face of convention will be denied opportunity for expression. 'Personalities' are not born in a social vacuum nor are they able to act in one. The 'great man hypothesis,' with its sin of oversimplification, is essentially similar to the 'search for the entrepreneural class' which was discussed earlier.

ANTHROPOLOGICAL HYPOTHESES

Orientation

Two preliminary comments are in order before starting a detailed discussion of anthropological approaches to development. Both have to do with the orientation of anthropologists and anthropological studies. Margaret Mead spoke for perhaps the majority of anthropologists in remarking that insofar as technical aid programs were concerned, anthropologists have come to symbolize conservative attitude and pessimistic outlook, that they view the changes desired by pragmatists as either difficult or impossible of attainment, and those that are achievable may be destructive.[1] Secondly, when anthropologists do manage to overcome their inner qualms to a point of carrying out active development research, their interests are found to center primarily upon cultural, rather than technological change. Ralph Linton made a distinction between the two types of change in noting that, 'There have been numerous periods of rapid cultural development which are not correlated with any such fundamental technological changes.'[2] He points to the great age of Athens and the earlier Egyptian dynasties as graphic illustrations of unilateral cultural change. In this writer's opinion both of these societies are prime examples of rapid advancement in man-machine organization at the pretechnological stage, but they were unable to sustain technological progress because of their failure to develop a power technology. At any rate, the foregoing is to say that anthro-

[1] 'Applied Anthropology, 1955.' in *Some Uses of Anthropology, Theoretical and Applied*, Washington, D.C.: The Anthropological Society of Washington, 1956, p. 98.

[2] Ralph Linton, *The Tree of Culture*, New York: Alfred A. Knopf, 1955, p. 46.

pological studies may shed light on some of the highly generalized processes of cultural change without contributing much to our knowledge of technological movement.

Anthropologists, like the other social scientists, also are plagued by the inconsistencies of the concepts by which they attempt to explain change. A classical example of anthropological hypotheses at loggerheads is mirrored in the philosophies of Radcliffe-Brown and E. R. Leach.[1] Radcliffe-Brown takes the position that a society tends to operate as a functional unit, that in order for it to maintain itself, its various groupings and associations must possess a certain degree of social integration. But, at times, integration ebbs to a low point and the society must grope for reintegration; and in the process it experiences change. Some of the conflicts producing disintegration are irresolvable, so in the process of recovering its posture the society will inevitably be forced through a certain amount of change in structure. Radcliffe-Brown draws an analogy between the society and an animal organism by pointing out how both may lapse into a pathological condition and then move toward the recovery of health.

Leach, for his part, does not regard change, or the conditions preceding it, as necessarily traumatic. People may sometimes set about modifying their culture and its structural organization with genuine enthusiasm and in anticipation of the benefits that this move will bring. Indeed, says Leach, the highly integrated society may be in a deadlocked state of equilibrium which, far from being a condition of good health, may lead to its extinction.[2]

Linton defines cultural change loosely and in connection with the steps by which a society adopts an innovation. First, the society acquires a potential additive to its culture which is then accepted or rejected. If the former alternative is chosen, the item will be modified to suit the accepting culture and integratively adjusted within its framework so as to preserve its internal balance. Finally, the older, displaced item will usually, but not always, be eliminated from the culture.

The anthropological field studies which are of interest to developers are of two types. One type, loosely referred to as theoretical, is represented by the descriptive studies that anthropologists make of the community or the greater society. Excellent examples of the descriptive type of study are those of Eglar, who describes the culture of a village in West Pakistan,[3] and Fraser, who recounts life in a

[1] Ian, Hogbin, *Social Change*, Watts, 1958, pp. 21–44.

[2] Ibid., pp. 41–48.

[3] Zekiye, Eglar, *A Punjabi Village in Pakistan*, New York: Columbia University Press, 1960.

Malay fishing village in Southern Thailand.[1] Properly utilized, these studies could be of value in planning technological development. A thorough knowledge of the society's folkways, its taboos, and some preliminary information as to its human and natural resources would be of great help in pinpointing the most expeditious modes for introducing technology. This type of study would not be expected to add to technological theory, but rather to provide practical information which is highly important to the earlier stages of operational planning. However, Sjoberg brings to attention the facts that the traditional folk society and the feudal society differ markedly in their behavioral and structural characteristics, and it is with the latter, which is much more likely to be a transitional type of society, that national planners most often will be called upon to deal.[2] The small folk society, when it does ask for outside aid, probably will continue to be dealt with under local, community development types of programming.

A second type of anthropological field study which is of interest here are those projects examining the causes and effects of community change, with anthropological field programs sometimes acting as the vehicles for introducing change. One of the most extensive series of field programs ever undertaken, and one that included both types of study, theoretical and applied, was that established by Cornell University in 1948 under the financial sponsorship of the Carnegie Corporation. These studies have been interested in the cultural processes and dynamics of spontaneous and planned cultural change among a variety of aboriginal and peasant cultures throughout the world. Members of the Cornell group, and of similar types of projects, have succeeded in introducing improved varieties of seed potatoes to Andean Indians, small-scale poultry raising enterprises to Indian families in a Mexican community, etc. The same may be said of these projects as of any type of community development program. Looked at in retrospect, after several years of intensive labor and study a group of social scientists succeeded in inducing a single, or at least a relatively isolated type of change in the lives of a few hundred Andean Indians. Out of this has come no broadly useful contribution to the knowledge of how to induce change or any necessarily permanent or far-reaching alteration in the life or technological prospects of the community where the experiment was carried out. An attempt at widespread change by

[1] Thomas M. Fraser, Jr., *Rusembilan: A Malay Fishing Village In Southern Thailand*, Ithica, N.Y.: Cornell University Press, 1960.

[2] Gideon Sjoberg, 'Folk and "Feudal" Societies,' *American Journal of Sociology*, 58, 231–239, November 1952.

this method probably would require almost as many administrators as there are Indians.

Another, and an important area of study in which anthropologists are just beginning to make an appearance is in the analysis, within primitive and, therefore, more easily studied social settings, of factors which until now have been accepted more or less at face value. An analysis of the functions of money among South Pacific Islanders, and detailed accounts of modes of trade between African tribesmen fall into this category. Paul Bohannan found, for example, that among the Tiv of Nigeria, the introduction of general purpose money tended to increase differentiation in the wealth of individuals, to introduce a secular indebtedness which was hitherto unknown, and to merge the Tiv economy with the world economy.[1] A better understanding of these types of variables might be of great assistance in the design and development of new modes of distribution and exchange. It is in this general area, and in providing descriptive materials for the groundwork of technological planning, that anthropological study promises to be most helpful.

POLITICAL HYPOTHESES

It would appear that an institution wielding the overall powers of government would be an ideal authority for working out and carrying through, the *grand design* of development. Very few political scientists dispute governments' having a definite role in development, but there is much difference of opinion regarding the degree of authority that it should be given in this area. At the one extreme are the spokesmen for the welfare state, for whom government and development are almost synonymous activities; and at the other are the advocates of free enterprise, who believe that government should content itself with carrying out only those background functions opening the way for private initiative. The two groups share with one another, and with economists, an implicit faith that, regardless of exactly how they are to be undertaken, their basic functions are those of establishing the preconditions for economic growth. The various institutional aspects of development, along with the political strategies for carrying it out, are discussed in nicety of detail in a symposium of writings recently edited by Finkle and Gable.[2]

[1] Paul Bohannan, 'The Impact of Money on African Subsistence Economy,' *The Journal of Economic History*, Vol. XIX, No. 4, December, 1959.

[2] Jason L. Finkle, and Richard W. Gable, (Eds.) *Political Development and Social Change*, New York: John Wiley and Sons, Inc., 1966.

One of the first problem areas addressed by political theorists is that of determining the type of government best suited for carrying out development. Whatever the answer, it will remain an abstraction since an underdeveloped society will not be likely to change its form of government at the suggestion of political scientists. But even before this *cul-de-sac* is reached, standing in the way of academic agreement are pronounced differences of opinion. Some political scientists are now inclining to the viewpoint that the problems are so great in most of the emerging societies that the developing government will have to be a strongly authoritarian one. They go on to say that this need not be a permanent condition, but as the economy progresses this government probably will be replaced, as in the case of Japan, by a more moderate one. However, the call for strong governments is a hollow one inasmuch as most of the world's transitional societies already are living under totalitarian governments, many of them absolute. Most of these governments are rigidly unyielding in their attitudes toward permitting change in the established order.

Another and more liberal school of political theorists maintains that totalitarian government almost always is conservatively inflexible, and as it combats the growth of political opposition, as has happened in Saudi Arabia and most other absolute rulerships, it simultaneously squelches technological development. An even more liberal group within the school maintains that a one-party system (and where there are only single parties they are usually under the control of the military) will usually be found in association with static economic conditions. They assert that the best prospects for development lie under a two-party system, and within a democratic framework allowing for flexibility in communications and for vibrant dissidence.

Leaving this impasse, and proceeding upon the happy assumption that political theorists were free to choose the type of government they wished, we would still find them in disagreement on the inner details of whether given *types of government action* would help, or hinder development. To one political theorist, state-created pressures to drive wages upward would seem to assist in saving and capital formation, while to another it would appear to be a costly welfare gesture which should be postponed until after it can be afforded, with the state, meantime, raising development revenues directly through taxation. Fortunately, there are a number of more general, and less controversial measures which political theorists agree that government *can* discreetly take in behalf of economic growth. They are: the establishment of national objectives and a program and time schedule for accomplishing these objectives; the creation of public systems for the collection and disbursement of revenues for development programming; giving aid in augmenting the available supply of people skilled in entrepreneurship; assistance in the importation of technology; and enforcement of the egalitarian measures needed in education and related institutions to draw forth a middle class that is strong enough to carry the society through the development program, etc.

One could go on, at great length, recounting the ways in which government could be of help in establishing the preconditions for economic growth. But this would be an idle recitation because it is a type of model building that results in nothing more in the end, than a description of the technologically advanced society. It does not realistically describe the means available to, or the development procedures that should be followed by the emerging society. The latter will not achieve government of the calibre desired by political scientists until it has built up a thriving technology. In modern industrial society the state is a bureaucracy of highly specialized and interlocking agencies which is produced and financially supported by technology. It takes great resources to develop a modern government, and the developing countries will be lacking for some time in this magnitude of wealth. Moreover, for the developing society to attempt to establish complex government as a lead-in to technology is to raise the question, 'Government for what?' Most government functions, as followers of Ogburn might point out, come about after technology begins growing, some in response to the social disturbance its growth is causing and others in answer to its further needs. Government action against monopoly or stream and air pollution, government regulation of communications and transportation, laws governing terms of employment, the legislation of protective tariffs and tax exemptions, and the levy of taxes on a massive enough scale to support all these government measures plainly presuppose both, means and purpose, and these two forces can arise only out of a vigorous existing technology. There is much to be said for planning ahead but, unfortunately, government programs of the grand scale usually felt necessary for 'economic development' must await the quickening reality of *technological development*. Those planners who attempt to push government too far ahead of physical development will find themselves working in a vacuum, without public interest or support.

Can the state realistically expect to provide universal education for the masses, or to somehow generate a large middle class from a feudal society? Again, these two conditions will not likely appear until technological growth, itself, creates new conditions of employment, a burgeoning commerce, a social fluidity breaking down old social controls, and a *need* for better educated employees. As these conditions come about, an educated middle class probably will begin to form. Paradoxically, it is where the situation is most inhospitable to development, where resources are shortest and where social barriers to development are greatest, that political theorists call for government to play the strongest role. It is in precisely these societies that government will be most indifferent, or even strongly opposed, to growth on any such scale as to bring general social improvement.

Many political theorists join economists in the belief that government can import a technology from abroad, and with it propel the society into an eventual prosperity. The *basic* quality of a technology cannot be imported. The all-important supporting skills and attitudes cannot be successfully brought in from abroad. They must be cultivated in the population. It is patently true that an industrial complex can be imported, and placed upon even the poorest of technological soils it can be made to work if it is automated or properly staffed with imported personnel. But this type of import by no means promotes domestic technological growth, nor will the imported complex achieve any real prospects for permanency until the domestic society cultivates the skills and managerial ability to carry it along. Until then, the physical production system will literally remain in the possession of whatever foreign group manages it.

It cannot be demonstrated that there is any one particular type of government that is best suited for carrying out development. The highly organized welfare state or any other type of government that presently may be in power may do equally well, providing that they know how to approach the problem of development directly and effectively, and providing that they are willing to come to grips with the problem with minimum delay. With these provisos, the private economy stands a chance of developing as fast as the welfare-directed state. At least it will be on a competitive footing with the latter so long as its attentions are kept riveted upon the production factor. A proper planning approach should allow the society to begin moving ahead without the trauma of revolution or radical change in government, meantime, leaving some of the more polemic questions of human and material resources management to be solved later as its people choose, or, more likely, as its evolving technology may dictate.

CONCLUSIONS

Like the concepts enunciated by economics, those thus far propounded by the other social sciences are of little assistance in development planning. Present social and cultural change hypotheses are vague, untestable, and, therefore, of undeterminable reliability; and they are inconsistent with one another. Sociologists appear to be confused in defining their mission in development. Some conceive of their task as the abstract study of values, others see themselves as grassroot fundamentalists in community development, and still others view their role as working closely with economists in laying a groundwork which will, hopefully, conjure up a live technology. Their general state of ambivalence is summed up in the frequently heard *non-sequitur*, 'the non-economic factors of economic development.' This phrase may eventually be amended to read, 'the non-economic factors of non-economic development.'

Development is, above all else, an acquisition of machines and a knowledge of how to employ them. In a broader sense, a beginning production technology means a mounting mechanization that is moving in the direction of industrialization and is firmly embedded in a domestic power technology. Hence, development planning calls for instruction in, and for the acquisition of, machine facilities. The major task of indoctrinating a society in technology falls to the educators, and the task of planning for, and creating physical facilities is the job of engineers. Incredibly, among the many books and articles on the theme of development there is virtually no contribution by educators or engineers, nor does it appear that either of these two groups of professionals have taken a first step toward creating a philosophy of development. Perhaps, it is because the others of us have not allowed them the opportunity.

Part Three

NEW PERSPECTIVES

6

HISTORICAL TRENDS IN PRODUCTION

The present and following chapters are concerned altogether with educing new hypotheses accounting for technological development. There are different ways in which a problem can be viewed, and sometimes it may be resolved more readily by using two or more approaches. A long-standing dual approach to social phenomena, and one that is applicable here, is independent analyses of function and structure. Functional analysis is applied in this chapter in studying the *historical* movement and interplay of technology's basic manifestations – its patterns of production. The next chapter will present an attempt to describe the underlying structure, or mechanics, which impart to an active technology its inner dynamic and tempo.

An excellent jumping off point in an analysis of the growth of technology is provided by the hypothesis of economic growth propounded by W. W. Rostow. As shaky as it is, this hypothesis stands virtually alone as the only noteworthy attempt that has been made to get at the process of 'growth.' Rostow postulates five stages of development, beginning with the traditional society and progressing through to 'the age of high mass consumption.'[1] He regards the vital transitional stage, 'take-off into self-sustained growth' as requiring three precursors: increased rate of investment, the development of one or more manufacturing sectors with a high rate of growth, and some triggering stimulus such as a radical political change. He adds that the foregoing must be accompanied by a considerable capacity for raising capital from domestic sources. While Professor Rostow's hypothesis may describe some of the economic concomitants of technological progression, it neither articulates nor sheds much light upon the basic underlying social and technical dynamics, nor does it yield much predictive utility. It is the thesis of this writing that *a more meaningful hypothesis for technological development can be derived by drawing*

[1] Walt W. Rostow, *The Stages of Economic Growth*, Cambridge University Press, 1960, pp. 17–58.

together social and technological data into a single analytical framework.

It is postulated here that through the interplay of a complex of processes developing societies, historically, have evolved normally through four overlapping, but distinctive, phases of productive activity. For lack of more appropriate terms I have labeled these four: Basic Production, Factory Production, Elaborative Production, and Automation. Each phase will be examined individually, and in some detail, on the following pages. However, so as to familiarize the reader, beforehand, with the fundamental meaning of each, it may be said that Basic Production is that enterprise which provides the elemental stuff of survival – food, shelter, and clothing. Every society must carry on, or have indirect access to the products of some form of agriculture, construction, and fabric production. Although everywhere recognized as necessities, the outputs of Basic Production do not, by social definition, constitute true wealth. Because of limitations inherent in its underlying social and technological characteristics, this phase of production will not bloom into high-volume, independent growth but must await, for full stimulus, the social and technical subsidies afforded by the second phase, Factory Production. However, one of the three basic enterprises, *fabric production*, because its processes lend themselves to mechanization and because its product is semi-durable and suitable for long range transportation, *historically provided the bridge for movement from Basic Production into Factory Production.*

The signal characteristic of Factory Production is an outpouring of a durable type of goods. These latter goods are in a realm apart from the items of Basic Production. The demand for durable goods steadily swells within the framework of the well-nigh infinitely expansive psychological desires, as opposed to the more readily sated physical appetites catered to by Basic Production. Durable goods can be collected, collated into specific configurations to suit the individual taste, merged, traded, and, in general, manipulated. They are freely negotiable; they represent true wealth.[1] The hallmark of Factory Production is the creation, by semi-mechanized or mechanized means, of a variety of durable items which are *not* universally known or available. Its main evolutionary feature is that it creates the surplus wealth and the techniques necessary to subsidize Basic Production, thus largely closing the growth loop by knitting the entire production complex into an *elaborative*, growing whole whose logical terminus is automation.

[1] Durable goods is used here in the conventional economic sense of its being a type of commodity whose purchase and consumption can be postponed and whose lifetime is at least one year.

PHASE I: BASIC PRODUCTION

Basic production centers upon those commodities that are everywhere necessary, in some form, to the domestic maintenance of the society. Whether they are obtained through conquest, provided by the society's own labor, or are in natural abundance is relatively unimportant here; suffice it to say that they are universal. Therefore, in meeting these basic needs the activities of the pre-industrial society, whether the society is nomadic or sedentary, are compressed into three general areas of activity: 1. Agriculture or other types of *food* provisioning; 2. The creation of fabrics for *clothing* and other household uses; and 3. The erection of crude structures for dwelling *shelter*, assembly places or storage. In addition there is, of course, a production of some durable items such as ceramics and metal wares, but in pre-industrial society these are usually in limited supply and do not enter into extensive commerce.

Socially and technically, these basic spheres of activity have two noteworthy features in common. First, their products are not in themselves, however abundant, determinants of a high standard of living. Many small pre-industrial societies have a surplus of all three, food, shelter and clothing, and although they live at a high level of physical comfort this alone is not construed as a high standard of living. These societies are classified as 'undeveloped.' Secondly, none of these three basic areas of activity is capable of being led into indefinitely sustained growth, although at least one of them, historically, must have acted as a springboard in initiating industrial growth in the West. A given sector's ability to grow and to produce growth in other sectors, originally, must have depended upon its ability to create enough surplus production to allow for exportation, upon some breakthrough in production efficiency providing at least a temporary competitive advantage on foreign markets, upon the attainment of enough trade volume on these markets to permit a return of significant added wealth into the domestic society, and upon a social tendency to recycle this wealth into further productive enterprise. Since these three basic endeavors comprise the platform from which most of the emerging societies will have to begin development, each should be examined carefully as to its potential for making contribution.

General Agriculture – Its Growth Potential

One way in which to lay bare agriculture's potential for contributing to development is by an appraisal of the role it has played in the growth of societies that are now in the vanguard of development or that are in transition. Earlier classical economists were of the conviction, and perhaps the majority of present day economists and social scientists still hold this view, that high agricultural productivity is a prerequisite to industrial development. This viewpoint rests upon the supposition that it is from agricultural surpluses that industrial capital is formed. If this assumption contains any truth at all, it has not been borne out in clear-cut fashion or on a very wide basis. Mexico, for example, came into an era of industrial progress initiated by a land reform in 1910 that, although democratically reapportioning land and releasing labor from serfdom by the terms of its land provisions, cut the former estates up into tiny parcels that lessened their absolute productivity. In this same year, while Mexican industry embarked upon an era of accelerative growth, agricultural production dipped into a trough of such severity that it did not regain its 1910 level of production until thirty years later.

Japan, in many ways a model of rapid development, between the years 1878 and 1937 increased the net income of her agriculture sevenfold; but during the same interval she increased the net income of her non-agricultural enterprises by about forty-seven times. During this period, government revenues realized through taxation of agriculture declined by one-half while those coming from non-agricultural enterprises increased by eighty-nine times. Obviously, support for Japan's development did not derive its main, or long-term sustenance, from the farmer.

The tempo of development did not increase markedly in the United States until just before the Civil War. During the seventy year period from 1799 to 1869, a predominantly rural (94 per cent, 74 per cent) U.S. society managed to advance its real per capita income by only ten per cent, or from $216 to $237.[1] But, during the decade immediately preceding the Civil War, U.S. production began to march, and in this movement the increase in manufactures to agricultural output ran at a ratio of about four and one-half to one. During the economic upsurges that occurred during the twenty year period following the Civil War, at the turn of the century, and again in the 1920's, agricultural production rose in response to such factors as the preceding development of railways or war-stimulated foreign demand, but agriculture never played the role of a leading sector in development. It is interesting that economic historians have variously attributed U.S. national growth to railroad expansion, iron and steel increases, and to the development of public utilities and street railways, but almost never to

[1] Barry E. Supple, *The Experience of Economic Growth*, Random House: New York, 1963, p. 265.

agriculture. Yet, these national growth periods were characterized by the formation of capital in agriculture and by increased agricultural output. However, the greater part of this agricultural expansion was stimulated by the homestead opening of new, tillable lands in the West rather than through improving the production methods used in farming settled lands.

It is a usual case in the plans of transitional societies that development funds are prorated over the production sectors in accordance with their stated needs. Each Ministry, or other development agency, designs plans of a sort and each contends for a share of the available funds, rather than the funds being allocated in the first instance on the basis of anticipatable returns. Because of the population pressure on most backward areas, food production always looms in the foreground as a development requisite and, thus, can command strong funding. Nigeria's six year plan, inaugurated in 1962, channeled almost equal funds into agriculture, and to trade and industry, and straightaway fell into trouble because of a drop in foreign demand and general market prices for its agricultural products.

In India, although great emphasis was placed upon agriculture during the period 1950 to 1961, while agricultural production increased by 3·6 per cent annually, industrial output, despite the handicap of its 'cottage craft' character, rose by 6·9 per cent. Russia has made phenomenal industrial progress but is perennially embarrassed by low agricultural productivity. With regularity she has experimented with new plans and incentives but without achieving noteworthy success until quite recently, and, in the wake of an established industrial base. Communist China, which has likewise soared ahead industrially, is plagued by an agricultural problem. In the United States the problem of obtaining agricultural output has been surmounted, but only through the largess of industry and the other sectors which, through government-sponsored measures introduced during the 1930s, now annually subsidize the farm producer through price supports.

So much for the broader patterns of agricultural movement. Now the question might be raised of how much vitality agriculture shows when it is examined *within* national settings, and when it is compared more directly with the industrial sector. In answer to this, one of the more disconcerting aspects of agriculture is its unevenness of development and its tendency to lag behind the other sectors, within even the most advanced agrarian societies. The average living standard of the richer one-third of the human population and the poorer one-half is at a ratio of approximately ten to one, and the difference is rapidly widening. This schism has captured the world's interest. But somewhat less obvious are the regional divisions in socio-economic well-being within the advanced nations, such as the differences between the north and the southeast of the United States or between the north and south of Italy. Thanks to vigorous federal intervention in both countries their southern areas have begun to emerge, but the disparity is still such as to make these areas classifiable developmentally, as backward ones.

To carry the analysis a step further, not only is development regionally uneven within the larger advanced nations, but there is considerable disparity *between occupational groups* within the 'have regions' of the 'have nations.' And at the lower end of the socio-economic spectrum are the agriculturalists and, in particular, agricultural laborers. In the United States, which is considered one of the world's more prosperous agricultural areas, for the amount of capital invested the farm proprietor still realizes a relatively low return; and the United States' farm laborer, as evidenced by the Table below, is, in many respects, on a standard-of-living parity with the peoples of the under-privileged societies. Throughout the world's nations, with a few exceptions such as Israel, England, and Australia, the income of farm laborers has trailed far behind the earnings of non-agricultural workers.

Vexed by such inconsistencies as those listed above, some observers seem to be veering away from the belief that agriculture is the anointed leader of development. Haselitz cautiously and somewhat erratically observes that

> It is theoretically possible that a country may experience rapid economic growth through perfection of its agriculture. Moreover, a few countries, e.g., Denmark and New Zealand, actually have reached high levels of per capita income largely on the basis of agricultural development and without intensive industrialization. However, the only known path to economic growth is industrial and selected tertiary development.[1]

Other points that Hazelitz might have brought out are that those nations having food sufficiency are almost exclusively industrially advanced nations, and that in all of these countries the *relative* importance of the agricultural sector has steadily declined. Canada, Denmark and New Zealand, sometimes erroneously cited (as above) as exceptions to the rule, are, in fact, primarily industrial nations; for none of the three does direct agricultural production constitute a share of more than one-fourth of their total output.

[1] Iowa State University Center for Agriculture and Economic Adjustment, *Food*, Iowa State University Press, 1962, p. 126.

TABLE 1

Ratio of Money Income in Agriculture Per Worker to Income of Nonagriculture Per Worker, United States

Year	*Ratio*
1870	·26
1880	·23
1890	·27
1900	·35
1910	·46
1920	·49
1930	·34
1940	·48
1950	·56
1960	·47

Source: Kuznets and agricultural outlook charts for 1960.

TABLE 2

Ratio of Income of Agriculture Per Worker to Income of Nonagriculture for Selected Countries

(Labor Force of 1950)

Country		*Ratio A/Non-A*	*Country*		*Ratio A/Non-A*
Australia	1939	·99	Israel		1·02
Austria	1951	·40	Italy	1954	·51
Belgian Congo	1952	·09	Japan		·34
Belgium	1947	·63	Mexico		·16
Bolivia		·48	Netherlands		·61
Brazil		·34	New Zealand	1951	·88
Bulgaria	1934	·18	Norway		·50
Canada	1951	·63	Pakistan	1951	·47
Ceylon	1946	1·07	Paraguay		·74
Chile	1952	·46	Philippines	1948	·28
Denmark		·77	Portugal		·43
Ecuador		·68	Puerto Rico		·41
Egypt	1947	·36	Sweden		·58
El Salvador		·66	Thailand	1947	·21
Finland		·42	Turkey		·16

TABLE 2 (*cont.*)

Country		*Ratio A/Non-A*	*Country*		*Ratio A/Non-A*
France	1946	·36	U.K.	1951	1·08
Germany		·44	United States		·56
Hungary	1941	·56	USSR	1939	·26
India	1951	·42	Yugoslavia	1953	·20
Ireland	1941	·73			

However, there are three members of the Western bloc – Denmark, New Zealand, and Australia – whose *exports* are primarily agricultural. And as may be seen in Table 3, the terms of trade for this trio are even worse than those experienced by the underdeveloped countries, in general. One might conjecture that if their main internal dependency was upon agricultural production, they would be in desperate straits, indeed. In general support of this point and in connection with the increasing of per capita income, West remarks, 'No solution is possible until economic and industrial development raises per capita output and increases individual earning power.'[1]

There seems to be a certain short-sightedness in promoting agricultural development as an intermediate step toward increased food production. Since, in most undeveloped countries, the great bulk of agricultural output is consumed domestically, agricultural increases must, therefore, depend upon the vitality of the home market, and these pristine markets lack the necessary initial buying power. The tendency in the advanced nations for agricultural development to lag behind industry indicates that it is first necessary to industrialize to the point that purchasing power is infused into the society, and that agricultural production then wells up to match the level of industrial prosperity. Without steady sustenance from the industrial sector, agriculture will slump. Export produce, notably coffee, has repeatedly climbed to impressive production volumes in response to increased foreign demand, but each time this has proven a short-term trend incapable of supporting long-term domestic growth.

The foregoing observations were not intended to disparage the importance of agricultural development but rather to stimulate critical inquiry into some of the current philosophies and practices *presumed* to promote food production. The insurance of an adequate

[1] Ibid., p. 110.

TABLE 3

Real Export Purchasing Power Index

(1937=100)

Group	1937	1948	1950	1951	1952	1953	1954	1955	1956	1957	1958	1919	1960
1. Developed countries, I	100	138	128	129	138	149	149	162	178	177	189	206	236
2. Underdeveloped countries	100	104	143	151	140	161	190	177	179	169	159	172	179
3. Developed countries, II	100	105	133	136	118	194	130	137	143	154	140	163	165

Notes: Developed countries I include U.S.A., Canada, Belgium, France, West Germany, Italy, Norway, Sweden, U.K. and Japan. The base year used for calculating import price indices for France and Sweden, West Germany, and Japan respectively are 1938, 1936 and 1934–36. The value index for Belgium is based on the total value of exports for Belgium–Luxemburg.

Underdeveloped countries include Bolivia, Colombia, Dominican Republic, El Salvador, Uruguay, Turkey, India, Burma, Ceylon and Philippines. The base year for Ceylon's import price index is 1938. As the import price indices for Bolivia, Dominican Republic and Uruguay are not available the import price index for Latin America is used. The import price index of Burma is based on unit value import price index. The value index for India is based on the 1937 estimate made taking into consideration the 1948 proportion of total value of exports of India and Pakistan.

Developed countries II include Australia, New Zealand and Denmark, whose total value of agricultural exports as a percentage of total exports exceed 60 per cent. Ireland has been excluded for the lack of 1937 value data. In the case of Denmark, 1938 import price index is used.

Sources: *International Financial Statistics*, Oct. 1957, 28–31 and 40–1; *International Financial Statistics*, June 1961, 34–9; *U.N. Monthly Bulletin of Statistics*, Oct. 1953, June and Dec. 1960.

food level probably is the most fundamental issue in technological development, and it is a primary goal of almost all developing nations. This being the case, the issue then becomes an important one of identifying more fully those factors which constrain agricultural development, so that agricultural planning can be incorporated more effectively into the overall development program.

Impediments to the Development of General Agriculture

If the relative production efficiency of agriculture is to be judged, appropriate yardsticks must be devised for the purpose. The general framework within which agriculture might be evaluated is by viewing it against the backdrop of factory industry, the other great moiety beside which it stands. However, the absolute outputs of the two endeavours cannot be compared because of the incommensurability of their output data. Economists regularly chart the individual outputs of each, factory industry and agriculture, and they frequently attempt to compare the two, but indices allowing *valid* cross-comparisons have yet to be invented. This leads us to a second type of analysis, and one which holds considerably more promise – systems evaluation. What are the differences between agriculture and factory industry in the methods they employ, the machines they use, the characteristics of their work forces, and the general social and physical environments within which they exist?

Agriculture and factory industry operate within radically different types of 'demand' environments. Factory industry, as it grows, steadily strengthens the base upon which it rests, while agriculture, however strong its potential, eventually encounters a production ceiling which limits its further growth. Factory production consists in large part, of durable goods. The market for this class of commodity is practically inexhaustible, and in the generally prospering society the factory system can go on indefinitely in pyramiding these goods layer upon layer, in making the society continuously richer. Agriculture, on the other hand, with the exception of those of its segments that are industry-linked, produces for *finite* physical needs. A society, like an individual, can consume only so much food stock, and even with extensive systems for food storage and preservation this fact imposes a production limit. In the wealthier countries agriculture tends to create production surpluses, the outcome of which is likely to be policies designed to curtail production to fit the immediate consumption pattern. Hence, even when it has a free rein, agriculture probably will be arrested in its growth by the capacity of the domestic market, well before it realizes its full potential. Those nations producing the greatest abundance of food are the great industrial nations, within which, significantly, the relative importance of agriculture has steadily declined.

It would seem that if an emerging nation of strong agricultural potential is to reach full stride it must look beyond the domestic market to the agriculture export trade. But again, the foreign markets for general agricultural produce also are limited, and this time by social, rather than physical factors. Food production is to a great extent every man's and every society's business; and practically all societies, however urbanized, have their own agriculture and are hypersensitive to a felt need to increase its adequacy and thus avoid food dependency on outsiders. Pressure to maintain an internal monopoly, plus generally low standards for defining food adequacy place the domestic food producer in the emerging society behind a protective screen of import tariffs which are let down only in the event of emergency, and then only until the food crisis has passed. This monopoly persists despite the continuing impotency of the domestic agriculture. To enter this trade arena from outside is to move against heavily shielded competition with a product which is characteristically bulky, depressed in price as compared with other types of goods, and much of which, especially for the technically backward exporter, is not preservable. A way around this impasse, and one which is resorted to by most of the underdeveloped countries, is through the cultivation and exportation of specialized, regionally peculiar agricultural commodities such as coffee and rubber. But this is highly unstable, plantation type of agriculture that usually runs directly athwart the society's food needs and other developmental interests.

The problem of maintaining internal production ceilings is not a matter of concern to most of the underdeveloped societies, only to those societies that have a viable agriculture. The majority of the world's present-day agricultural nations do not produce enough food to meet their home needs. Although most of the world's materially retarded societies are agricultural, their farm production is barely keeping pace with, or is falling behind population increase. The poorer one-fifth of these nations reap a per-acre yield that is approximately one-fifth that of the richer one-fifth of the community of nations. In large part, this is testimony to a retarded agricultural technology. However, in even the most agriculturally advanced societies the efficiency of agricultural methods seems to suffer in comparison with those of industry. Agriculture is universally handicapped, in comparison with industry, by its less efficient methods and by the many other internal problems with which it is beset.

When the production methods of agriculture and factory industry are compared, several factors seem to point to the conclusion that those used in the factory are significantly the more efficient of the two. The factory process is the epitome of 'tight organization,' in which even the humans who are retained in the 'production loop' are made to perform very much as mechanisms. Once the industrial processing of a given item has been initiated, it flows in a smoothly controlled peristaltic ripple in which the output of one machine becomes, almost instantaneously, the input to another. The overall process is paced to the slowest processing point, and, since these bottlenecks are easily detected, the machines or human actions accounting for them can be improved, or two or more such production segments may be set in the loop in parallel. This work at improvement is systematic and unrelenting. Design engineers strive continuously to break bottlenecks wherever they are found to occur. The factory employs relatively many employees who carry out one, or a few highly specialized tasks in which, by sheer repetition, they develop great speed and finesse.

In agriculture, on the other hand, work must be phased to the three differing rhythms of planting, cultivating and harvesting. Each stage requires specialized techniques and machinery, and this, with other tasks interspersed, makes for a frequent changing of work techniques and equipment configurations. A seed planter must be laboriously removed from a tractor which is then refitted with a crop cultivator which, in its turn, may be removed one or more times to allow the temporary mounting of an auger, mower, manure loader, etc., to fit the demands of the work day. Although there are differences between cereal growing, vegetable growing, and animal husbandry, they all share the feature of having their tasks grouped into seasonally determined waves. In most farm operations the machine must have an extra quality – mobility. Work cannot be articulated to flow along a 'factory type' of machine line; instead a single type of machine is moved against the material being processed. The agricultural picture is one of relatively few men carrying out relatively generalized operations of three differing, and successive, classes.

A special stimulant to industrial growth that is not found in agriculture is the direct and sustained effort of the hired, full-time innovator. Schumpeter and others have discussed the role of the innovator in industry. They have given him special stress as a stimulus to production activity and rank him, in this connection, significantly above the inventor or entrepreneur. In some cases the inventor and the innovator may be one and the same person, but the two functions are quite distinct. Innovation is an action program; it translates a heretofore inert idea, an idle invention, into a working reality. One might conjecture that the innovator is a by-product of the corporate system, that the latter setting provides an especially friendly home for his talents because it allows him to occupy a position in the system that is protectively offset from the line organization.

It is an oversimplification to say that the innovator is the basic factor making for technological change. It is probably more valid to observe that a certain type of socio-technical structure will educe innovators, and innovation. The organizational characteristics inviting such experimentation are not fully identifiable but it is a reasonable assumption that sheer organization *size* will function as one factor in creating the specialization and differentiation calling forth creative planning. A large organization will not only tend to draw out innovative skills but it will grant them an especially effective organizational niche within which to work, a special staff position.

This is not to ignore the importance of changes made casually, while working, and through the suggestion-box, by operational personnel. However, even though the aggregate value of these types of changes is appreciable they usually appertain to modifications of a single machine, task, or limited work situation. They do not have the broad compass for organizational revisions which grow out of the analyses of systems planners.

Generally speaking, the innovator is not an administrator, supervisor or executive, but an analyst and advisor. He can function effectively only in an organization large enough, and sufficiently specialized, to allow him to apply himself full-time to experimentation with methods for increasing productivity, and in making consequent recommendations. His is a continuous business of engineering improvement through promoting change. Regular operational personnel will sometimes inaugurate changes voluntarily, and sometimes quite sweeping ones, but once the change from this source has been effected, rigidity sets in. Continuous change causes continuous psychological perturbation, and when it is perceived to originate with some, one person within the immediate work organization resistence can be aggressively channeled against this person, and the would-be author of change soon loses his effectiveness. More, after an individual who belongs to the line organization introduces change, his reputation is somewhat at stake, he is thus confined to making a 'one time' change followed by relatively minor revisions. After 'the change,' his main concern becomes one of justifying the change by obtaining immediate production dividends.

In the large organization, the innovators usually are members of a regular systems engineering group whose full-time assignment is experimentation. In the smaller organization, this role may be filled, in part, by the hired consultant, the cost accountant or others in positions of overview where they can observe technical or organizational impediments. In the larger organization, the physical presence of the innovator is to a great extent invisible to the work force affected, but his influence is pronounced. The individual worker is informed with little prior notice that his desk is to be moved; that he is to be attached temporarily to another organization; that he is to be given another assignment working on a new project; that the company is embarking upon a whole new type of production program; that he is to be transferred geographically to work in a subsidiary organization in a distant part of the country; or that because of an anticipated production slump he is to be discharged. These continuous reverberations undoubtedly entrain psychological hardships, but in the long run they also expedite production.

In comparison, the limited manpower on even the largest of farms and the very nature of farm industry preclude the innovator from being effectively installed. As a member of industry, he may persuade the top leadership to abandon a relatively new multi-million-dollar plant and build an even more costly one in its place. He accomplishes this by hard-and-fast calculations demonstrating differences in future output volume and costs. The farm manager, on the other hand, will 'trade in' an expensive machine only after long deliberation. As sociologists have pointed out, agricultural methods are crystallized by tradition and even the communistic, collectively operated farms do not physically uproot the worker or physically move him far enough, or frequently enough, to eliminate the effects of provincialism. Patriarchal lines of control and traditional community relationships are merely transferred to a more mechanized setting. Israel has been more successful than most societies in agricultural innovation; and, not surprisingly, the state has taken a quite 'industrialized' approach to agricultural development. But as for the professional innovator, who has so heavily influenced industrial progress, he cannot be injected into the subculture of agriculture under even the most highly mechanized conditions presently attainable.

Another constraint upon agriculture is the relatively high cost of equipment. The low ratio of equipment cost to actual use-time makes capitalization much more difficult for agriculture than for industry. In industry, a turret lathe may have an installation cost of $25,000 and an operating lifetime that may easily extend to ten years, or 2,600 work days. A sixteen-foot self-propelled combine may cost a farmer $10,000, but be employed no more than five work days per annum and require replacement at the end of ten years due more to age deterioration than wear. It has, meantime, served a useful working life of only fifty days, a factor driving its cost to over twenty times that of the industrial lathe. It should be added that the anticipated lifetime of farm machinery is aptly reflected in its construction – in light-gauge metals, low-grade alloys, an absence of safety features, and in a generally poor quality of engineering that would be altogether unacceptable to the buyer of industrial equipment. One possible conclusion that might be drawn here is that before there is a significant movement toward farm mechanization, industrial competition for labor must have reached a point where it creates the agricultural labor shortages and higher labor costs that will force the farmer to make these high capital investments in equipment. So long as there is a plentitude of cheap manual labor available he will avoid capital investment, despite the much lower output rate obtained by manual methods.

Another impediment to agricultural development lies in the nature of the agricultural product and the humanistic relationship it has to the market. While agricultural prices do vary with place and time, they have a certain inelasticity that sets them somewhat apart from durable products. Since the farmer's products are essential for human survival they must somehow be kept within reach of the poorest spectrum of society. There is, conceivably, a little-inown ethic at work here which saps agricultural output of the supply-demand elasticity enjoyed by the less essential manufactured goods, and which forbids prices to soar to the levels that might be predicted by economists, even in time of severe famine. This is not to deny that food prices sometimes are callously manipulated, but rather to point out that the practice could be carried to greater extremes and allowed to become much more abusive.

Another factor inhibiting agriculture, particularly in the poorer undeveloped nations, which characteristically are predominantly agricultural in enterprise, is inability to drive the submarginal producer permanently off the market. In industry, the submarginal producer necessarily goes out of business. This is not true in agricultural societies, in some of which as many as sixty per cent of the farm families are engaged in subsistence farming. These producers, however low the prices, will always have something to offer the market. Their latent ability to increase production can react very strongly to dampen a market that is beginning an upturn, and certainly this, as well as the sheer number of agricultural producers, bars the farmer from the privilege of oligopolistic price-setting enjoyed by the combines of big industries. Whereas, the corporate entity approaches the market place with a predetermined 'price tag,' the farmer is much more subject to the market place's appraisal of the worth of his labors and investment. The industrialists present a final product fabricated through multitudinous operations whose nature and costs are something of an enigma to the buying public; the operations involved in farming are better understood, less camouflageable, and prices are more likely to be driven in line with costs. Moreover, agriculture does not have the rapid production response-time that permits industry, almost spontaneously, to increase production to take advantage of currently high market prices, nor does it have a nearly comparable ability to maintain a finished inventory that can be incrementally released to take maximum advantage of market changes.

In contrast with the relative inelasticity in *demand* for agricultural produce, is a conspicuous elasticity in supply. Unlike manufacture, agriculture is a field of crude skills such that in time of economic pinch virtually every man can become a backyard farmer. For this reason the correlation between farm mechanization and productivity is a loose one. This is particularly evident in the specialized cropping of undeveloped areas, where production will sometimes move radically upward, as in the frequent coffee production booms, with no discernible concomitant increase in mechanization. This manual production surge may spring, in part, from the behavior of the subsistence farmer, who is coaxed back into the market by rising prices, and in part by greater utilization of an omnipresent and ubiquitous surplus agricultural labor force.

Coupled with the foregoing impediments to agricultural production are a whole range of negatives usually pointed to as 'acts of God.' The annually recurrent possibilities of crop loss through drought, flood, hail, wind damage, unseasonal freeze, and insect depredation makes agriculture a hazardous business. Added to these imponderables is another which historians view as having been especially detrimental to the economic health of agriculture – wide price oscillation. What are at first moderate price variations become greatly exaggerated shifts caused by the *en masse* tendency of farm producers to plan next year's crop uniformly in relation to this year's market. There must be insurance against undue drop in at least this one factor, price, before agriculture may be expected to show steady growth; and, significantly, it is in those nations proffering this type of insurance that agricultural output has been moving steadily upward.

Agriculture may be supported by domestic government insurance derived from taxation upon the more prosperous sectors of production, or through market guarantees by foreign buyers who, again, if they are able to afford such guarantees, in all likelihood will be members of one of the industrially advanced societies. Prior to its subsidization in the West, agriculture enjoyed 'boom' times again and again, but these periods were always of too limited duration to sustain growth. Following the great agricultural depression of the 1920's, Western nations, from the largest to the smallest, set about subsidizing agriculture in one way or another. This action historically signalled the maturation of what we have labelled here as Phase II, Elaborative Production. There followed in the 1940's an unprecedented increase in all fields of production.

The fact that agriculture cannot forge ahead without the aid of a vigorous industrial sector is the dilemma of the poor agrarian society. It seems almost as though a society must be able to produce fine dinner ware before it can have bread. Not only does industry create the surplus wealth from which agriculture receives financial subsidy, but as it broadens its own base it draws increasingly upon agriculture for raw materials, thereby allowing the latter sector to variegate its output just as the growing industry itself does.

Textile Production

The production of fabrics is of special interest here because it is this area of endeavor that appears, historically, to have been the springboard to Phase II, Factory Production. The sedentary, repetitious nature of its processes and the relative durability and transportability of its product make it, of the three basic productions, the first logical candidate for mechanization. Although it suffers some limitation by seasonality in the production of its raw materials and in the consumption of its finished goods, it has virtues which single it out to initiate (but not to sustain) long-term growth in material output. In its more exotic fabrics, textile production allows for the investment of an enormous, and therefore more economically transportable, concentration of labor. This was especially the case of the textiles to form the early vanguard of foreign trade – silks, linens, rugs, and tapestries – which often had to be delivered by arduous overland caravan routes. The uniqueness and ornateness of these fabrics were sufficient to allow them to compete successfully in foreign market places even though they were in the general class of being universals. Perhaps, the greatest of fabrics' early discovered virtues was its durability, or at least semi-durability. It was exportable and, therefore, could recruit wealth from sources external to the society to augment that derivable from within. Because of its relative compactness, and durability in storage, it could reach out for distant marts. It was a much more suitable trade good than were agricultural products, being less subject to spoilage during transportation than even oil or grain produce. Like the more sophisticated manufacturers which it initiated, fabric-making is a sedentary process in which raw materials are concentrated at a point of input and then flowed from machine to machine.

Early mechanization in textiles was to gain its first great impetus in the production of cotton goods. Whereas the earlier fabrics found a limited export market on the basis of their originality as a semi-art form, because of a technological breakthrough allowing for their cheap manufacture, cotton goods were enabled to compete on foreign markets as genuine consumer goods. Cotton weaving, like silk and linen work, dates back at least three millenia B.C., and although the basic tasks of carding, spinning, and weaving had been carried out by simple appliances from earliest times, it was not until the mid-1700's that the industry began to make a radical transformation to mechanical methods. In so doing, it became the *progenitor* of the factory system, of mass production techniques, and of the industrial revolution itself. The early cost of capitalizing this type of industry was relatively low and, as opposed to much of the hard-goods production which later followed, textile manufacture could be powered by water. It did not have to await the development of steam power for its inception. A rapid succession of innovations – the 'fly' shuttle, the spinning jenny, the spinning 'mule' and the cotton gin – were combined with high-volume, low-cost water transport by a few nations, which were, thus, temporarily enabled to dominate a significant part of the foreign market. Those nations that enjoined factory textile production with water transportation most successfully were England (in particular), the Netherlands, France, Belgium, Germany, and the United States. In 1835, England produced over sixty per cent of the cotton goods consumed by the world, while the remainder of the countries just cited jointly produced about twenty-four per cent of the world's supply. By this time Spain and Portugal, both of which had textile producing facilities, had declined as maritime powers; and Italy, another producer, had never been a particularly strong seafarer. None of the three had the mass transportational means to compete seriously in export markets.

In the face of the ubiquitous production of cotton textiles and a rapid adaptation to the new production methods of the West by some of the outlier nations such as India and Japan, this Western commercial gambit yielded only short-term advantages, but they were sufficient to establish the conditions for transition to the high-volume manufacture of fully durable types of goods. Britain, regarded as the heartland and nerve center of the industrial revolution and the point from which early mechanization diffused, provides a classical example of technological evolution which was later approximated, but never really fully matched by other Western nations.

By the middle of the eighteenth century, England had reached a point at which about half her production was carried out in centralized work places. The metal-ware industry had begun spawning new machines, and by this time a few factories employing a hundred or more men had appeared. Much impetus was given to iron works development by the mechanization of the early, pre-steam textile industry. The elaborate translational linkage needed for water powering soon demanded a material stronger than wood, and, in the production of the textile machines themselves, metal was soon used to replace wood.

While there, at first, appears to have been a somewhat concurrent development between textile and hard-goods manufacture, a closer analysis of the two trends in England shows textiles, during the early period of the industrial revolution, well out in the lead and eventually feeding back into hard-goods production. Between 1720 and 1788, the production of pig iron in England increased 272 per cent; but during an interval eighteen years shorter (1741 to 1791), textile production increased 523 per cent. During the next five decades, a crossover in trends occurred with textile production continuing to expand, but at a decreasing rate, while iron prodution mushroomed. Between 1788 and 1839, textile production increased another 285 per cent but pig iron output, meantime, jumped 2,000 per cent.[1] Pig iron is an important production factor because it lies at the base of a significant part of all durable-goods production, particularly for the time period under discussion.

By 1850, after a long evolution in mechanization, the cotton industry stood forth as a prime example of complete factory mechanization. It initiated the manufacture of machines; and the machine industry it spawned hastened the development of the supporting metal industries and entrained a rapid spread of mechanization within other types of industries.

A significant part of the surpluses needed for the general expansion of British industry was born from export profits. Exports, particularly in cotton goods, reached phenomenal proportions. Between 1870 and 1913, Britain's exports amounted to about one-third of her

[1] E. Barnes, *History of the Cotton Manufacture*, London, 1835, p. 343.

total industrial production. In way of comparison, the United States, whose gross output amounts to forty per cent of the world's total, typically exports only about five per cent, and imports at a rate of about four per cent, of her national income. In British export, the proportion going into cotton goods rose from fifty-seven per cent of the total, in the early 1840s, to account for eighty per cent of Britain's total export trade by 1850, thus bringing about great increases in the national product and inducing general industrial expansion. After the 1860s, the growth rates of exportation and general industrial expansion began to decline, along with a steady fall in the output of agriculture. As these factors declined, however, pig-iron production, which provides a fair index of metal manufacturers, showed the rapid increase illustrated in Figure 1, below, which shows growth relationships between the basic productions.

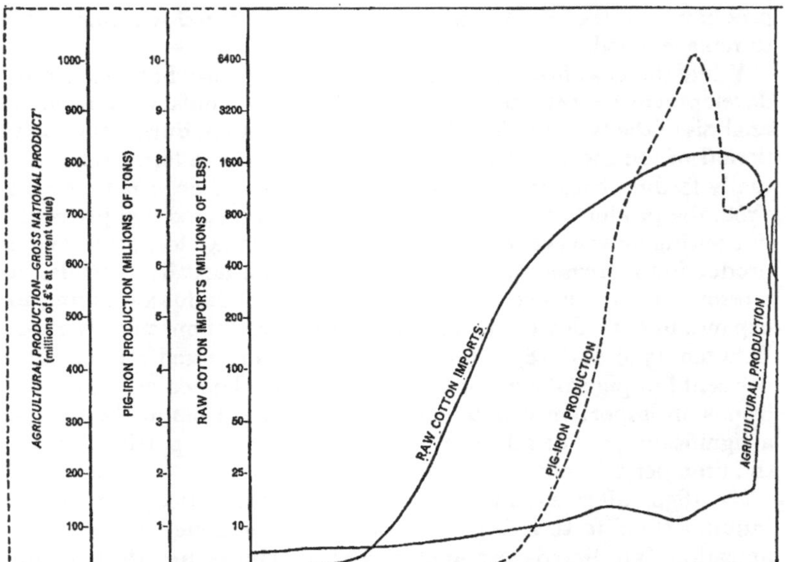

Figure 1. Growth trends in England in Cotton Textiles, Pig-Iron and Agriculture during the period 1700 to 1950.

Sources: G. W. Daniels, *The Early English Cotton Industry*, Manchester, 1920; E. Baines, 'History of the Cotton Manufacture in Great Britain' *Tattersall's Cotton Trade Review;* T. S. Ashton, *Iron and Steel in the Industrial Revolution*; Phyllis Deane and W. A. Cole, *British Economic Growth 1688–1959*.

Fully reliable or complete census statistics on manufactured goods do not date back in any country before 1850. Data describing trends for the construction industry are even more limited. Table 7 illustrates the infant status of Contract Construction in the United States in 1870 and its elevenfold increase by 1950.

The crossover point between cotton textile and hard-goods manufacture outputs appears to have occurred around 1875 in England, and to have followed between the years 1895 to 1900 in the United States. In England, as textile exports hit their peak growth rate between 1850 and 1870, pig iron and steel exports, which had constituted only twenty-seven per cent of total export in the early 1840's, jumped to forty-five per cent, in the 1870's. The relationship between textiles and metal and engineering exports is illustrated in Table 4 below.

TABLE 4

Composition of the United Kingdom's Exports

Year	*Textile exports as per cent of total exports*	*Metal and engineering exports as per cent of total exports*
1830	67	11
1850	63	18
1870	56	21
1890	43	25
1913	34	27
1937	24	35
1951	19	49

Source: E. A. G. Robinson, 'The Changing Structure of the British Economy,' *Economic Journal*, LXIV, no. 255, p. 460, (Sept. 1954).

By the 1920's, British textile production had begun an absolute decline in which, between 1925 and 1950, it fell about twenty-five per cent. The same trend was paralleled in the United States, Holland, Belgium, Germany, Italy, and the other textile producing countries, bringing their output more in line with their domestic requirements. The emerging nations had, meantime, mechanized to a point where, during this same period, their collective output more than tripled, and the former competitive edge enjoyed by the Western textile producers was lost. These later nations quickly shifted to the exportation of textile-making *machines* in support of the domestication of textiles in the emergent group. In the 1950s, twenty-five per cent of the total of U.S. industrial exports were in the form of textile machinery.

Meantime, in England, as durable goods production had grown and textile output had declined, another fundamental structural change had set in. As a portion of national income, agricultural income successively fell from slightly more than twenty per cent in 1867–1869, to seven per cent in 1911–1913, and to only four per cent by 1939. From a former position of world leadership in agriculture, Britain's farm production acceded to the fact that through the more efficient manufacture and extensive export of industrial goods, the output, of the individual worker, could be exchanged for significantly more foodstock than he could produce in the direct employ of agriculture.

England, early recognizing the importance of mechanical invention, jealously hoarded this knowledge by forbidding the export of machinery or machine designs, or the migration of artisans knowledgeable of machine construction. Inevitably all three diffused, and with a lag of, perhaps, a couple of decades, the factory method spread to western and central Europe and the United States. The developmental trend in these later countries, from textiles to hardwares, was similar to that in England, but less conspicuous. Although in all these countries textile manufacture is still an important industry, in none of them is it now a dominant sector. Directly or indirectly, the other early textile manufacturing countries were heavily indebted to England's lead in machine invention as well as to her initiation of the building of a general European industrial-commercial complex. The United States drew heavily upon the British surpluses, made in textiles, in the borrowed finance of its nineteenth century railway and industrial development. By the mid-1800s, the United States, lacking skilled labor and preoccupied with offsetting this dilemma through invention and through the integration of manufacture under one roof (as opposed to England's separately specialized plants), had moved to the forefront in factory production. By now, the United States, together with England and central and western Europe, was solidly on the road to an expanding development which, in its full bloom, became Phase III, Elaborative Production.

Whether *transition* from the easily capitalized and temporarily profitable enterprise of cotton textiles to durable-goods, historically came about because of the rapid accumulation of wealth for capital formation, whether the prospering textile industry wheted a commercial appetite to expand trade through a broader employment of mechanization, or whether mechanization, once launched, became a cultural pattern carried forward of its own inertia are all interesting points for speculation. It is edifying, however, that nations of one-time wealth, such as Spain and Portugal, did not convert the surpluses coming from their colonies to capital formation, and it has been a common observation in undeveloped societies that a marked economic upturn may accomplish nothing more than increase the rate of investment in land. Apparently, the growth of mechanization is dependent upon deeper seated socio-technical processes than those exhibited in the bare behavior of the market.

Construction

Crude construction, the third factor of Basic Production, seems to have played a small role in *early* Western development. The transition to the more sophisticated building programs is conspicuously dependent upon a forerunning source of wealth which is not normally forthcoming until the factory movement of Phase II is well underway. By construction at the sophisticated level is meant luxury dwellings, commercial buildings, systematically designed manufacturing and processing plants, highways, bridges, port facilities, and, in general, those units subsumed under housing and basic provisions for transport. Unlike prime industrial capital, the products of construction are assets whose cost can be amortized only as they contribute to a greater efficiency in industry; and industry can afford them only after it has, itself, entered a genuine growth period.

For the housing of the early stages of manufacture, crude existing structures converted from other uses, or temporary shelters, were usually sufficient. These early structures clustered along water transportation lines and rude roadways. More elaborate construction, such as roads for the purpose of easing manufacturing's access to raw materials and the market, and large warehouses, became later addenda. With the addition of these latter types of facilities, construction finally burgeoned, although, as we have now learned through the success of Tel Aviv, the industrial cities of the Urals, etc., the order of the process can be inverted by implanting population points in advance of industry so as to mother its growth. However, left to a course of normal development, elaborative construction is the last of the three basic enterprises to evolve because of its heavy dependence on external funding. Its appearance is the best gauge of a society's achievement of a positive position on the sustained growth curve, since grand scale construction ordinarily will not come to flower until entry upon Phase III has been realized.

PHASE II: FACTORY PRODUCTION

Phase II might be described as the blooming period of manufacture. It marks the appearance of 'standard of living' goods, items whose purchase can be postponed and which are classifiable as luxuries rather than necessities. These items are distinguished by their diversity. The first goods to fall into this classification were paper products, ceramics, glass, metal ware, engines and machines; and the basic socio-technical feature of the period that produced them was rational mechanization. The factory system's unrivaled ability to integrate men, machines, and material made it the wellspring of a growing age of productivity and the criterion for judging efficiency in most other types of production. Those factors contributing to its capabilities, such as rational innovation and the development of more effective types of mechanization, were described indirectly in the preceding section in assaying the inherent technological limitations of agricultural production.

The products of manufacture which are socially significant are the durable consumer goods. Producer goods are of importance only insofar as they contribute to consumer production, being, in themselves, incapable of attaining sustained growth, particularly if their sale is confined to the domestic market. For example, although the many secondary activities and goods consumed in railway construction have caused this type of enterprise to be regarded as a multiple stimulus to prosperity, in reality it must be classified as an internal consumption cost which will have to be reckoned with, eventually, from out of the public pocket.

Durable consumer goods, on the other hand, are the wellspring of economic well-being, the *raison d'être* of the entire production system. They can be arrayed as the buyer or the seller chooses. Their diversity places them apart from the universals of Basic Production. They are limited only by the subtler psychological appetites; and their variety not only offers greater buying inducement by allowing the buyer to select property configurations in an individualistic blend of his own election, but they avoid, in their production, the gradually narrowing competition deadlock inherent in the naturally *limited* variety of the universal products, particularly those of agriculture. The great variegation characteristic of manufacturing output is continuously augmented by new inventions and elaborated upon by brand variations backed by special merchandizing and sales techniques.

Certainly a major feature of the factory phase of production is the enrichment of the society by the importation of added varieties of durable goods from external sources. The real value of foreign market resides not so much in its serving as a merchandize outlet as in its providing an exchange mart, one upon which Western entrepreneurs have traded to great advantage. This trade, mostly in raw materials, builds up the domestic inventory. Its return flow runs the gamut from ivory, apes and peacocks to rice and rosewood, from azurite to zaratite, and the enterprising industrial nations have been quick in converting even the most exotic of these imports to factors of further production. The nations and empires historically eschewing this type of wealth for the more specious riches of gems and palaces failed to bridge over into a substantive growth process.

From the early 1700's onward, the world factory trend deepened. It has increased its total output perhaps as much as fortyfold during the last one hundred years. It struck a new plateau when assembly line techniques, which had been under serious experimentation for the preceding fifty years, were introduced after the turn of the 20th century to industries already having an inherently high growth potential. So great were the increased efficiencies of mass manufacture that one giant manufacturer, who pioneered in its application, could soon make the industrially jarring announcement of a minimum five-dollar per day wage rate.

Just as during the 1700's pig iron production trailed in the wake of textile manufacture to finally surpass the latter in the early 1800s, agricultural output in the materially advancing societies has trailed consistently along behind industrial growth. While early pig iron production grew phenomenally, until the depression of the 1930's world agriculture was never able to achieve anything approaching a breakthrough. Among the industrially advancing nations its rate of growth has been no more than a third of that of industry, and its share in the total national output has steadily declined. Between 1870 and 1960, United States agricultural production as a proportion of total national output declined from 20·5 per cent to 4·5 per cent. During the 1920s, while industry enjoyed an unprecedented boom, agriculture languished in a world-wide depression. By this time a number of factors had added to its mechanical efficiency, but the action needed to give it stability – price support – was not to come about until the great depression demonstrated to the advanced nations the necessity for this type of support, and until these same societies had achieved the means for supporting farm produce price insurance through the tariffs realized from industrialization.

Most of the technologically advanced nations, beginning in the 1930's, developed, during the next few years, active agriculture income insurance and price policies. Although these policies differed from country to country, the objective was the same, to strip the uncertainty out of the agricultural market. In the Western food-importing nations, subsidy was employed to achieve national self-sufficiency in food production. In other Western nations, guaranteed prices or income were backed by programs to increase consumption and to reduce production enough to deplete the surpluses. Needless to say, although the effort to stimulate production succeeded handsomely, the effort to stem production has not been successful in any of these countries.[1] This period in which financial subsidy was injected into the agricultural process, marked the beginning of Phase III, a doubling back of industrial surpluses to pick up the basic production sectors of agriculture and construction and to integrate the whole into one great reciprocating, proliferating sphere of production.

There are many ways, in addition to direct financial aid, by which agricultural production draws benefits from the forerunning development of a healthy industrial base. Industry offers agriculture certain gratuities, and creates within it particular types of growth-inducing stresses. Industry, which is the springboard for innovation, invents for agriculture. The traditionalism of the pristine farm community and the open field are not favorable to invention. The reaper, the tractor, and the hammermill were the casual inventions, not of farmers, but of earlier day mechanics, artisans, or just plain inventors plying their skills in the atelier or the laboratory. Nowadays, farm equipment design is the work of corps of engineers employed by industries who perceive an enormous market in farm capital.

The area in which agriculture would seem to have its heaviest dependency upon industry is in the production of its facilities for mechanization. It is inconceivable that farm machinery could be made and disseminated on any appreciable scale without first having a vigorous and extensive base of manufacture by which to carry out this function. Industry, in its own growth siphons off labor from agriculture, and by its competition raises the wages of those laborers remaining in agriculture. But to maintain that labor scarcity and a strong labor seller's market alone will force the farm into mechanization is something of an oversimplification. Beyond the two foregoing

[1] Karl Fox, *The Contribution of Farm Price Support Programs to General Economic Stability*, National Bureau of Economic Research, Inc., 5 April, 1954.

factors, industry inadvertently lays the groundwork for farm mechanization by the example of its own methods. In its methods and machinery it extolls speed, power, bigness, and efficiency – ideas that come to permeate the society. Industry subsequently produces new types of farm machinery which fulfill this ideal, and presents these equipments to the farm community with new merchandizing techniques backed with credit arrangements and the 'hard sell.' Even at the beginning of the recent trend toward advanced mechanization, when a farmer was forced to replace an old plow by electing between a single-share, horse-drawn walking-plow and a large two-bottom sulky, his choice of the latter largely already was made for him. There is reason to believe that social prestige is as important a determinant of choice as is the motive to survive the competition through improved efficiency. The farmers who have 'gone broke trying to stay out in front' are legion. Thus does industry invent and produce equipment for the farmer, by its own growth create the labor scarcity helping induce the farmer to buy it, and by the propagation of its own production ethos and the use of established merchandizing techniques assure that he buys it.

The infusion of industry-like techniques into agriculture is aptly reflected in the differences in comparative output rates (for whatever these figures may be worth) between agricultural and non-agricultural sectors in high and low per capita income societies. The ratio of national output per worker, between agricultural and non-agricultural sectors in countries with a per capita output index of $1,700, is approximately equal (0·86), while in those societies with an output index as low as $100, the industrial output is approximately triple (0·31) that of agriculture.[1]

Industry gives indirect subsidy to agriculture by the creation of agriculture-based enterprises. During the past forty years, for example, raw rubber production has approximately quadrupled, despite the appearance of synthetic materials. Large-scale industrial demand for farm products comes rather late in the process of industrial mechanization. To early agriculture-based industries, such as alcohol manufacture, have been added great soya bean-supported plastics industries. Slaughter houses have been replaced by huge packing plant complexes processing everything from ham to hormone extracts.

Commerce, taking its cue from established techniques and pursuant of its own ends, performs still other services important to farm production. Merchandizing through new, supermarket methods

[1] Iowa State University Center for Agriculture and Economic Adjustment, *Food*, Iowa State University Press, 1962, p. 136.

provides the farmer with a mass outlet making it possible for him to sell contractually and on a volume basis. Prior to the advent of this type of marketing service, he was forced to take time off during one of the most pressing times of the year, the harvest season, to vend from door-to-door, from a market stall, or in small quantities to small grocers. The marketing process under those conditions cut deeply into time and profits. Mass selling, modern warehousing, and the resultant contractual arrangements they made possible, paved the way in Western society for larger and more efficiently managed farm holdings and for farm mechanization.

The majority of the world's peoples still live in societies existing under Phase I. Most of those who have advanced sufficiently to have instituted development programming are either in the last period or Phase I or in the opening period of the Factory Phase. These societies, in establishing development formal plans are subscribing to procedures which have been long characteristic of the technologically advanced societies, where there is a profusion of public and private development agencies – industrial commissions, government boards, chambers of commerce, departments of the interior, etc – of such long standing that their existence is generally overlooked by those countries that have put them into such effective play.

PHASE III: ELABORATIVE PRODUCTION

Phase III might be described as the integration and proliferation of all types of human enterprise. The surpluses, inventions, and social currents generated in factory production now had been back-linked to sponsor the basic productions and to begin lifting them to a development level commensurate with that of industry. Like its predecessor stage, Phase III was a consequence of long evolving trends. As mentioned before, the signal event marking off its full-blown appearance was the financial subsidization of the 1930's which saved agriculture from disaster and stabilized it for the sustained surge that it later began exhibiting with the opening of World War II.

The general agricultural legislative measures enacted in practically all the materially advanced countries at the time of the world depression are best exemplified in the policies of the United States. Although there had been faint legislative actions intended to aid in the stabilization of farm prices and production that dated back to the colonial tobacco allotments, the first thoroughgoing federal attempt to steady prices, to adjust acreages, and to enter into marketing agreements was in the Agricultural Adjustment Act of 1933. This act was later nullified, but was succeeded by similar types of legislation which were extended by the War Food Administration through World War II, and later were pressed into the service of providing food for a large part of post-war Europe. Despite some conflict of policies, it had become apparent by 1950 that agriculture could not function satisfactorily without controls and substantive aid, and that government subsidization was here to stay. Throughout this period not only financial subsidy, but other forms of world-wide government paternalism were shown the farmer in the form of new and easier credit arrangements as well as publicly and privately supported, and sometimes compulsory, types of crop insurance. By this time, the problem facing agriculture in the United States was not one of building up production, but of safeguarding against overproduction. The main points of interest in this chapter have been the broad processes which led to this high state of productivity. They might be summed up as the impact of industry as an organizational model upon agriculture, the advent of the tractor during the 1920's, and the financial subsidization of agriculture during the 1930's. Although the statistics cited here are for the United States, it is noteworthy that the pattern for development was similar for the other industrially advanced countries, including Russia, even though she operated, in part, under a quite different system.

The statistics for agricultural activity over the past hundred and forty-five years show recurrent growth periods which, in the aggregate, reflect both increased land use and heightened efficiency. For example, a bushel of wheat that required three man hour's input for its production in 1830 could be produced in 1950 with one-eighth of a man hour's input. The picture through the nineteenth century up to the decades of the 1900's, was one of paralleling growth in numbers of farms, of farm operators and laborers, and of the amount of land under cultivation. However, after about 1910 a number of interesting countervailing trends set in. Between 1910 and 1960, the number of farm workers declined by almost exactly half, but the output per remaining worker quadrupled. During this same period, total farm output increased over one hundred per cent (and this with very little further expansion of land); the absolute number of farms declined by one-sixth; average farm size increased by about fifty per cent; and agriculture's share in the total national output declined from 16·7 per cent to 4·5 per cent. Between the years 1940 to 1960, inclusively, the value of physical farm assets more than quadrupled by climbing from forty-eight billion to 203 billion dollars.

Taken altogether, the decline in farm manpower and the increase in capital and production were results of a rapid drive toward

TABLE 5

U.S. Farm Resources and Income as Proportion of Nation

	*Labor force**		*Capital**		*Net product or Income**		*Agriculture as per cent of Nation*		
Year	*Nation*	*Farm*	*Nation*	*Farm*	*Nation*	*Farm*	*Labor*	*Capital*	*Income*
1820	2·9	2·1	—	—	·9	·3	71·8	—	34·4
1840	5·4	3·7	—	—	1·6	·5	68·6	—	34·6
1860	10·5	6·2	16·1	8·0	4·1	1·3	58·9	55·6	30·8
1880	17·4	8.6	43·6	12·2	6·6	1·4	49·4	27·9	20·7
1890	23·3	9·9	65·0	16·1	9·6	1·5	42·7	24·7	15·8
1900	29·1	10·9	87·7	20·4	14·6	3·0	37·5	23·3	20·9
1910	37·4	11·6	152·0	43·3	25·6	5·6	31·0	28·5	21·7
1920	42·4	11·4	374·4	83·8	79·1	10·6	27·0	22·4	13·4
1930	48·8	10·5	410·1	60·5	75·7	4·3	21·5	14·8	5·6
1940	55·6	9·5	424·2	43·9	81·9	4·6	17·2	10·4	5·6
1950	63·1	7·5	1,054·7	107·4	241·9	14·0	11·9	10·2	5·6
1960	68·4	4·5	—	—	416·9	12·0	6·7	9·1	2·9

*Million for labor and billion for capital and income. Income figures are disposable consumer's income and net income from farming. Farm capital includes land.

Source: 'Historical Statistics of the United States. Colonial Times to 1957,' Series F 22–33 and USDA Statistics.
Taken from: Earl O. Heady, *Agricultural Policy under Economic Development*, Iowa State University Press, 1962, p. 42.

agricultural mechanization, a ground swell that started rolling during the decade of the 1920's. This wave was initiated by the U.S. automobile industry. In the early 1800s, American prairie farming gave rise to the first massive employment, in history, of draft animals. By the time of World War I, thirty-horse teams were pulling giant reapers, and steam-powered tractors were pulling five-bottom plows. But the ponderousness of the steam engine limited it to traction in heavy field work and to sedentary, belt-driven operations. In 1919 the Ford Motor Company, which had first experimented with placing an automobile engine on a tractor chassis in 1908, now turned its assembly line techniques to the mass production of light, general purpose, gasoline-engine-powered farm tractors. Ford's sales for that year mounted to three-quarters of that for the entire tractor-producing industry, and, despite the following two decades of agricultural depression, Ford initiated a tide of tractor buying that was to equip agriculture with a prime power source for the unprecedented production demands of the 1940's.

TABLE 6

Tractors on U.S. Farms between 1910 and 1955

Year	*No. of Tractors*
1900	1,000
1920	246,000
1930	920,000
1940	1,545,000
1950	3,615,000
1955	4,490,000

The first implements drawn by the tractor were of a hold-over type designed for draft animals. The addition to the tractor of the hydraulic lift, lights, battery ignition, rubber tires and greater steering maneuverability entrained the follow-on purchase, during the 1930's, of a great variety of tractor-mounted and self-propelled tilling, cultivating and harvesting equipments. During this period, and concomitant with the dearth of labor that followed during World War II. farming became mechanized; it became a changed way of life. The shell of the folk society had been broken and from now on agriculture was to steadily increase in specialization, mechanization, and in its resultant productivity. The massive impacts of farm mechanization and crop subsidization became manifest in a number of ways,

Between 1920 and 1950, more than twenty-five million people migrated from farms to urban areas, and to urban types of occupations. 'Although the farm population in 1950 was only about two-thirds that of 1920, the absolute number of migrants during the past decade has been above earlier periods.'[1] Other effects no less impressive accompanied this outpouring of population from the farm community. Between 1930 and 1960, the proportion of owner-operators increased from fifty-seven per cent to seventy-nine per cent, the proportion of tenants declined by one-half, and farm output per man-hour increased four times over.[2]

The rate of construction activity also underwent dramatic change during this, the second quarter of the twentieth century and the period of Elaborative Production. The erection of structures of great size and durability dated back through civilized history, as witnessed by the Egyptian monuments, Roman highways and aqueduct systems, medieval cathedrals, etc. But the building of large structures of utilitarian design was not to originate on any general scale until the industrial revolution had laid its technical base and created a need for such facilities. The invention of Portland cement, in 1824, and the combining of this material with a structural steel framework – a process made possible by new, mechanized building techniques – laid the base for urban commercial building expansion in the late 1800's. However, construction did not enter a strong growth period until the turn of the twentieth century. After that time, in the United States during the first half of the twentieth century the total non-farm mortgaged *building* indebtedness increased over thirteen times (from 4·7 to 68·5 billion dollars), and by 1950 came to constitute over half of the nation's long-term debt. For this period, as an average, construction, along with maintenance, amounted to twelve per cent of the Gross National Product, and by mid-century, if those engaged in processing materials are included with direct construction workers, the industry employed about ten per cent of the country's total work force. Within a very short period it had risen to approximately *equal* the declining work force in agriculture.

Again, one of the strongest fillips to construction in the United States was the automobile industry. It had, through its product, created a well-nigh insatiable need for roadways. The years, 1910 to 1920, were a period of preparation for large-scale road building

[1] Dale E. Hathaway, 'Migration from Agriculture: The Historical Record and Its Meaning,' *American Economic Review, Papers and Proceedings*, Vol, 50, May, 1960, pp. 371–391.

[2] Theodore W. Schultz, *Transforming Traditional Agriculture*, New Haven, Connecticut: Yale University Press, 1964, p. 120.

TABLE 7

Contract Construction in the United States

(1929=100)

Year	*Output index*
1870	11·8
1880	18·4
1890	33·4
1900	43·5
1910	75·7
1920	56·3
1930	100·0
1940	61·4
1950	138·0

enriched by the development of new types of road-building machinery and the passage of the Federal-Aid Road Act in 1916. From 1919 to 1950, the number of motor vehicles increased about seven times, from seven and one-half million to fifty-two million, and the amount of hard-surfaced roadage increased five-fold to reach 1·7 million miles.

Perhaps, the most far-reaching effects for construction came from a general wave of legislation, passed during the 1930s, establishing the federal government's right to initiate works programs in the public interest during periods of economic recession. This belated recognition of the importance of construction to the national economy, the giant subsidies appropriated to it through each succeeding administration, and the recency of growth in all phases of the building industry clearly denote construction's dependence upon the development of a preceding industrial base; and demonstrate its reliance for full fruition upon both, an industrial demand for its facilities and industrial subsidization.

Phase III is a period of elaborated production and wealth. The household's first television set is complemented by a second one, and both may be equipped with remote electronic station-selectors and viewed from specially designed chairs while eating a specially prepared 'TV' dinner. The secondary possession enjoins the third, etc. Phase III is the age of the second and third family car, the backyard swimming pool, the towed luxury boat, electronic controls, high-speed digital computation, automation, jet aircraft transportation, and space exploration. It is also, for many of the Western societies that have failed to keep their social planning abreast with technical progress, a time of social unrest and radical readjustment. As much as thirty per cent of the people of some of these richer societies are still poor, deprived of participation in general benefits; and whole societies, for lack of proper social provisioning and educational orientation, face the prospects of deepening disemployment as a threat rather than as a promise of liberation. As Galbraith and others have commented, in the technologically advanced countries basic concern is shifting from issues connected with increasing production to issues of planning and utilizing the already realizable wealth and leisure. Unfortunately, this is a problem obtaining for fewer than one-tenth of the world's population. The other three billion must first find the socio-technical pathway that leads to this secondary tier of non-technological problems.

PHASE IV: FULL AUTOMATION

The degree to which it may be ultimately possible to attain automation, and the time interval involved, are much debated topics toward which reactions are usually more emotional than objective. Whatever the individual's preference may be, it is evident that automation is a movement already well underway, accelerating, and causing mounting social stresses. It is a live issue which places questions having to do with – 'whether some machine designers and maintenance workers will always be needed in the work situation,' or 'the psychic values of cottage-craft industry,' – all in the class of rather idle polemics. The facts that the movement toward automation has *not* been brought under systematic study, and that we are *not* in a better position to predict and plan for its effects, should provide some pause for thought and cause for action. This is an area requiring multi-disciplinary study, and one in which sociological inquiry and leadership are especially pertinent.

As for its broad characteristics, automation might be viewed, in some respects, as a movement marking a full turn in the cycle of material development. Primitive societies that were originally provided for out of a natural abundance, owing to migration to temperate climes and to other environmental changes were confronted, in time, with scarcity; and somehow they began offsetting this condition by technological innovation. In this final stage—automation—invention's prospects would appear to be ultimately so successful as to reduce man's problems in caring for his basic needs to the same plane of simplicity as that enjoyed by his early forebears. The social universe in which he lives, however, has become a vastly different one, and it may be expected that its form will undergo still further changes not envisioned by any of the present day political systems. Peoples and governments heretofore unaccustomed to ministering to social needs save from a conventional economic frame of reference, must develop and apply new ways of thinking.

7

SOCIO-TECHNICS: A NEW SET OF HYPOTHESES FOR DEVELOPMENT

The basic proposition facing developers everywhere is that of increasing per capita material wealth, and it is almost axiomatic that, for the new, struggling countries, material improvement will depend upon the increasing of internal productivity. Ideally, increased output will be sought through those production systems which best organize the natural and human resources of the society. Since increased productivity in almost all cases will call for technological innovation, development principles must be made to strike at the heart of the problem by the isolation of new methods for injecting technological innovation into the society.

Most of the hypotheses discussed in the preceding chapter are *not* applicable directly or in meaningful detail to development programming. That chapter presented an attempt, by an analysis of ponderous and slow moving historical processes, to plot *production growth trends* as they have occurred in the industrially advanced nations. Underlying these crude production patterns, and accounting for them, are clearly discernible *technologies*. It is in the succession and interaction of these technologies that we are interested here.

As they have grown, the Western nations have given birth to a number of technologies. There is a technology of education, of medicine, of law, and so forth, but these are derivative technologies. They take on growth as the society can afford them, and in order to afford them the society must first develop its *production technologies*. It is the production technologies, and those other technologies such as power and transportation which surround them and attend their immediate needs, that will, above all else, set the general tempo of progress within the developing society. They are the very essence of development. In their dynamics they are basically social movements and in composition they are clearly articulate systems whose behaviours can be predicted and controlled. They are the root stock of development planning.

SPECIFIC STAGES OF TECHNOLOGICAL PROGRESSION

The production patterns described in Chapter 6 historically evolved from five successive levels of technological growth. Beginning with what is invariably a settled agricultural society, in its growth that society moves through five stages of technological attainment, the first of which is really a pre-technological stage, and the second of which, once the society has made full entry into it, makes possible the realization of sustained technological growth. These five stages are:

1. Man-machine Organization
2. Power Technology
3. Transportation Technology
4. Agricultural Technology
5. General Automation

1. *Man-machine Organization*

At the outset it would be useful to draw a distinction between the machine and the engine, a distinction that is an important one for the purposes of this discussion. A machine is a set of reciprocally interacting and moving parts designed to carry out a given function or set of functions. The engine, while it is also a machine is more than merely a machine. It is, in particular, the energizing factor lying at the heart of every advanced machine system.

The English factories of the early 1700's, before the advent of steam power, were primarily an improved manner of social organization. The power systems employed in the early eighteenth century were weak, undeveloped members of the man-machine-power trilogy. Early factory machines were energized either by harnessing water power or by the direct application of human or animal power. Nonetheless, the early factory was at a plateau of efficiency distinctly above that obtainable in the pre-industrial agricultural village, in that it concentrated raw materials, labor, and machinery at, or near, a single geographical point. This improved type of organization permitted a centralized and effective management. So superior was this systematic alignment of the factors of production to the older cottage craft industries that the latter gradually succumbed to the new and better organized industrial methods.

It is highly questionable, however, that the early crude factory system would have grown, or even survived, without the later breakthrough in power technology that followed in the second half of the eighteenth century. Time and again, earlier civilized powers had developed highly efficient methods of man-machine organization only to have the movement reach the highest plateau that was attainable in the absence of effective power systems, then having served society for a time they went into eclipse. Excellent examples of early pre-technological achievement were the ancient slave-powered gallies maintained by most of the Mediterranean civilizations over 2,000 years ago, man-machine organizations created by the great monument builders of Egypt, and the superb city-state organization built by Greece during the Hellenic Age and within which the mathematical and scientific bases for technology had been laid but failed to give root to permanent technological growth. Although a great deal can be accomplished by the better disposition of the factors of production, this is a stage having limitations beyond which further improvement ordinarily is not attainable, and one which in the past has never proven itself capable of sustained growth. Continuing technological growth beyond the stage of man-machine organization is dependent upon discovery of, and the wholesale indoctrination of the society in *power systems*.

2. *Power Technology*

Although power in its present-day form takes on the broad aspects of electricity, chemicals, and nuclear energy, early power technology was almost synonymous with steam engine development. Even today, *engines* (of the petroleum-fueled type) provide most of the world's energy. The power unit, whatever its form, is the beating heart of advanced technology. Without it the heavy machine would be impractical, the machine's great advantage of conserving upon the expenditure of human energy would be lost, and the type of systems progression which eventually culminates in automation would be unrealizable. The attainment of the power stage of technology in Western society may have come about through nothing more than historical accident; but in the practical matter of a society's maintaining a firm purchase on this second ledge of technology, once it is reached, it will need a large corps of general machinists, engine technicians, and engineers. The achievement of the power plateau is signalled by an ability within the society to do more than simply operate and maintain machine systems. The society must have developed an internal capability for repairing and overhauling engines, for producing replacement parts and even manufacturing whole engines.

When a society reaches the power stage of technology it no longer thinks in terms of outer form, as it did during the preceding stage of man-machine organization, but in terms of inner working principle.

The society now becomes *systems* oriented, and as its knowledge of power technology reaches a critical mass it becomes capable of sustained technological growth. The power unit provides an energy source around which a multitude of applied machines may be invented and built. Once it understands the principles of power creation, the society next sets to work on problems of devising new types of applied machines, designing the appropriate powering units, and fashioning the transmission systems required to link the two. Once it is in possession of engine knowledge it is predictable that the society will next begin thinking about ways in which the engine may be advantageously employed. New machines of an advanced type are almost always invented *around* the power system. When this point of inventiveness has been reached, the society has become one of builders of machines, of innovators.

Any attempt to stimulate growth in a society's technology which falls short of a thorough indoctrination of the members of that society in power technology will likely achieve only temporary and limited goals. The fact that advanced methods and complex machines can be feasibly employed in backward areas is amply demonstrated by the large foreign owned and managed fruit producing companies, and the many specialized plantations, logging industries and other types of specialized enterprises found there. These enterprises usually train indigenous personnel in machine operation and basic maintenance, but they seldom school them above these levels. As a consequence, when the colonists withdraw, when the skilled mechanics and engineers depart as they did in parts of Africa and Southeast Asia, tractors are abandoned by the roadside and irrigation complexes fall into complete disrepair. This is not out of willful neglect, but from sheer inability to keep these systems in operation because members of the undeveloped society do not understand them as *systems*, nor will they until they have penetrated to the heart of the system, to its power technology.

The 'cargo cult' of New Guinea provides an example of a people completely unable to distinguish between outer form and inner principle. This group has witnessed the functioning of the aircraft transportation complex, but at a distance. It has been observed that cargo-carrying airplanes arrive from somewhere and that upon landing they disgorge all types of exotic merchandise. The group has surmised that this same type of magic can be invoked on their own tribal grounds under the proper conditions of mimicry. Consequently, they have developed a primitive replica of a landing field, and nearby it they have built a signal fire which is attended night and day. Situated at one side of the landing field is a crude mock-up of an aircraft. This primitive complex has been developed for the purpose of enticing the great iron bird, with its apparently precious cargo, to land. And in the process of this animation the tribe imputes an independent role-playing ability to the machine and displays a complete ignorance of the physical principles which motivate it. Not only does this example point out the readiness with which extremely technologically retarded societies will ascribe a role-playing ability to the machine, but it offers the inference that even the more progressive of the emerging societies will not successfully intermesh with technology until they have been indoctrinatively lifted to the stage of power technology, and thereby given an understanding of the systems principle.

As the early leader of Western technological development, England did not reach the threshold of power technology until the latter half of the eighteenth century with the development of Watt's steam engine, an event which occurred a full eight decades after the onset of the early factory system in England. In 1782, James Watt produced a steam engine, which improved upon its toy-like predecessors to achieve a mechanically feasible full-scale power system. This engine brought a new flexibility to the industrial system which greatly accelerated its growth. Formerly chained to the banks of rivers by its dependence upon water power, the industrial plant was now free to move inland near its raw resources, or nearer to the center of its markets, or, taking transportation facilities and labor distribution into account, it could locate at some point within optimum reach of all these factors. Just as importantly, *new forms* of industry could not be developed which were formerly prohibited by the logistics problems involved in transporting their raw materials

Following hard upon Watt's invention, in 1787 the first workable steam boat was built, and by the beginning of the nineteenth century, England's technology, fed by lavish textile profits, had expanded to the production of engines and engine-powered machinery. As mentioned earlier, England recognized this latter industry as being so important a profit and growth factor that she forbade the exportation of this type of technical knowledge under severe penalty. However, it was not until the last quarter of the 19th century that the four-cycle reciprocating *gasoline* engine was sufficiently developed for general use. This power unit together with electricity, was soon to revolutionize the factory and to push the early industrial nations of Western society into a sustained technological growth.

It is hardly surprising that strong technological growth does not set in until a society reaches the power, or systems, level. Psychologists have long pointed out that a full knowledge of any kind of system with which the individual must deal generates a greater breadth of understanding, capability, and enthusiasm on his part than does a partial, fragmentary knowledge. This same principle seems to hold for the society as well as for individual behavior. It is at the stage of power technology that the engineer makes his appearance. The engineer is a professional innovator whose business it is, in large part, to find new applications for power.

3. *Transportation Technology*

Traditional society obtains its transportation by ox-cart, pack animal, human porterage, or by sail vessel. Transportation underwent no significant advancement in Western society until after the invention of the steam engine. By the 1830's, screw propelled steam ships were plying the Atlantic, and following the introduction of the first successful steam-propelled land locomotive in 1814, overland rail commerce grew so rapidly as to span the entire continental United States by 1869. The great jump-off point in transportation came, however, with the development of the internal combustion engine and the advent of the automobile. Made workable in 1885, and brought under mass production methods by Ford in 1909, the motor vehicle was to become, in the space of a single generation, the economical means for 'every man's transportation.' In time it was to provide a means for massive personal conveyance, a source of overpowering competition for railway transportation, and it was to form the base for the field-roving tractor unit which was soon to revolutionize agriculture.

Just as power technology is a logical successor of man-machine organization, transportation technology in its turn must have awaited, historically, a successful power technology. Transportation clearly is at a next higher level of technical sophistication. The factory may be powered by relatively simple, stationary engines, but land transportation makes the more difficult demand that the power unit be made capable of propelling itself and the larger vehicular system of which it is a part. This entails reducing engine bulk and weight to feasible proportions, giving the engine variable thrust controls in order that it may respond to differing power requirements, and equipping the vehicular system with sensitive and reliable transmission, guidance, and braking sub-systems.

As it has evolved mechanically, the motor vehicle has brought in its wake a great battery of social inventions. The many improvements that have gone into roadways and the enactment of traffic regulations are only a few of these. It is doubtful that any technological advancement makes for more social change than does motor transport. Rapid transit opens the possibilities for a vast reaggregation of places of residence, it forces change in the conventional institutional controls over such momentous matters as courtship, recreation, and general family behavior, and it converts a once provincial neighbourhood group into an anonymous intermingling of peoples.

4. *Agricultural Technology*

Agriculture, historically, was the last of the basic production specialities to reach an advanced stage of development, and, again, this was because of its higher level of mechanical complexity. It had to have available a reliable and transportable engine unit as well as a chassis capable of accomodating both the engine unit and the complicated machine system which the engine powered. Thus, it had to add to the facility of the transport vehicle an ability to carry out special machine operations. Compare the complexity of the specialized production machine, such as the metal lathe, to the self-propelled cotton picker. Although the former must have a high operating precision, in terms of total number of parts and complexity of movement the cotton picker is far the more complicated of the two machine systems.

Rudimentary mechanization and improvement in farm techniques occurring during the eighteenth and nineteenth centuries had enabled agriculture to accrue enough production surplus to provide some small aid to the development of early industry. The mid-nineteenth century development of horse-powered equipment, such as the grain reaper, improved harvesting efficiency by several orders of magnitude. By the time of World War I, huge harvesting rigs drawn by steam engines or multiple horse teams helped make the U.S., temporarily, a cereal supplier for a considerable part of Europe. But, again, it was not until after the development of the internal combustion engine, the automobile, and methods of mass manufacture, that agricultural technology surged into a truly advanced stage of productivity. Once the transportation industry had acquired the ability to manufacture a reliable motorized transportation vehicle, it was only a short step in re-design from this vehicle to a farm tractor. And by applying already existing mass manufacturing methods and facilities to their production from 1919 onward, it was possible, during the ensuing thirty-five years, to flood the United States with four and one half million tractor units.

Almost immediately behind this outpouring of power units came a variety of advanced, special-purpose planting, cultivating, and harvesting machines. These ranged from the Lister plow to celery pickers carrying crews of two dozen men and performing all harvesting operations from the digging of the product to its final grading and crating for the market.

5. *General Automation*

Automation is a generalized technological movement which is attainable, potentially, for practically all fields of production as well as for the service industries. Its latent possibilities and effects are just now becoming apparent. It is the end goal of technicians and the crowning point of technological development. Since our primary concern here is with those technological stages preceding and leading toward automation, and since the effects of automation have been discussed at length elsewhere in this book, no more need be said on the subject at this time.

IDENTIFYING THE 'CHANGE-AGENT'

It is appropriate at this point to re-examine and restate the basic objective of development. The prime goal of development is generally conceded by social scientists to be that of introducing benevolent social change, a type of change conducive to 'economic growth,' into the backward society. Despite the large current following enjoyed by this school, it is a questionable, piecemeal method which will bring segmented, and often only temporary change. Perhaps this prologue should be rephrased to state that, *The main objective of development is that of converting a traditional or transitional society into a society of technical innovators.* If the foregoing socio-technological hypothesis for development is valid, then the approach should be one of delineating the most expedient avenues by which the emerging society can be precipitated into the mainstream of power technology. The next issue, and a crucial one, becomes that of determining ways by which power technology can be made to penetrate the developing society's cultural shell. In brief, who, or what, are the change agents by which this penetration may be made realizable?

One must ask whether it is reasonable to talk about urging a society toward institutional change in divorcement from, or prior to the appearance of the new behaviour or physical item which is to be socially accomodated. What will be accomplished, for example, by seeking community consensus and supporting legislation to bring about an amalgamation of small free-holdings unless modern machinery and its potential for increasing productivity are already known and appreciated by the community? And it is not likely that they *will* be appreciated unless they are an incorporate part of the society's technological organization. When this becomes the case they will create their own stresses for change. It is questionable that institutional change is ever a fully deliberate, consciously planned event. Rather, at that point when physical invention or new physical item is introduced into a society it takes on its own special social clothing, distorting custom and forcing institutional change by its own forward-driving momentum.

The term 'change agent' is interchangeably used to describe an individual, institution, or a certain social stratum. A society's prospects for development are sometimes viewed against a background of its social class system. Kurt Lewin maintained that a relatively affluent people within the community act as its 'gate keepers.'[1] They provide the behavioral cues, direction, and censorship for the social rank-and-file members of the community, who, as a group, desire to emulate their behavior. They are the community's leaders, by whom it would appear that any type of change under contemplation would have to be first-passed upon and blessed. But in the technologically handicapped society the elite class forms a major stumbling block to change. It is they who own and control the society's assets, and it is they who have most to lose, and perhaps least to gain, by radical change. Although some few liberal dissidents within their number are generally presumed to eventually act as the society's *prime* change agents, this assumption is far from an established, quantifiably demonstrable fact.

In most of the transitional societies there are, in reality, only two social classes, the elite and the proletariat, the latter comprising the great bulk of the population. It is the proletariat who ultimately have most to gain by benevolent technological change, but under ordinary circumstances it is this group that has been most indifferent, and oftentimes most opposed, to change. This is due in good part to the fact that the working class became the early, and as Marx pointed out, frequent butt of technological change. In numerous instances, seeing their jobs jeopardized by a physical innovation they struck back by damaging machinery and at times even putting whole factories to the torch. The word 'sabotage' originated in the early Dutch textile factories and is a term quite descriptive of the relationship of the worker to the industrial system

[1] Kurt Lewin, 'Frontiers in Group Dynamics: II Channels of Group Life: Social planning and action research,' *Human Relations*, 1 (1947), 143–153.

of that day. 'As early as 1779 a mob of eight thousand workers had attacked a mill and burned it to the ground in unreasoning defiance of its cold, implacable mechanical efficiency, and by 1811 such protests against technology were sweeping England.'[1] In modern society it has been the worker who has been most resistant to technological change and who has stoutly resisted it through unionization and every other means at his disposal. Such innovations as have been introduced by the blue collar class in Western society have been cumulatively valuable but they have been circumscribed types of innovation. As its operator, a blue collar worker may make or suggest particularized changes in the machine but he will seldom analyze or comment on the broader socio-technological context. A bulldozer operator may be instrumental in the design of an improved scraping blade but it is unlikely that he will introduce a machine that improves upon the bulldozer. The development, manufacture, and distribution of a significant new invention requires knowledge, capital, and organizational abilities far beyond the grasp of the average blue collar worker. This magnitude of enterprise must come either from the elite or from an emergent, adventuresome middle class. And neither group of sponsors can be educed in a technological vacuum; they will appear only *after* the technological dynamic has been implanted in the society.

The economic approach to development has already been reviewed and found of little help. Change is not likely to issue initially from any of the secondary, economic sources. Thus, if it is improbable that change will come from the society's individuals, social groups or institutions, then it must radiate from a special set of relationships existing between the society and its physical artifacts. *It well may be that technological growth occurs as a series of changes in the ways in which men interact with the machines with which they work.* It may be this relationship that, as it grows, acts as the prime agent for change. If so, the solution to technological development lies in discovering how these relationships are patterned and in finding means by which man-machine interaction in the backward society may be actuated and intensified.

TECHNIQUES, TOOLS, AND MACHINES

These three categories – techniques, tools, and machines – are the sum and substance of technology. In any discussion of technology one necessarily deals in terms of one, or some combination of these

[1] Robert L. Heilbroner, *The Worldly Philosophers*, New York: Time Inc. Book Division, 1961, p. 103.

three factors. Each of the three is distinctive but their interrelationships are such that, for the moment, it is preferable to mix the order of their treatment.

A tool is a physical object, usually simple in structure, which has been designed to aid in achieving some cultural end. It is a device which goes beyond the mechanical definition of being an instrument of manual operation or a means for concentrating energy at a given point. A fish weir, a wood chisel, or a contraceptive may all fit the definition of 'tool.' But in every case it will be subject to some standardized procedure or set of procedures – 'techniques' – in its employment. It may consist physically of one or more inert, rigidly related parts.

A machine is a more complex device. It is a system of reciprocally and dynamically interacting parts designed to carry out a function or a series of functions, and in the process it is capable of taking over some of the tasks of providing its own guidance in the delivery of energy, carrying out repetition of action, and so forth.

A technique, on the other hand, differs markedly from either of the foregoing two. Techniques are exclusively social or socio-psychological in nature. Techniques are social prescriptions or *procedures* for carrying out any and all types of cultural functions, from the beating of flax to the offering of prayer. As such they find their expression in overt physical patterns of human behavior. They may operate in relative isolation, being little more than a sequence of straight, undiluted, work procedures; or they may serve as the interface between humans and tools or machines, clothing the latter two with a social fabric that confers upon them direction, guidance, and a special meaning within the context of the culture.

The argument now to be advanced is that in most cases where tools and machines are found actively employed within a society they become social extensions of the human beings who employ them. As such, they may be classified as actors, as having a capability for carrying out a social role. The role is determined by the types of functions which a machine has been built to perform; and a machine's acceptance and *status* within a society will depend upon the consonance between its role-playing and that society's present socio-technological system. Newly introduced machines will be accepted, in general, when they are perceived not to be in direct conflict with established techniques, or as not having a strong potential for creating dislocative effects among the techniques of institutions other than that one for which they are intended; and they will be rejected when their prospective behaviors are dislocative or disopprobrious. Of overweening importance in this line of analysis is the fact that machine-using societies *do* react toward tools, and especially machines, as though they were discrete social entities. This fact makes them amenable to treatment by social theory, and gives them special relevance to development planning.

1. *Techniques* As defined here, techniques are purely social in nature. They may enshroud tools or machines or they may operate in isolation from these two physical vehicles. The process of shelling peas is illustrative of the latter case. Being socio-psychological behavior patterns, techniques are especially obdurate to change. They are, as time and motion study men have discovered, almost hopelessly difficult to change without altering a number of other social factors in which they are almost always embedded. Experimentation conducted at Western Electric's plant at Hawthorne, Illinois during the 1920s and 1930s revealed that within a social climate in which the plant's management gave them attention, workers' productivity increased markedly although they continued to use the same general techniques. The work pace simply speeded up. However, attempting to increase the work pace by a bare rational appeal (the type of appeal made by time and motion study) will avail little. Going beyond to raise the entire order of productivity by the introduction of an altogether *new* technique will prove to be an even more difficult undertaking. Established techniques become, for the worker, pockets of habit and custom. For a given technique the worker learns specific skills, and even more importantly, within this technique he can vary the rhythm of work so as to parasitize a certain amount of individual free time on the job. Under unusual work conditions human labor can be seen to be highly elastic. Wartime emergency conditions represent one of the few occasions when the worker will voluntarily change techniques in order to effect speed-up, or will tolerate procedural changes when they are recommended by management. After the emergency has passed, the output level will tend to resettle to its former norm. The enduring and significant past changes that have come about in productivity have come as a result of a change in an entire machine regimen and, consequently, as a result of forcibly, but indirectly creating change in the work technique. It is at the machine juncture, rather than within the technique that change is most easily effected.

Ironically, because improved techniques appear to be the first logical step toward improvement, and because changing the technique would appear to be an economical approach calling only for instruction and not for materiel, it is at this point that change is most frequently attempted. It is doubtless much easier to carry out the less direct, obverse approach in which techniques are forcibly changed later as a result of the calculated intrusion of a new tool or machine and its accompanying demand for new technique. Despite the commendable efforts of people associated with the Peace Corps and the like, in terms of long range and enduring social change, one 'Ugly American' with real engineering skills probably achieves more lasting results than an army of Peace Corpsmen.

2. *Tools* A tool that is in active use within the society is never found to be a socially inert object. It will be used through well defined techniques and it will have social and psychological relationships radiating far beyond these prescriptions for its use. It will become an extension of the user's personality. So manifest is this tendency that in many cases the man-tool relationship will run to a complete animism. A simple hand loom used by a Middle Eastern rugmaker has become, through long use and accommodation on the user's part, especially 'suited to my body.' It is 'an especially willing loom,' one whose parts, out of tradition, must not be replaced even though they are badly worn. This loom is not only satisfying in its psychological dimensions, but since it was constructed more than two centuries ago by the operator's forefathers, it has become a social mortar bonding the generations. Whosoever attempts to induce this weaver to substitute a technically superior loom for this eighteenth-century model will not only face a formidable task, but, if successful he will likely upset a deepseated social rhythm.

The tendency to form a social relationship with the tools he uses is not confined alone to the primitive, but is observable in the technologically advanced society. When the individual is reduced to reliance on just a few tools he will begin forming a special rapprochement with them and will begin imputing to them certain desirable traits. He comes to accommodate to them physically, psychologically, and socially.

There is no society so primitive that it does not employ some type of tool, if only the digging stick. But the tools used by primitive groups are few in number and of limited type. They are cared for slavishly and are sometimes made the object of religious veneration. *Machines*, on the other hand, *are seldom in evidence in pre-literate societies.*

New tools and techniques may originate from within the society, or they may diffuse from some external source. There is no society so static that it does not engage in a certain amount of invention. In fact, as men go about their work the process of innovation can hardly be avoided. Very often it will occur inadvertently, with a new and better piece being substituted for an old one, or with a short-cut in prodecure being arrived at subconsciously. But from whatever source they may originate, the greater part of the stream of new material items and ideas that flow through a society are treated with indifference. They simply remain inert objects that fail to propagate. This holds equally for the more advanced technological societies, for it is recounted that of the total number of inventions registered at the patent office archives, fewer than two per cent ever become utilized by the society. That is to say, that no society, not even the most innovative, will be receptive to a new type of physical innovation unless its manifest social role is especially compatible with the enveloping culture. And in traditional society, where the relationship between man and existing tools is an especially close one, the cultural shell will be even more impenetrable.

3. *Machines* The social characteristics of the machine go much beyond those of the tool. Though it is still an extension of the user's personality, in its more complex forms the machine takes on a semi-autonomous role-playing ability of its own. A machete or a war club may be almost completely incorporated into the ego of the user, while the machine has an imputed personality that makes it a much more individualistic entity. It has no capability for self-identification, but within the social plasma it becomes the 'generalized other.' As such it has some qualities that are human-like, that make it socially acceptable, and that give it a certain social identity within the society. Additionally, it is *devoid* of some of the more negative human characteristics, and this fact even further enhances its social desirability and utility.

The grounds for viewing the machine as a social entity are severalfold. The machine is an actor. It is capable of carrying out socially approved and useful functions. It sometimes has structural members that mimic the human anatomy, and its style of movement may resemble that employed in human work behavior. The machine has a quality that is essential to any social interaction and one especially prized by the tightly organized industrial societies. Its behavior is highly predictable. Except for cases of mechanical malfunction, it can always be depended upon; it will not defect on psychological grounds. It has, by human standards, incredible power, speed, and endurance. These three features, which from earliest times have always been the fundamental human qualities under trial in athletic contests, may now find expression in a competition between whole man-machine complexes in which, as in the case of automobile racing, the *combined qualities* of a human operator and machine now go on trial.

Certain classes of machines are credited with having a type of individual personality. Because of its exceptionally high mobility and its susceptibility to being stolen and spirited away into the anonymity of secondary society, the automobile is made party to formal contract. It is given legal title. Although it may be abducted and temporarily maltreated by someone other than the legal owner, it can be illegally disposed of only with great difficulty. Under still another type of contract called the 'warranty,' the new automobile and the owner are entered into a provisional 'get acquainted period.' Automobiles may be 'traded in' but never without some feeling of regret on the part of the owner. As every car owner well knows, every auto has its idiosyncrasies and these often persist throughout its lifetime. There is no automobile so close to the heart as one that was owned in the past. One often hears, 'I wish I hadn't traded in the old clinker, they just don't make them like that any more.' At another level of mechanization, production machines are anthropomorphologically regarded as 'putting people out of work' or 'taking the place of human beings' and this causes people to 'turn against the machine' – the 'infernal machine' – that is. One of the more remarkable human-like apparatuses is the computer, which is widely looked upon as having near-human functional capabilities but is pityingly regarded as being devoid of that most necessary of all human qualities, 'feeling.'

Nonetheless, machines are treated in Western society as though they actually *did* have feelings. They are sometimes said to be 'abused.' Technologically unsophisticated peoples tend to misuse machinery when allowed to operate it, and those from technologically advanced societies look down upon this malpractice. Although the reaction to machine abuse is not as sharp as that against horse-beating, it nevertheless is expressed in an attitude of strong social disapproval. Practiced by another upon one's own mechanical possessions, this not only is irritating because of the damage and inconvenience it causes, but it also betokens lack of proper respect for the owner. Technically unskilled peoples abuse machines because they do not have a clear knowledge of how they work, and they do not identify with them socially. Indeed, they may actively *hate* them.

Machines are invested with social status. The ermine-upholstered royal carriage or the Rolls-Royce are poles apart from the 'tin lizzy.' The type and quality of machines that an individual intereacts with are taken as basic social indicators of his own 'quality.' A man driving a Cadillac is in a quite different role situation than would be the same man walking alongside the road barefoot and in tatters.

Perhaps most importantly from the standpoint of its human-like characteristics, a machine can be heavily exploited. It has all, and more, of the potential for subjugation offered by slavery and the other forms of enforced servitude. In a world historically patterned along lines of human subjugation and exploitation, the machine can be substituted readily as an uncomplaining victim through which (or whom) its master may enjoy increased freedom and luxury. And by making types of innovation that improve the machine, its operator is enabled to enjoy ever increasing quantities of both.

As for its more important *non-human* characteristics, *the machine can be exploited without objection or protest on its part.* It can be made a party to reciprocity; but only in a limited sense can it demand reciprocation of the human. One such exception is the alarm clock, thousands of which fall victim to fits of human fury each year. But, by and large, the machine stands by, responding only when called upon and otherwise not usurping its owner's attentions. In many of its characteristics it goes far beyond the limits of human capability. It can work with extremely high precision and can sustain a high and even output without flagging.

In the broad scientific context within which the term 'communication' is now used, machines *do* communicate with their human operators. Although this communication does not occur at a verbal level, it is nonetheless positive. As an operator directs a machine he receives continuous feedback which he uses in judging its behavior and in taking corrective action. If a malfunction should appear suddenly in the machine, this is quickly reflected in the attitude and physical reaction of the operator. When the behavior of the machine is crisp and spritely, the psychological temper of the operator will likely correspond. In summary, some form of communication, however crude, must always exist between the machine and its operator if the machine is to be controlled.

The question of whether a machine is, or is not, an independent, or at least a semi-independent social entity, is aside from the point that it is *treated* as though it were a social entity. The social world is a labile domain wherein, for example, despite all biological argument to the contrary, if a racial group has what are generally considered to be biologically inferior characteristics, such as dark skin color or kinky hair texture, it will be accorded discriminatory treatment and separate status. For the minority group member this situation becomes a very definite 'social reality.' And so it is that the social treatment and status accorded the machine also constitute a 'social reality.'

In the early stages of a society's technological movement, the adoption of new machines will depend upon how well the roles performed by these machines fit into the social structure, and upon the discovery of special avenues by which they may be introduced obliquely. Once the socio-technology of a society starts moving, it begins creating new forms of social interaction which will give it a dynamic all its own. Institutional change will follow as an inevitable result of socio-technological movement. One machine will create new role segments that will invite the creation of still other machines. These unfilled gaps we refer to as 'bottle-necks'; and they are filled only to create, endlessly, still other gaps. Once machines acquire a momentum as relatively independent role-players, the types of roles they play, and their subsequent physical number tend to multiply rapidly.

Out of the preceding discussion of techniques, tools, and machines, one set of factors emerges dominant over all the others, and this is the social character of machines. Greater insight into the relationships between man and machine could contribute greatly to forging useful new concepts for development theory and planning. Accordingly, discussion now continues of the many ways in which the machine interacts socially with man, and of how the machine itself becomes a powerful instrument for technological change.

ROLE-PLAYING INTERACTION BETWEEN MAN AND MACHINE

It is quite obvious, and inescapable, that role-playing between a machine and its human operator is reciprocal; each conditions the behavior of the other. Under the direction of a human, the machine begins displaying evidence of intelligence in its behavior, changing its activity in adjustment to changes in its environment. On the other hand, in interfacing with the machine the human becomes more rigidly machine-like in his behavior. For best production results the operator's behavior must be clear-cut and monotonously repetitive, and it is this type of role-playing that the human objects to most strenuously. It is these same repetition-demanding areas that are likely to be first mechanized.

But whatever the particular configuration of the man-machine relationship, each draws from the characteristics of the other in carrying out overall role-playing. Many of the undeveloped areas of the world demand of their people a drudging, monotonous, work routine which admirably prepares them for intermeshing with the machine. Other societies, and these are groups relatively free from the conventional work process, experience great difficulty in this type of role articulation.

As machines begin proliferating within a society their roles, like those of human beings, become integrated into the various social institutions. Some machines are narrowly specialized, while others carry out generalized functions that enable them to integrate with virtually all the institutions and to interface with human behavior over a broad range. The stationary lathe is a specialized apparatus. It is an artist. It has incredible finesse for translating lateral movement into an eye-pleasing symmetry that could never be achieved by the unaided human hand. The motor vehicle, on the other hand, is a highly generalized machine that, with some mechanical modification and change in dressing, performs functions which cause it to relate to practically *all* the social institutions.

In its versatility, the motor vehicle has done far more than simply replace the horse. As the family sedan, it creates and supports a new configuration of role obligations for each member of the family. It attends that unit's needs by providing transport from one social function to another, conveying its members to and from the place of work, aiding in the assembly of groceries and other consumption goods, etc. With some modification, it can be made into an elegant racing apparatus which, replete with its own costumery and social vestments (such as rallies), brings the athletic contest to a new and highly specialized arena. As a closed van, it may become a roving library waiting upon the educational institution; or it may be made into a bus transporting children to and from school. With a flat bed, it may be made to serve the needs of agriculture and forestry as a produce or logging truck; and this same flat bed, elongated and reinforced, may make it a mover of heavy industrial supplies. Again, equipped with a van of fitting decorum the motor vehicle becomes a part of the undertaking establishment, and in this capacity of serving as a hearse it becomes a role-player integral to the institution of religion. Fitted with tracks enabling it to negotiate difficult terrain, mounting a weapon, and outfitted in armor it becomes a successor to the war horse, conveying men to combat in distant places and in massive marshallings that would never have been achievable in the era of the horse. The florist's pick-up; the wailing red fire truck trailing its wildly careening hook and ladder; the black sedan with its top-mounted, red turret light identifying it as the dread police cruiser; each play differing roles and each evoke distinctly different human emotions. Machines have 'personalities' in ways compatible with some definitions of this phenomenon, along with the accompanying social roles.

Vehicles are further distinctive by the sound their engines make, the engine fairly crying out the identity of the vehicle of which it is a part. Depending upon the type and vintage of the vehicle, the engine will variously 'putt,' 'cough and sputter,' 'whine,' 'hum.' 'purr,' 'snarl,' 'roar,' or 'thunder.' Almost everyone upon hearing its sound will be able to identify instantly the general type of vehicle.

The number of role constellations embraced by the largest types of vehicles, the great sea and airborne transports, is even more impressive. The seagoing airport has made it physically possible to telescope transportation system within transportation system. In addition to aircraft, the aircraft carrier may even carry various types of land transportation vehicles on board. And in its overall social configuration the great ocean ship of today is literally a floating city. The pleasure resort has taken to the open seas, equipped with most of its formerly land-locked pastimes (with the possible exception of horse racing) and with the same deck-staggered social *status* system that differentiates land-based resorts into their different classes. We now have the beginnings of floating hospitals serving an international clientele in port-to-port calls, and the beginnings of floating universities which carry their student body around the world and give them accredited college instruction in the process. These giant vehicles interact with humans in a highly detailed type of role-playing.

Transportation, because of the multiplicity of individual desires and social needs that it satisfies, is not only a means, but an end in technological development. Some types of transportation are essential to the early stages of development, and others make their appearance only when the society has achieved the riches to indulge them as luxuries. And certainly, because of the great number of roles that it plays and because of the importance of these roles, transportation is the prime ingredient in any development program. It acquires a very early importance on two grounds: expediting mobility and so conferring an organic wholeness upon the society; and serving as a medium for the indoctrination of the society in the principle of power technology.

The ways in which machines interface with humans in social role-playing varies greatly. At the one extreme is full automation, in which machines simply relate to one another. The basic social attributes of this type of machine complex become manifest only as the product emerges and finds its place in the processes of distribution, marketing, style pacing, etc., which processes are basically social. It should be mentioned in passing that the automated complex, in its independence and remoteness from human society, poses few observable role conflicts, and therefore is one of the easiest pathways for the injection of change into an emerging society. But it should be noted that precisely because of its alien nature within the society, because it fails to become culturally integrated into the society as a role-player, the automated complex does little to aid the society in becoming technologically self-sustaining. It merely provides immediate wealth. However, this in itself is a great boon to most emerging societies and makes the imported automated complex a factor which must be considered in planning for development.

At the other pole of sociality are mechanisms so intimately related to human behavior that it is sometimes difficult or impossible to distinguish the role-playing of the mechanism from that of the human. Prosthetics are a case in point. An ingeniously designed mechanical arm may succeed in passing as a living member of a living organism and will leave undisturbed the image of totality in an individual's role-playing. On the other hand, a flesh and blood arm hypothetically grafted onto a human-like robot would still carry out social roles but against a different, a mechanical, setting. In both cases the role of the arm will differ markedly from that where the stump is mechanically attenuated with a steel shaft ending in a razor-sharp, pointed hook.

Most of the processes of recording are essentially a mechanical mimicry of human, or of some other type of mechanical behavior. The degree to which the mechanism can ape human behavior (through reenacting it) is so uncanny that it escapes notice. The moving picture, television, and radio, are processes by which human behavior is recorded through an optico-mechanical or an electro-mechanical system of encoding and is electro-mechanically transmitted and decoded in front of a human audience. The results, which are mechanical mimicry of a human mimicry (drama), can evoke laughter or tears, anger or tenderness, a broad range of human emotions. It is only when the transmission is mechanically faulty, when a record is cracked or begins a sequence of unending repetition that the observer is pulled back into full awareness that what he is witnessing is an entirely mechanically conveyed type of role-playing.

The machine as a direct, total extension of the human body is well exemplified in a type of operator-controlled robot now under development. This apparatus is anatomically structured along the lines of a colossal human body, with the human operator suspended in the head, or hypothetical brain center. The operator's body is encased in a sensitive electro-mechanical harness which transmits information as to his every movement to a control center which causes the movements of the machine's body members to duplicate exactly those of its human operator. The result is a Gargantuan apparatus capable of much of the generalized flexibility of human behavior but, most importantly, surcharging this behavior with the Titanic powers of a machine.

Thus, the degree of *behavioral reciprocation* between man and machine will vary from the intimate interaction just described to the almost complete separation between man and machine found in the automated complex. Extremes in role-playing will follow, of course, this same pattern, ranging from a situation in which the roles of man and machine intimately reinforce one another, to the machine's carrying out role-playing in virtual independence. As a society advances technologically its machines, especially those used in production, become more specialized, more highly inter-linked, and more systemically autonomous. In Spencerian terms, they undergo processes of differentiation and specialization that broaden the social base and lend it added stability.

There are many ways in which the machine exercises a profound and, sometimes, what seems to be a one-sided influence on the role-playing of its human operator. Consider, for instance, the differences in attitude, work pattern, and manner of dress between the railway locomotive engineer, the fireman, and the sailor. Each of these three performs on definite schedules, deals with different elements and on different terms, and each is easily distinguishable from the other. In terms of the similarities between members *within* each of these three occupational classes, one discovers that they are remarkably alike even across national and cultural boundaries. The engineers, firemen, and sailors of diverse societies behave and dress much alike. It is by no means entirely out of arbitrary choice that the locomotive engineer wears a tall and visored striped cap, coveralls of a similar material and, formerly, but no longer, a neckerchief. These features are largely elicited by the operating characteristics which sometimes will be shared by a number of machines. The operators of motorcycles, open cock-pit aircraft, speed boats, or racing autos, will wear headgear, goggles, and uniforms that are much alike, and yet are still distinguishable in certain details because of the basic dissimilarities of the machine systems of which they are a part and also because of deliberate social intent to stamp each with a distinct symbolism.

Just as there are machines that play what are considered to be socially benevolent roles, there are others that play socially disapproved roles. 'Respectable' machines may be put to perverted role uses, and some machines may be specifically created for pernicious ends. Using the family sedan for an illicit rendezvous illustrates the first case and the clandestine manufacture of firearms for criminal use bears out the second example. Military weapons, from tanks to agents of bacterial warfare, burglar tools and 'love potions' are all intended to subvert convention. The 'hot rod' and the public execution chamber are less directly threatening but are, nonetheless, menacing to the entire society where they are found. And, of course, a technological item that is accepted as morally impeccable by one society may be found morally repugnant by another.

The degree to which the machine becomes, in the Freudian sense, a real projection of subconscious desire, the extent to which it is made an instrument for libido gratification, makes for interesting speculation. Its ability to provide multiform communications undoubtedly makes celibacy and other types of personal isolation more bearable than they once were. Many, like Daedalus, have perished in an attempt to fulfill the desire to fly, a wish that later materialized with aircraft. At a more fundamental level, the Masters-Johnson study and other projects designed to analyze sexual response have developed machines which are used as copulatory partners by human subjects. The acceptance of the machine in this last capacity calls for, on the part of the human, a very definite type of role-playing projection.[1]

Machines exert a powerful influence in coordinating the activities of individuals. Punctuality, so painfully lacking in the pretechnological societies, is just as painfully evident in the technologically advanced societies. Punctuality and its associated forms of social coordination cannot be established simply through a transfer of the normative structure of the technologically advanced to the emergent society. It cannot be implanted through example, request, or preachment. It is built into, and is a part of the fabric of technology. The machine system is faceless, impersonal in operation. It will not go out of its way to await a particular individual's needs and its size and impersonality make it impervious to threat of retaliation by those whom its regularity thwarts. If an air passenger is late in arriving at the terminal, the system, which transcends the will or control of a few individuals whether clients or members of officialdom, cannot be bent to accommodate the fancy of the passenger even though this may mean his waiting another day or two for another flight. Whatever momentary resentment the passenger may have at its obduracy is smothered by the machine-like formality of the system, and the individual soon resigns himself to making his behavior comply with its workings. If the system did yield to such exceptions their effects would prove to be reverberatory, inflicting heavy penalties upon the

[1] William H. Masters and Virginia E. Johnson, *Human Sexual Response*, Little Brown and Co., 1966.

system throughout its reaches. Its operation would be not merely slowed down, it would be dragged to a complete standstill. In contrast, the small, relatively unmechanized and independent systems characterizing pre-technological society will yield readily to exception, often going to great extreme in restyling their operations to suit the irregularities of a few influential clients. This tendency to cater to the individual case will diminish as these organizations increase in the mechanization of their operations and in size – and size is ultimately a function of mechanization.

Taken in its overall form, the production process, particularly at the factory level, is in itself a super-machine demanding the utmost of behavior rigidity in individual human performance. Within this overall machine, great stress is placed upon a tight synchronization of activities so as to achieve minimum time waste in the mergence of collateral activities, and this same economy is enforced in the steps between sequential activities. This man-machine interdependence is a product of the work complex; and the strain toward finer co-ordination (called 'efficiency') is the hallmark of modern industrial society. In this setting, job incumbents are impersonally selected for their abilities to intermesh as a part of the system. Authority is narrowly channelled to the single end of maintaining or increasing production, and communications are employed sparingly and to the same end. The factory environment strikingly presents a situation in which the machine calls forth in its human operators a set of standardized behaviors much like its own. Within such environments there is a trend toward increasing rigor and a constriction of human activity until the individual worker is finally expelled altogether from the machine system.

Machines change in design, and the role of the human operator must change accordingly. The superseding of the horse-drawn buggy by the automobile, the replacement of the steam railway locomotive with the diesel powered one, the abolition of certain forms of manual, white-collar, clerical work resulting from the use of computers are but a part of a great procession of changes in human life styles occasioned by prior changes in machine roles. The human discomfort which this has caused has been the subject of many texts by social scientists, but, being somewhat aside from the point here, will not be further pursued.

Machines exist in, and create for their human users, a world of radically new dimensions, and as they are advanced by the hand of man they literally lift him into this new world. Tools are limited by the capacity of the human body and, therefore, tool-using cultures will remain relatively static. But machine-using cultures are pulled into new domains of habit and thought that will percussively help drive their technologies forward.

Machines behave in a radically contracted time dimension. By even the most commonplace comparisons, the speed standards of the technologically advanced nations are incredibly advanced over those of the primitive society. The equivalent of a journey requiring a full day by ox-cart may be completed in minutes in Western society. As a society moves deeper into technology its technical thinking, and even its social planning, are increasingly couched in 'machine time,' from the speed of internal movement of engine parts to the external velocity of the overall system. These times, until they become familiar to a society through contact with technology, lie outside human experience. Artificial illumination is obtained by an electrical impulse designed to alternate at fifty or sixty cycles per second; new types of air bearings make it possible to rotate small shafts thousands of revolutions per minute; and advanced types of aircraft enable mankind to fly at velocities of two or three thousand miles per hour. Projected into space in special vehicles, man already has traveled at a velocity of around twenty thousand miles per hour; and the computers which he designs are now being calibrated to act upon information in nanoseconds (billionths of a second). Once he has carried his activities into the machine time-dimension, it seems that there is no conceivable design limit to speed attainment short of the velocity of light. When mechanical movement proves to be a limiting time-factor, engineers counter by turning to electronics.

Machines behave in a radically expanded power dimension. Whereas the human body is capable of a sustained power output of approximately one-twentieth of a horsepower, mechanical or chemical power units in the range of two or three thousand horsepower are common, and the thrust of the giant space engines dwarfs even those power monsters. Even by the most mundane of machine standards, machine power eclipses the physical powers of the human body; and even in their smallest sizes machines are capable of a sustained endurance that is far beyond human capacities.

It should be added that machine power and machine time interact within radically and rapidly changing physical dimensions. Closer design tolerances, higher operating speeds, and super velocities are rescaling the physical universe. Man now tends to think of tolerances in terms of thousandths of an inch, of physical lengths and diameters in angstroms, and of velocities in thousands of miles per hour. It is because they dwell in pre-technological dimensions that traditional societies stand in such strong temporal contrast to the modern nations. As they begin bridging from the old to the new, the resulting cultural dualism is even more starkly apparent. These are societies in transition to new dimensions of behavior.

The machine lends itself handsomely as a competitive agent, and in this capacity it has a further, and potent, effect in promoting technological advancement. Although it is impossible to draw a hard-and-fast line between competitive and cooperative behaviors, to some degree men tend universally to compete with one another. Competition may be almost completely suppressed in some institutional areas and given long leash in others, the permissible directions of competition varying with the society. In Western groups, certain competitions may be more or less open and encouraged (different work groups vying for the highest production record), and others may be somewhat covert ('keeping up with the Joneses'). In general, in all societies, depending upon where one looks – in work, warfare, the hunt, courtship, the giving away of family riches, etc. – he will find certain elements of competition. And, as was mentioned earlier, in most societies there exists the custom of testing the competence or capacity of one individual against others through carefully formalized athletic contests, a type of behavior that tends to carry over in modern society into various types of competition between man-machine systems. It is at this point that an important distinction can be made between nakedly competing human beings, and humans who are competing with one another as parts of a man-machine system. Unaided human physical capabilities fall closely about a norm, and whatever the type of competition and however intense the opposition, beyond what slight gains he may make in physical conditioning or prowess there is little the human can do to improve his performance. He cannot have added muscle grafted onto his body.

In the man-machine system, on the other hand, competition may spur a significant improvement in performance because the *machine can be modified* physically. An innovator in a man-machine system will likely stimulate a race, between competing man-machine systems, for continuing functional improvement. In those respects in which man's presence as an operator is perceived as being a dead weight to the system, his functions will tend to be eliminated by mechanical substitutes. This trend in modification ultimately may lead to a situation where, as in the industrial process, machine will be made to compete against machine. And when the human has been stripped entirely from the system, machines will be pressed into competition with one another in their own peculiar style and dimensions. The weaker competitors ('bottle-necks') will be given added speed and sinew or they will be replaced (and in every system, however well balanced and efficient, there will always be bottlenecks).

It is interesting to speculate upon the degree to which machine improvement in modern industrial society may have been either the cause or the effect of intensified competition. Man and machine doubtlessly have been reciprocally interactive in this progression. There is no special evidence of there having been unduly competitive behaviors in preindustrial European society, but since the advent of engine-powered mechanization competition has been ubiquitous and undeniably intensive in all those societies, including the most socialistic ones.

The development dynamic described above will not become operative until the society reaches the power level of technology. Tools usually can be improved somewhat in design but the change this will make in their performance clearly is constrained by an upper limit – the strength, speed, and skill of the human who wields them and must supply the power for their application. This same constraint is apparent in primitive, muscle-powered machines. A Leonardo Da Vinci may design the chassis and gearing for a highly sophisticated machine, but without an engine to power it, it will likely come to naught. It will be arrested in the design stage.

The preceding paragraphs described direct ways in which machines act as agents of change. Machines also promote change in less direct ways, and one of these is by the depreciatory effect they have upon the status of a job once they take it over. As machines pre-empt a given type of work this alters the status attributes of the work in much the same manner as encroachment upon the occupational area by a class which is considered socially inferior. The higher status males formerly active in occupations that are under mechanization soon abandon them or change to positions of managership, and the prospect of returning to their former position is viewed with distaste. After all, 'A man is foolish to do work that can be done by a machine.'

One of a vast number of rapid occupational changes of the sort just described took place in the rural U.S. after the introduction of the chain saw. In those areas where it appeared, the chain saw soon displaced the crosscut saw and its manual appurtenances. Within a short time the farmer began turning over wood-cutting tasks to the owners of chain saws. But this group, most of whom were laborers, enjoyed only a temporary advantage. As chain saws improved, were manufactured in greater quantity and thus fell in price, farmers began buying them and carrying out their own wood-cutting chores. To digress for a moment, the foregoing process also describes a well established trend that has been triggered by innovation time-and-again in the rural areas – custom hiring followed gradually by an acquisition of the new production machine by farm operators. Needless to say, farmers would return to the old manual methods only under duress (perhaps war-time machine shortages) and then grudgingly and in the knowledge that the reversion was temporary. Once it has been demonstrated, in a society accustomed to mechanization, that a machine has been developed that is capable of carrying out a given type of work, there is a rapid abandonment of former manual methods and a growing aversion to them. This change in attitude (and its effects are anything but mild) is in large part caused by the changed status of the job. It secures the place of the machine wherever it may have happened to lodge, and thus helps in stimulating technological movement.

We have discussed the machine as a change agent but we have neglected the human reciprocal of this equation. There are two occupational classes, engineers and machine operators, who, in the course of interacting with machines, are led into prime roles as change agents. The engineer creates change by applying new time and power yardsticks (standards derived by assessing the machine's potential capabilities) to the whole production complex, from making improvement in the speed of individual machines ('breaking bottlenecks'), to making broad design changes in the overall system. Machine systems, out of their very nature set a new social tempo. And so it is that man, in his relationship to the machine, is led increasingly into a world of different dimensions, a transition in which the midwife is the engineer. Often accused of being a socially insensitive group, in terms of the long-range consequences of their behavior, engineers are, inadvertently, society's greatest agitators.

The machine operator also effects change, although, as pointed out earlier, less consciously than does the engineer and on a less spectacular scale. Indeed, many of the innovations he makes will attain only local significance unless the engineer seizes upon, and propagates them. Just as they interact in the process of doing work, operator and machine will also interact in the process of innovation. In its unrelenting demands on his vigilance, and in the shadow of the monotony created in its attendance, the machine will literally compel its operator to attend its functional problems, to experiment with modifications in both techniques and mechanism. He will do this, in part, to lighten his own responsibilities of operation and surveillance. The next significant step in innovation comes when the managing element becomes aware of this local improvement and propagates it by making like modifications in similar types of machines.

On a macro-scale, the various technologies, each of which is a vast aggregate of machines, because of their interdependencies induce growth strains in one another. Each helps to roll back the frontiers of the others and each creates certain reference points for the further development of the others. The first great technology to develop in the West was its system for goods production, its factory-industrial technology. Because transportation technology was so rudimentary at this time, there was necessitated a wholesale re-settling of peoples so as to bring them conveniently close to the place of work. Building technology and community planning, because they, also, were in primitive states, proved incapable of coping with growing slum congestion, much less in eliminating it. Hence, the much later development of transportation made possible a resurgence of population, particularly in the middle and upper classes, from urban to semi-rural residential areas. The middle class in the vicinity of the great *metropoli* has exploited technical advancement in transportation to its limit, moving far out into the countryside and into distant satellite towns. This movement has recently so overloaded the transportation system that the problem can be solved now only by radical new transportation techniques such as air shuttle and ultra-high speed rail conveyance. But meantime, as these new techniques are developing, compromise is being effected in other and related technologies. Not only has industry begun decentralizing, moving out nearer to the new population sites, but its mercantile outlets are also relocating in shopping centers adjacent to these outlier settlements. And at the same time, the center of the city is being refurbished by innovations in building technology which makes realizable more livable types of architecture in more natural, park-like settings. Thus does one technology, as it nears its technical parameters, self-protractively expand these parameters; and in so doing it creates strains for compromising innovation in the technologies with which it is associated. This is an area deserving further study from the standpoint of identifying cardinal technologies or technological sub-patterns which might be used as lead-in approaches in development planning.

The question will arise as to the relationship between technology and science, or more specifically, since, in this writing, technology is made almost synonymous with mechanization, 'How does science relate to the machine?' Past distinctions that have been made between science and technology, like some of the attempts to distinguish between invention and discovery, have been rather superficial. Science and technology go hand-in-hand. Early astronomers had first to build a telescope before they could observe the heavens.

It is improbable that any society will develop an appreciable science, and certainly it will not build an *institutionalized* science, until it has begun the creation of a modern technology. In the same sense that a developmental engineer is a scientist, scientists help plug the gaps in technology. Science interacts within, and as a part of the machine complex. The atomic bomb, which is generally regarded as a product of science would never have been brought into existence without, nor would it have much present meaning outside, the machine complex. Machines of various sorts were necessary in cradling the development of this weapon. Basic machines, such as the atomic pile, had first to be developed, along with special consoles and intricate robotry for the indirect handling of 'hot,' fissionable, input materials and by-products. Without these machine systems the bomb could not have been developed. And without the pre-existence of some means for its delivery, in this case the highly intricate machine known as the 'aircraft,' there would have been no *reason* for its development. The bomb's final testing was carried out remotely by still other types of mechanisms. Even had it been possible to create the atomic bomb without the assistance of machines, without a subsequent supporting machine context it would have had little, if any significance, and it would be an object presently creating little concern. It is not the atomic bomb, in itself that is terrifying; rather it is of the entire machine complex of which it is a *part*, the gigantic, awesome rocket systems which are capable of carrying this projectile around the world, that nations stand in dread. This inseverable relationship between scientific discovery and machine will be found, in virtually all instances, either in the early stages of a scientific product's development, in its later production, or in its final utilization. Thus, neither science nor technological research are likely to occur outside the nurturing and supporting shell of an ongoing technology. Technological growth molds the interests and activities of scientist and engineer alike.

The foregoing treatment of man-machine relationships should not be confused with that usually accorded this subject by scholars of cybernetics. The relationships being examined here are of a different type. Weiner, who revived the Greek term 'cybernetics,' succinctly described the viewpoint of that approach in the statement that the 'operation of living individuals and the operation of some of the newer communication machines are precisely parallel.'[1] In the present writing there is no interest in demonstrating the similarities between man and machine but rather in tracing out their far more

[1] Norbert Wiener, *The Human Use of Human Beings: Cybernetics and Society*, Boston, 1950, pp. 9–16.

important complementary features. The 'mentality' of the computer may, or may not, be analogous to the human brain; in some limited respects (accuracy of retention and speed of calculation) it is manifestly superior, and in other ways (storage capacity and ability to relate information) it is obviously inferior. But these questions are aside from the point. The far more important issue is that the computer *is a part of the human cultural complex*. Both human and computer types of mentalities coexist within a given culture, and both are used by human society. The two interact, and quite effectively, in problem solving and this high effectiveness derives from their *complementary* natures. Those capacities in which the computer excels are precisely the complementary high performance characteristics which were sought for and created by its human designers. The possibility of building a life-size human-like robot might be scientifically intriguing, but except for the possibilities it would offer for man to study himself or to carry out functions hazardous to flesh-and-blood humans, it would be of relatively limited utility. In an already overpopulated world, creating a life-size robot could result in merely adding one more client to the public relief roll. But to accomplish something that the human *cannot* do, such as flying through the air, adds vastly and profitably to the repertoire of human capabilities. And it seems most logical that man first built an aircraft because he did not have wings; he built it to carry out functions that he, as a human being, desired but was physically unable to carry out. Man achieves, not by the creation of highly generalized systems, because he has this characteristic abundantly in himself. He, instead, builds highly specialized sub-systems of enormous capabilities and then interlocks these into self-regulatory wholes. And he goes on to interact with all the mechanisms which he builds in a most intimate social manner.

SUMMARY

The past two chapters have attempted to uncover historical patterns of technological growth, to extrapolate from these patterns guiding hypotheses within which development programming could be carried out with maximum effectiveness, and to establish a set of sub-hypotheses which would specify a particular approach in instigating development in the emerging society. Viewed against the backdrop of Western history, the production patterns described in Chapter 6 are fairly evident. And the corrollary stages of technological development described in Chapter 7 are even less arguable; they appear as an orderly and logical succession of cumulative *strata* each of which is marked by successively greater complexity, and each of which was historically dependent upon antecedent supporting strata. They are clearly discernible as development stages in the history of the West. They are:

1. *Man-machine Organization* This period characterized the crude factory system as it operated from the beginning of the 1700's throughout the greater part of that century, at least until the development of steam-engine-powered systems. Man-machine organization achieved greatly improved efficiency, but primarily because of improved social organization. Men, machines, and raw materials were brought together under a single management and in one location. This antecedent to an advanced and enduring technology had blossomed historically many times and withered. But the massive factory system existing in the eighteenth-century Europe laid the groundwork for, and encouraged the advent of, level number two, power technology.

2. *Power Technology* This period marked the beginning of self-sustaining and proliferating industrial development. While level one was marked by crude and inefficient types of power – human, animal, water, and wind – level two is clearly identifiable by the advent of the engine. This enormous and flexible new source of power made it possible to meet the energy demands of large factories; it eventually led to the development and utilization of rare metals and new alloys; and the processes and output of factory production spilled over to construction and, eventually, to the laying of a base for a new and advanced agricultural technology. The engine supplied not only an unprecedented source of power, but it came to create a new way of social thinking. It established the basis for the systems approach, causing the members of society to begin studying the various ways in which the energies of the engine might be put to useful work. This entrained a whole new regime of engine-powered machines. Level two, power technology, must be fully assimilated by a society before technology growth can become a sustained process. While it is not necessary for the emerging society to duplicate, in its development planning, the exact stages through which Western society evolved, nonetheless, it will not be assured of sustained growth until it has internalized stage two. Meantime, the society might employ the strategy of attempting to inculcate level two through the prior implantation of level three, or parts of levels four and five.

3. *Transportation Technology* Transportation technology falls in the third order of development because it must await the creation of a power unit and, in addition, it must have a relatively sophisticated type of carrier vehicle. Advanced transportation will have an enormous social impact on the society and, like each of the other technologies, can be considered, in itself, a major social movement.

4. *Agricultural Technology* Advanced agriculture development depends upon the invention of the power unit, the carrier vehicle, and complex types of machinery capable of operating while in physical movement. The coming of advanced agriculture marks the beginning of an era of basic plenty for the society.

5. *Automation* At the present time this would appear an end-point in technological evolution. It is a direction in which the more advanced societies are rapidly moving and one which is creating for them an even greater number of problems and changes.

Just as the driving force for technological growth is power technology, the guiding agents which make it finally realizable must be the instruments of production which the power principle sustains. These instruments were divided into three categories – tools, machines, and techniques – and around them another tier of development hypotheses were woven. Tools are an extension of the social identity of their user. Techniques are the social fiber binding the total complex of a society's activities; and it is with these psychologically ingrained physical patterns of activity that developers must contend when they attempt to introduce change. The machine, however, stands apart in a social and physical domain of its own. To a degree all machines, like the puppet (which is a simple machine), are imputed with certain personality-like characteristics. They have their own social status aura, and they interact with their human operators with a reciprocity which powerfully affects the behavior of both, man and machine. In playing the supplementary roles fitting them into the overall social order, they draw the society into new and powerful dimensions whose sheer speeds and magnitudes are unknowable to the non-technological society.

As a mode for introducing technological change, as well as a means for obtaining a better understanding of the dynamics of the structure of the advanced technological society, it is suggested that closer attention be given to the social character of machines; to how they play supplementary roles fitting them into the overall social order and how they draw the society, functionally, into new domains of thought and action. A complete analysis of man-machine role-playing might well produce information which would be highly useful in introducing advanced technology to those many undeveloped societies that aspire to it and to whom it is still alien.

From the viewpoint of this writer, social change, technological advancement, and mechanization are, in a broad sense, synonymous. Societies may change over long periods of time on the basis of shifts in techniques alone. But when machines begin making an appearance, this is the beginning of a social process leading to rapid, profound, and a rather rectilinear type of social change. The machine will be accepted or rejected by the society for which it is intended on the basis of how well its role-playing dynamics integrate with those already existing in the society. Thus, role-playing theory may be directly applicable to introducing technological change. Through indoctrination in power technology, a society may be made to acquire the interest in, and the knowledge of machines necessary for its becoming a society of innovators. Innovation comes about when an individual learns the principles that allow him to innovate, when he understands power technology and develops an aptitude for systems analysis. Once familiar with the process of engineering invention, he will use it to expand upon his own powers. By augmenting his own abilities with machine attributes he will be enabled to increase his physical powers, his capacity for social dominance, and, consequently, his social status. And the society, once it does become firmly engaged with the growth of technology will be in somewhat the position of the dancer of Hans Christian Andersen's *Red Shoes*. Once these slippers were donned it was impossible to remove them, or to control the tempo of the dance.

8

PRACTICAL APPROACHES IN DEVELOPMENT PLANNING

A program for development, to be useful must meet a number of criteria with which present programs are failing to comply. First, it must be based upon theoretical principles which give it positive direction; principles which assure it maximum opportunity for success and which inspire a reasonable confidence in both its executives and those including the public, who must lend it general support. If it has these qualities it will be enabled to achieve another essential objective – it can provide a framework for unanimity of action. At present, program resources are allocated on a general basis and expended without a central guiding theme. The result is a welter of uncoordinated and often conflicting activities which consume funds without discernible returns. An operable program must be certain enough in method to permit the assignment of priorities of action so that planners, who will be almost always working under fund limitations, can achieve at least those objectives that are basic, that are logically prerequisite to further stages of programming as funds become available, and that will give those basic parts of the program that are initiated maximum forward thrust. Needless to say, the degrees to which further funds *do* become available will be heavily dependent upon the initial success shown by the program. Present trial-and-error methods, in their lack of clarity of purpose, numb the initiative of planners and alienate outside support as the program drifts aimlessly along.

The developing society, in supporting its programming will have to depend almost entirely upon its own resources. This, most emphatically, forces it to concentrate its efforts on well defined objectives and, where required, to divert funds which are presently not winning satisfactory returns into more profitable channels. This is not to say that plans should be laid along immutably rigid lines, for the realities of everyday living, the need for maintaining reasonable balance in the system and coping with unexpected future contingencies will force some compromise. However, compromise should be effectible upon rational grounds and within areas which generally serve the public interest. Thus, sound planning principles should greatly reduce the area for conflict when compromise of interests is unavoidable.

Since it is not possible in the space of a single chapter to give a fully rounded treatment to the empirics of development, this chapter will be confined to a discussion of basic prescriptions – the taboos and imperatives of planning, the ordering of objectives into priorities, and the creation of administrative bodies within which development planning can be amalgamated and its programming given co-ordinated guidance. Discussion will turn about the theme that development planning is fundamentally a matter of creating technological growth, and this amounts to attaining a basic mechanization within the society in the shortest time period possible. Hence, in discussing development we will be describing the means by which the aspiring society can acquire the machines, the work shops, and the supporting technical skills which are everywhere in evidence in the materially advanced nations, and which are the main features setting them apart from their struggling neighbors.

GENERAL PRINCIPLES – TABOOS AND IMPERATIVES

Taboos

Since there are so many potential pitfalls in development planning, it is, perhaps, more appropriate to begin with a discussion of these negatives, arriving at the imperatives through a process of elimination. The major taboos are as follows.

Programs aimed at achieving economic growth alone should be avoided. For reasons mentioned earlier, this broad, ill-defined objective is too amorphous to offer a platform for aggressive planning, and worse, in its philosophy it confounds cause with effect. It is not advisable to attempt to trigger growth by the simple expedient of pumping finance into the society. However great it may be, in all probability this wealth will in time vanish, leaving little trace behind. The flown riches of ancient empires are mute evidence that wealth alone will not create technology and that wealth without technological knowledge is an ephemeral possession. During the great depression of the thirties, it was discovered that even in the technologically advanced nations several years of steady 'pump-priming' showed little evidence of moving these technologies out of the financial doldrum into which they had slipped. A country that does not even have a technology to begin with can offer no rallying point for funds. They will dissipate aimlessly.

A development program should make no further expenditures in behalf of agriculture than those needed to hold food production to its present per capita level. In following this principle, most developing countries will find it necessary to expand agriculture somewhat to compensate for population growth. Major agricultural programs, however, if started prematurely squander funds and bring little or no return. A really burgeoning agriculture will not be attainable until a heavy industrial base has been laid and general industry has made its appearance. Most societies are managing to get by on the food stocks they now produce and they must, by austere management, continue to do so until they have succeeded in instrumenting an advanced technology. Since it will not be possible to bring advanced mechanization to agriculture until the later stages of technological development, it would be much more profitable, in the interim, to funnel development resources into industrialization and related forms of general mechanization.

Early planning should avoid placing its resources, beyond a minor extent, in the improvement of commerce. Occasionally a planner appears who takes the contrary position that in order for agriculture and industry to grow there first must be a general improvement in the facilities of commerce. It is maintained that improved rail lines and highways will increase the efficiency of movement of farm produce and industrial materials, and that up-to-date mercantile establishments supported by more liberal credit policy and technical advisory services will further expedite distribution. This overlooks the facts that the technologically retarded regions of the advanced nations are surrounded with excellent transportation facilities with many of these facilities traversing their very heartland, but the commerce moved within these regions is relatively light. These regions also have modern mercantile outlets, but the business they transact is of a relatively low volume as compared to the rate of transaction in the prosperous regions. These areas are deficient in production facilities and because of this they are weak in commerce. Much of their commercial life centers about the movement of raw or semi-finished materials. As production facilities increase they tend to create pipeline pressures that will demand improved methods of distribution and better outlets. This proposition will hold even truer for the underdeveloped society, which is in a more isolated, self-dependent position than the retarded region of advanced society. For these societies, it is far more likely that improved production will bring about an expansion of commerce than that an invigorated commerce will expand the production system. Thus, at the beginning of its development program, a country would do well to defer action on its commerce and to concentrate on increasing production. There are, however, a few junctures lying between the two where action could be taken that would benefit both. One of the more prominent of these is the storage and preservation of agricultural produce. It is maintained that in some of the underdeveloped countries as much as fifty per cent of the annual harvest is lost to spoilage or pests before it can be gotten into the hands of the consuming public. Measures safeguarding and preserving this output would benefit the public by attenuating the food supply and would aid the producer and distributor by minimizing their losses and by smoothing the flow of production.

The society should not initiate a broadside program ('the big push') which attempts to move ahead all aspects of development simultaneously. Funds will be limited in almost all cases and must, therefore, be rigidly prorated to those specific areas where they will have genuine effectiveness. Under the big push heading, also fall the various 'motivational programs' which have an objective of creating within the developing population a 'desire for the better things of life.' The attainment of the so-called 'better things,' which are primarily of a material nature, are not responsive to a simple wish on the part of the society. To secure them requires the technological knowledge, physical facilities and a cultural habit systems characteristic of technology advanced peoples. An individual reared in a machine culture habitually sets about solving a harvesting problem with machines; a person living in a machete-level technology habitually confronts this same problem by trying to determine how many men wielding machetes will be required to do the job. The latter, lacking a more advanced technical knowledge can do no better. Hence, a society should not expend funds in attempts to engineer social change, as antecedents to growth, except for those changes which will unequivocally clear the pathway for technological movement. Land redistribution may create great social disturbance with little to show in way of later accomplishment, whereas extensive skills training may eventually achieve a great deal.

Often treated as a separate program in itself, and also to be avoided, is the total drive to develop social overhead capital. The resources required to create full systems of transportation, communications, and power generation would bankrupt most development programs at the outset. These facilities can, and undoubtedly should, be built piecemeal or sectionally around the installation of prime production facilities, as they are built, and from whose output they would later receive still further impetus. When social overhead facilities have been pushed too far in advance of the general technology, the lag between the two has been reflected in their low rate of use and poor maintenance. First-class, hard-surfaced highways, usually built under the direction of foreign road-building firms and with limited amounts of imported equipment soon become undermined with water erosion, and pitted. The road condition soon drops to a point which is at a level with the society's limited interest, need, and maintenance capability, the latter of which is confined to manual patching techniques. On the other hand, first-class road trunk-lines, facilities which have been built expressly to link industrial complexes to urban centers, will perform immediately needed services and probably will be kept in reasonably good condition. The industrial nations of the West did not initiate development by the wholesale creation of social overhead facilities. These grew along with the rest of the technology as normally evolving parts of the whole.

Planners should avoid increased commitment to the service technologies. Although there will be an immediate public clamor for the benefits of these technologies, they cannot be adequately supported until the production technologies have been first established, and to divert a significant quantity of funds to them will cripple the development of the latter. Two of the service technologies most likely to receive premature attention are general education and medicine. Although this will raise an outcry from the many who consider general education to be a panacea for all ills, it probably will be necessary to forego liberal education, the development of secondary and college facilities, and perhaps even universal elementary education in those areas not already offering it, until the production technologies have become strong enough to bear the burden of such services. It is difficult to demonstrate a relationship between the more advanced types of education and technological growth, but for the narrower forms of technical training and their supplementation by lower-level elementary education the connection is clear and unmistakable. The ability to read a blue-print, to follow written operating instructions, or to issue the type of work communiques essential to technology *require* that basic elementary and technical education be given to the potential urban-industrial population; and it is here that developers must concentrate their attentions and resources. The scant exception would be in the educating of engineers and higher-level technicians.

Medical services will have to be brought under the same programming austerity as that to which education is subjected. This is truly unfortunate, in that, like education, medicine is considered one of the basic gauges of a society's standard of living and internal well-being. But until it can be adequately supported, medical attention probably will have to be confined primarily to the more urgent types of cases, to chronic childhood diseases and the like, that would be much more costly to defer than to treat. The greatest positive contribution that medical science can make to develop, and it is a monumental one, is in helping to curb the birth rate. Many of the underdeveloped societies are now giving frank recognition to uncontrolled population growth as a problem which must be dealt with frontally, thus opening the way for active programming. It has been the medical sciences, in their own steady expansion and contribution to increased life expectance, that have been primarily responsible for the population increases occurring in most of the underdeveloped countries. In many countries this prolongation of life will mean, unless there soon are radical decreases in birth rate and increases in production capacity, that more people are being enabled to survive only to face later the spectre of death by starvation.

There should not be any large-scale attempt made to promote development by the introduction of new production techniques alone. Techniques are deeply entrenched habit patterns which are particularly difficult to change by the direct method of merely substituting one technique for another. Rather than confronting techniques on an individual basis, if an effort were made to overlay the old manual system with an entire new mechanized one, whole complexes of outmoded techniques could now be forced into discard by the new techniques dictated by mechanization. In brief, techniques yield most easily under the pressures created by new forms of mechanization. It is the opposite approach, however, that has been hewn to by programs in community development, the Peace Corps, and by independent agricultural aid programs. It seems to these groups that by simple indoctrination, alone, they should be able to achieve considerable improvement in production and, of course, instruction is not nearly as expensive as mechanization. Granting that its cost may appear to be relatively low, the direct technique-substitution approach is not 'worth the candle.'

Imperatives

The first stop in a development program is the prosaic but, nonetheless, important one of providing an administrative framework for the management of the planners, field workers, and materiel that will be involved in the program's prosecution.

Technological development will call for a special type of administrative body, one that is quite distinct and separate from the conventional ministries, and like agencies, which are presently responsible for managing development and are trying to do so through economic media. Technological development will require a highly specialized planning agency and one that is articulated by punctilious scheduling procedures. Planning for near-future industrial development will require particularly close-knit scheduling; and even the rather amorphous process of propagating mechanization cannot be left to chance. It is in the realm of establishing goals and precise schedules leading to their attainment that most of the developing nations are now falling short.

In the truly technologically backward society, one lacking almost altogether in technical skills and physical appurtenances, hope for development will rest primarily upon the generation now in its childhood. But, with an administrative apparatus that assures appropriate training and machine dissemination, a country can be moved to a plateau of technological growth within a period of about twenty-five years, a relatively short time as the affairs of nations go. If intensive technological indoctrination is aimed at the group now in its early teens, by the time they are of an average age of thirty-five years they should have begun a widespread translation of the skills they have acquired into practical technical channels. When this point has been reached, the society is on the threshold of sustained technological growth. This time estimate is conservatively more than the time involved in which one technically trained generation succeeds another in the materially advanced societies. However, in order to attain this goal all the processes of development, the long-term as well as the short, will require close administrative management and scheduling.

A second imperative in a development program is a comprehensive evaluation of the society's resources. This will require the assembly of an inter-disciplinary team of scientists who have had the experience and abilities to carry out a complete exploration and mapping of the society's natural, cultural, and human resources, and to assist in the analyses of these data. Most of the underdeveloped societies have only a hazy idea of the types, quantities or geographic disposition of resources at their command. For example, the United States has the most comprehensive geological mapping program in the Western Hemisphere but still has four-fifths of its total land area left unmapped. Resource information is essential to the establishment of basic guidelines for a development program and in determining the particular directions in which mechanization should be planned. Resources evaluation, like the development of an administrative framework for the program, is not a part of development planning proper, but is a *prerequisite* to planning. Since its processes will consume considerable time, it is advantageous to have resources evaluation initiated well in advance of the establishment of the basic planning organization.

The promotion of technological growth will come primarily from two broad sources. The society must bend its efforts toward the physical proposition of achieving a general mechanization, and along with this it must acquire a sure grasp of power technology. A knowledge of power systems, how to operate, maintain, repair, and *build* them, is the key to success in expanding a technology. Therefore, every development project must contribute as directly as possible to indoctrinating the society in power technology. This is a broad area covering all types of power units from internal combustion engines to electric motors.

In consonance with the foregoing, technological development programming will require large quantities of 'hardware.' Technical knowledge cannot be cultivated in the absence of physical equipment, and this knowledge should radiate as the society acquires machinery. This changes the usual procedure of conducting theoretical instruction as a prelude to technological growth, and makes the physical diffusion of mechanical items and the mastery of mechanical skills interactive and concomitant processes. This is to say that mechanization and the technical culture will have to be implanted side-by-side. It also signifies that in order that they may attain a meaningfully broad propagation, those types of machines will have to be singled out for promotion that best combine economy, learning experience, and immediate contribution to productivity. Obviously, no one class of mechanisms can be expected to meet all these criteria if only because a growing technology requires balanced expansion. However, there are certain *sets* of mechanisms that can be singled out and ordered into a system of priorities which can cumulatively, and by stages, force technological growth in a balanced direction.

Technical development will require field and planning cadres of special composition and adequate size. The practical work of laying the base for technology should be primarily the responsibility of educators and of an assortment of engineers. In general, the engineers should be given responsibility for the *physical* dissemination of mechanization, and the educators should be called upon to design special programs for the regular school system and for adult education, which will lead to the speediest possible inculcation of technological knowledge. This hard core of 'work cadre' should be supported and guided by a nuclear group of planners whose members are recruited from both the physical and social sciences. Both types of scientists will figure prominently in any comprehensive physical and social resources evaluation, and both will be required in drafting into a development program, the data that grow out of an evaluation of resources.

The developing nation will have to plan so as to, eventually, develop a full system of industry. It will have to produce the bulk of its own consumer goods if it is to prosper, and in order to do this it will have to create its own base of heavy industry. This is indeed a 'tall order,' but historical evidence and present day realities attest overwhelmingly to its necessity. First, there is the inferential evidence. All the nations of relatively high per capita wealth are predominantly industrial nations. There are specific reasons as to why this rule holds, and as to why its observance is particularly binding upon today's emerging societies. It seems that no nation is able to create a vital agriculture until it first has developed a prosperous industrial base by which to support it. The underdeveloped societies are already predominantely agricultural and most of them are not able to produce enough food for their own needs. The terms of trade under which they must exchange their own labor and crude resources for consumer goods and production capital are very unfavourable and are steadily worsening. Almost without exception, they lack adequate financial resources and they labor under strained balance of payment ratios which place further limits on the quantity of capital they can import. These factors, plus the magnitude of their needs, virtually dictate that the developing countries follow the examples historically set by the technologically advanced nations and, by importation and domestic austerity, improvise ways in which to build their own capital.

Behind the foregoing difficulties are subtler and even more ominous straws in the wind for those societies that would specialize in non-industrial types of production. There is an evident trend toward production involution in the technologically advanced nations. As their production increases, a greater share of this output is retained in the society for home consumption. As their production grows, these societies tend to decrease their total external traffic (both exports and imports) relative to their total production. This trend suggests that as societies mechanize they are enabled to bring their total resources into a closer ecological relationship and, by their fuller exploitation, to achieve increasing self-sufficiency. The society that fails to mechanize will not realize this ability to 'super-organize' its assets, and as this trend occurs in other countries it will encounter increasing difficulty in maintaining satisfactory foreign trade relations with them. Thus, industrialization seems to be an imperative regardless of the state of a nation's natural resources or its geographical location. After all, what sensible observer of 200 years ago would have ever been so foolish as to predict that Switzerland, Sweden, or Japan would become great industrial sites? The tiny nations or those with badly imbalanced natural resources, have no choice but to form the closest possible trade relationships with adjacent societies. For them to seek patronage indiscriminately from just any nation would prove to be a gross error. They must form relationships with proximate groups with whom, as they mutually mature, they can merge into more harmonious ecological wholes.

In its technological development, a society must accept the fact that it will have to proceed primarily upon its own resources. Despite the publicity given international assistance programs, in comparison with the needs they must meet their offerings are so scanty as to be of very little help, and unless this aid is used judiciously it may be of negative value. The time spent in fruitlessly awaiting assistance, and the political entrammelment that may result from its acceptance may prove to be a highly disappointing experience to its recipients. Reliance upon food imports and generalized types of material and should be minimized, these services being waived, when they are offered, in favor of obtaining technical instruction and machine imports, and in developing machine and engine manufacturing plants. It is in these latter areas, in helping the backward societies to mechanize, that the materially advanced nations have the strongest knowledge and can be of greatest service. And, to the extent that assistance is available, this is the form in which it should be sought by the developing society.

Most of the points which have been briefly described in the preceding paragraphs under 'imperatives' will be treated in detail later in this chapter. First, however, before discussing these issues and the specifics of assigning goals and priorities, it would be appropriate to examine the generalities of program administration: the types of administrative bodies and substructures that will be required in formulating and guiding the program, and the responsibilities with which they should be charged.

ADMINISTRATIVE ORGANIZATION

One method by which a society may give greater clarity to its development goals and identify their order of importance is by making a clean-cut separation between those programs which it presently has in effect, and which are usually labeled 'development projects,' and a new system of programming which would have the *exclusive* objective of technological growth.

The great bulk of development resources are presently going into strengthening agriculture and existing industry, the latter being mostly of the small, privately owned, cottage-craft type. These two sectors are conspicuous in virtually all the developing societies. They clamor for attention, and even with the most expedient type of technological development programming the society is going to be highly dependent upon these two sectors for some years to come. Because of their interim importance, not to mention the entrenched interests centering around them, continued attention must be given these two sectors, not from the viewpoint of expanding them but of enabling them to maintain their present per capita levels of production. However, more judicious planning might allow a portion of the funds presently going into these two areas to be diverted, without lowering their present production levels, to projects more directly relevant to technological development. The task of providing administrative guidance to these basic, life-sustaining activities might be turned over to a consolidated organization which will be referred to hereinafter in this writing as 'Domestic Maintenance Administration.' It is this *stratum* that would comprise the foundation for development. Resting upon this steady-state base, there should be a second layer of functions and responsibilities which are invested in a separate administrative office that is here termed 'Technological Development.' It is proposed that the Domestic Maintenance program carry out a holding action while the second level, Technological Development, be designed to operate as a *growth* program in the true sense of the word. For a better appreciation of the potential of this double-tiered approach let us examine each of its two levels in greater detail.

Domestic Maintenance Programming

By Domestic Maintenance Administration is meant the type of conventional 'development' programming that is already underway in most of the emerging societies. These programs attempt to encourage greater production on the part of agriculture and private industry and to bring about general improvement in the community by group and 'self-help' projects. They offer encouragement through social incentive plans, small loans, and technical advisory assistance. The supporting funds diffuse through many channels with the hope that they will provide a broad stimulus which will bring accumulative benefits to the entire society. These projects go just as far as the available funds will carry them. They seldom have clear goals or underlying schedules.

The majority of these programs are not succeeding in even maintaining indigenous standards of living, much less in improving them. The reasons for their failure are severalfold. Such production increases as are made are often swallowed up by uncontrolled population growth, although there are indications that this factor may have been unrealistically exaggerated in the past. In those societies having *low* rates of natural increase, production rates are still badly in arrears, thus indicating the possibility that these programs are not inherently capable of real growth. Agricultural programs are based upon highly specialized export crops which are in over-supply, and perenially depressed in price. They are produced by a manually laboring population which is likewise in oversupply, and working for depressed wages. Local industry, in its attempts to grow, is dependent for capital and capital accretion upon internal sources of finance which are too weak to provide them. Industry is dependent upon sales on the local market, and this market is in poor health. Competition from foreign, machine-produced goods, which are superior in quality and sometimes lower in price, further discourages the growth of local enterprise. Local industrial concerns are so small, and of such a diversity of types, that they cannot be coordinated to produce the volume and quality necessary for successful entry into the international market. But despite the limitations of extreme fragmentation, tiny nations persist in the attempt to duplicate, in miniature and spotty fashion, the full spectrum of industry existing in the giant, multiregional, technologically advanced nations.

Cottage-craft programming has been encouraged because it is highly favored by some of the outside assisting nations, who prefer to grant aid on the basis of 'teaching their less fortunate neighbors in making better use of what they already have.' Administered as a part of community development programming, it has been undertaken on a fairly lavish scale in India. There the program has had to face down competition in both trade arenas – domestic and foreign. The general policy in India has been to encourage village industry by the restraint of factory production. The result has been a generally low rate of production, relatively high unit cost, and a general failure to absorb the unemployed, this latter also being a major program objective.[1] If cottage industry cannot compete on the

[1] *Measures for the Economic Development of Under-Developed Countries*, New York: United Nations, 1957.

domestic scene, it is a safe assumption that it will be completely impotent in international competition. It will become further disadvantaged as the advanced societies continue to reduce costs through mechanization until, eventually, the developing society will be forced to subsidize home industry at an exorbitant rate against the cheaper imports, or abandon the cottage-craft scheme altogether. Truckling to small industry or the small farm plot is to go counter to the very currents which have increased production in the materially advanced societies. In these societies, farm and industrial facilities have steadily *increased* in size.

Taking their cue from mistakes consistently made in the past, Domestic Maintenance Administrators will have to aim for increased productivity by different methods. Programming which has had the major objective of reducing unemployment has not succeeded in this respect, nor has it increased productivity. Nor will sheer size alone by any means insure a project's success. Grand scale irrigation projects often succeed only in placing hundreds of thousands of additional acres under obsolete, and sometimes ruinous, methods of farming. Great tracts of irrigated farmland (about five million acres) in the Punjab now lie fallow, waterlogged and choked with saline while, in the shadow of what has been described as one of the world's most modern hydroelectric dams, farmers still work the arable lands watered by this gigantic complex with wooden plows drawn by oxen. And land reform, certainly a sweepingly drastic type of programming, has promised much but yielded little. All the foregoing types of programming have consumed great amounts of funds, funds which, in retrospect, could have been used to much greater advantage in bringing a power technology to the society and in promoting general modernization. In attaining these two goals, it will be necessary for Domestic Maintenance administrators to work closely with the next level of planners, those responsible for inaugurating technological development.

BASICS OF PROGRAMMING FOR TECHNOLOGICAL DEVELOPMENT

A program for technological development might be visualized, at its simplest, as consisting of three interdependent endeavors. First, there is the task of *identifying* the country's physical, cultural, and human *resources* in order to plan mechanization along the most efficacious lines. Secondly, lying at the heart of the entire program is the development of methods for the physical *propagation of machines* throughout the developing society, and these plans will differ, depending upon whether the society is of a traditional or an urban transitional type. Thirdly, simultaneously with the dissemination of 'hardware' there must be a supporting program of *skills development*.

Resources Evaluation

A nation's resources may be classified as physical, cultural, or human. A reasonably precise tabulation of all three of these classes of assets is a necessary prelude to development planning.

Resource surveys are usually carried out in developing societies by outsiders who are hired on flat contract terms, or by a group of experienced domestic personnel who are temporarily brought together for this purpose. The objective is, conventionally, one of gathering whatever information is decided beforehand to be relevant to the project under contemplation, and rendering these data into reports and appropriate types of displays. Ideally, the work of this group should precede and, in most cases, help originate development plans, rather than follow in the wake of major development decisions. Although the resources evaluation group will vary in size with the geographical size of the region it analyzes, it should, in all instances, house a diversity of skills, and it should sustain its cartographic and exploratory activities throughout the entire period of development.

Assuming that a nation's resources are relatively unknown, survey work should proceed through four successive phases: 1. An overall study of the country to isolate its most promising development areas; 2. A general investigation of the area, or areas, singled out as prime for development; 3. A detailed study of these same areas; 4. Continuing survey work concomitant with the development program. After the first step of overall study has been completed, analysis and decision-making will be required. The particular area to be surveyed, its size and dimensions, the time at which the survey must be completed, and the personnel and material for carrying it out should be worked out cooperatively by top planning and government officials. An elementary survey may be carried out in as little as one year. A survey in depth may require three or more years even with a relatively stong complement of survey personnel. The cost may range from two per cent of the total cost of the program to a figure significantly higher. The larger the program, the smaller will be the relative amount consumed in survey. However, because good survey work will yield enduring and generally valuable social and technological benefits, its cost should not be charged altogether to the development program.

The lead work in resources survey should be carried out by the Surface Survey group, whose broad-ranging activities defy compression into any more precise classification, such as 'land survey.' The Surface Survey group should be composed of a mixed force of geographers, ecologists, biologists, agriculturists, civil engineers, survey technicians, and aerial photogrammetrists. It would be their responsibility to *gather* a major part of the field data which would later be rendered into reports and cartographic displays. The information gathered through Surface Survey would eventuate in a subset of separate field maps and photomosaics for climate, soils, vegetation, surface water, cultural resources, and topography. Together with the maps developed by the Sub-surface and Human Resources groups, they would provide the 'resource classification' data needed by development planners for appraising the relative values of all geographically classifiable resources and for further studying these for tendencies to fall into certain integrated patterns.

The volume of cultural resources charting and bookkeeping that will be required is extensive. Under this heading falls all the man-made facilities that are usually referred to as 'capital.' This charting would entail a detailed account of all transportation facilities, for example, the mileage of existing rail lines, their cartographic layout, annual maintenance requirements, types and quantities of rolling stock, total transport capacity, etc. Similar types of information should be obtained for roadway networks and for public and private conveyances. Communications, electrical facilities, private and public buildings, would all be tabulated and mapped in as much detail as possible. In summarizing the types of facilities that should be classified under this rubric, they should include all the artifacts, public and private, that may be expected to enter into a study of the industrial development of the area. Such statistics are highly useful in making maximum use of those assets already at hand.

Sub-surface survey would require a highly specialized complement of earth scientists and engineers. Such a group would be staffed with mineral geologists, hydrologists, geomorphologists, marine biologists, and petroleum and mining engineers. Its objective would be the development of reporting maps which show: the earth's sub-surface morphology; the type, extent and location of mineral deposits; the positioning, depth, volume, and chemical characteristics of sub-surface water reservoirs and streams, along with reports on the feasibility of using these water resources for industrial and agricultural purposes. For littoral countries, a map should be prepared which plots the disposition and quantity of those types of marine life that are of potential commercial value – oyster beds, fishing, shrimp, and lobster grounds, usable kelp, etc. These assets, if identified, can take a significant place in the development of the smaller societies. The search for petroleum deposits has become well-nigh world-wide; the geologies of most of the emerging areas would warrant at least a broad, cursory, petroleum exploration. Iron and coal deposits, notably short in the tropics and in developing nations in general, are also items deserving of special exploration.

Human resources survey involves the taking of a social type of inventory. In many ways more important than the natural resources of a region, are the characteristics of its human population – their density, distribution, education, standard of living, and specific skills. In taking this inventory, the society's deficiencies as well as its assets should be pinpointed. The demographers responsible for this survey should determine the numbers and types of occupational categories employed and unemployed; compile statistics on the number who are, at any one time, in the educational pipeline and when they are expected to complete their training; and make projections of future skills requirements which then may be presented to education planners. Much of these data already may be available from census statistics, employment records, etc., but it is improbable that they would have been consolidated so as to be useful for planning purposes.

It is apparent in the range of scientific and engineering skills involved in resources survey that, in all probability, a developing society will find it necessary to import these talents from other countries. Although the initiation of programming at this high level of sophistication might seem to be somewhat unrealistic, its cost relative to the overall program is modest, and, without the intelligence it provides, development planners will be unable to work effectively. A knowledge of resources is essential in a society-wide development program, and it is no less so for the development of an isolated region. The direction of planning for mechanization may be changed radically as a result of the society's having obtained fuller information regarding its available resources and their relative potentials for long-term contribution to development.

Planning Mechanization for the Traditional Type of Society

It will be difficult to maintain a clear-cut operational separation between the traditional and the transitional society because most of the larger underdeveloped societies present a mixture of both, with the transitional, feudal-like structure apparent in the urban and more advanced agricultural areas, while the traditional type of organization is characteristic of the more isolated outlier communities. For the sake of brevity, in distinguishing between the two it might be said that the traditional society is generally one without machinery, whereas the transitional society has begun mechanization but is still badly in arrears, in this respect, when measured by such technological criteria as per capita horsepower and the number of held-over manual tasks that could be converted easily to mechanized methods. In any event, the problems of technological development will differ for each of the two societies, and different plans will have to be drafted for each. For the transitional society, which is already on the road to mechanization, the problem is not so much one of familiarizing the population with the basics of mechanization, or overcoming resistance to it, as of accelerating its rate of progress. Technological planning for the traditional society, on the other hand, as was pointed out in the preceding chapter, must begin the process of innovation at the grass root by analyses of the role-playing interactions between established and new (and presumably improved) techniques, as they stand alone, or as they evolve about tools and machines.

One way by which the prospects for introducing change into a traditional society can be assessed is by listing each of the possible permutations between the established and potential, new techniques, and appraising the probability that the new will be accepted. In this case, the appraisal is based upon two hypotheses: 1. Resistance to a proposed innovation will vary directly with the number of old techniques that would be displaced by its adoption; 2. And resistance will vary in proportion to the directness of the method of displacement. Put another way, those innovations threatening to undo a great number of established habit patterns (techniques), many of which will cross institutional lines, will be difficult to introduce; but this will be qualified to a great extent by whether the first step in innovation is one calling for direct, deliberate change of technique, or whether change in technique is forced upon the individual indirectly as a consequence of a preceding commitment to a new tool or machine.

It will be noted that the master concept about which innovation turns is 'technique.' Techniques are the human factor in the man-tool-machine equation and in order to inject innovation into any society it is this living, volitional side of the equation that must be *led* to change. Techniques, in terms of types of interaction and their breadth and intensity, may be classified as falling upon three gradients: 1. *Straight techniques* (unaided manual procedures); 2. *Tool-centered techniques;* and 3. *Machine-centered techniques.* These three categories form a hierarchy of increasing ease and flexibility for innovation. As one moves upward from straight techniques to man-machine interaction, techniques become increasingly diluted by the behaviours of the non-human entities in the interactional pattern and they become correspondingly less resistant to change. Whereas, in the bare substitution of straight, new techniques for old the sequence is one of new skills mastery as a prerequisite to operation, when the machine has been introduced, and accepted, the sequence becomes one of subsequent mastery *through* operation (or 'learning through doing').

The following are a listing of the various possible permutations between old (established) and new techniques, along with a description of their probable modes of interaction:

1. The substitution of straight improved techniques for established ones. This is the most difficult type of change to effect. It entails heavy role conflict because it is a type of change occurring entirely on the personal plane. It calls for the voluntary surrender of entire packets of personal habit patterns, and the learning of new ones.

2. The superimposition of tools upon straight techniques. This method will be approximately as difficult as the preceding one, but if the innovation does 'take,' its after effects will be more sweeping because of the indirectness with which old techniques will be displaced. The tool will help by playing a partial role as change agent, and it will aid in rationalizing the changes in technique.

3. The substitution of improved tools for established tools. In general, it may be said that the less the new tool disturbs the old tool-using techniques, that is, the higher the rate of transfer, the more readily it will be accepted. However, there are a number of other factors that may intrude. Tools are much more likely than machines, since they are much more direct projections of the personality of the user, to be invested with special social significance. The difficulty of displacing them will be proportional to the extent to which they are surrounded by the techniques of religion and of other institutions. The people of a preliterate society will react to a new tool very much as they would to a newly arrived human stranger. They will express toward it attitudes of acceptance, indifference or rejection, depending upon the interpretation placed upon its behaviors. If an incoming tool bears close physical resemblance and functional similarity to an established tool, it probably will be readily accepted. There will be, of course, certain exceptions to this rule. If the society is of a type that invests a property value in the device, an incoming flood of similar items would depress the established item's value and would have negative effects for those engaged in its distribution and sale. Like immigrants coming into a country who are of the same ethnic and cultural background as the

original settlers, these *material* newcomers will be welcomed so long as they do not enter in excessive numbers. However, the closer the new tool resembles the old one, the less likely it will be to improve upon the latter.

4. The superimposition of mechanization upon straight, established techniques. This endeavor will encounter many of the same difficulties described two steps earlier in substituting new tools for established techniques. However, since the effects of the substitution will be less obvious than they would be in the case of substituting the tool, it will be easier, psychologically, to introduce the machine. The technical difficulties will be considerably greater, on the other hand, because of the radically different techniques that will be required in machine operation. This is an approach often tried by visiting engineers. If it is to succeed it must be backed by a strong training program.

5. The superimposition of mechanization upon established tool systems. Since, in this area of change the society's people are already tool users, they will have already taken one step forward in skills acquisition. The tool system will be more easily displaced than would straight techniques, and the change, once effected, would bring radical, indirect improvement and place the society squarely on the path to technological growth.

6. The substitution of improved mechanization for established mechanization. This is a proposition not likely to be applicable to the traditional society. It is only in the more advanced sectors of transitional society that rudimentary forms of mechanization already will be in existence. And where this situation does exist, change will come easier but still not entirely without worker resistance, as the experience of the West bears out. In general, however, when this stage has been reached the society is in a state of technological growth. Innovation now takes in more massive proportions and becomes more expensive, so that it becomes increasingly tempered by financial considerations.

7. The introduction of new techniques, tools, or machines which are of an *unfamiliar* type, and which carry out functions previously *unknown* to the society. This is an important and often wide-open possibility that is usually overlooked by development planners. Where there are no established, competing systems, the way is sometimes clear for a transilient movement in which the society can make the leap from the primitive level of straight techniques to the simpler forms of mechanization. This type of movement is evidenced at its extreme, by the jet-fighter pilot who bears the ancient tribal scars on his face. Innovation, under these circumstances, will

encounter relatively less opposition, but will require a thoroughly comprehensive program of technical instruction in parallel with the introduction of mechanization.

The last step listed above is so important as to warrant further exploration, especially because these functions are new to the society and will, therefore, require particularly deft management by those attempting to introduce the innovation. If a new device enters a society, which carries out 'new' functions hitherto unknown to its members, unless those functions are foreseen to conflict with the culture it will probably be treated with indifference, or, if its introduction is pressed by outsiders it will be passively accepted. But if the innovation is properly prosecuted it may be easier to introduce whole new forms of agriculture, from new types of agricultural products on through to new types of tending devices, than it would be, ordinarily, to effect one, or a few changes in an existing agricultural complex. The same would obtain for industry; it might prove to be easier to introduce factories producing new types of products than to convert existing cottage-craft industries into more efficient industrial settings. This general principle might be applied with high utility by developers.

If a new device which is interpreted to be hostile to the interests or values of the society threatens to infiltrate it, then, regardless of its apparent technical superiority there will be attempts to reject and, perhaps, even destroy it. For example, even though it were placed within their financial means, an artillery piece would doubtlessly be pre-emptorally rejected by a peace-loving society. But there could be extenuating circumstances in this case, too. If a society finds itself under severe threat from outside aggression, its institutions might, under this exigency, temporarily join forces in sponsoring a new type of weapon system. Possibly more than any one other factor, foreign aggression by Western forces has influenced rapid technological growth in some of the emerging societies. These latter societies have been forced to the use of the same weapons as are used by the aggressors, and are thereby catapulted, almost overnight, from a machete monoculture to the manning of complex antiaircraft networks.

If a new device is introduced which carries out functions that are unknown to the society, or that cannot be made intelligible to the society, it will probably be treated with indifference. This situation has its analogy in the behaviors of some of the Australian Aborigines who assume that there is a similar type of kinship pattern existing among all the adjacent tribes and who, upon the arrival of a newcomer, either assign him a set of roles based upon his status in his own tribe or, unable to do this, ignore him. A strange tool or machine, like a human who has no decipherable role-playing characteristics, will remain socially inert. This situation often crops up when outsiders attempt to proselyte a society but do not go far enough in carrying out indoctrination. A new tool is simply brought in with the expectation that the superiority of its characteristics will make themselves manifest, and the device is 'left to demonstrate itself.' The upshot is that it goes unused. The Western observer frequently notes parallels to this when he visits the emerging area. Deserted naval craft, destroyed in wars long past, lie grounded and unmolested on the beaches. Tanks and other vehicles rust away by the roadside, their engines and fittings left intact because they are of no interest to members of the indigenous culture.

Even in those societies where physical work is not socially approved, there are always some functions which the group feels *must* be carried out, and these are usually susceptible to some form of mechanization. The prayer wheel, and similar devices which enable people to escape work, may come to be prized for their aptitude in taking over essential but, distasteful, tasks. Each culture has its particular points of emphasis and it is at these points that innovation is most likely to occur. Food and the other accouterments of physical survival were of only passing interest to the early Buddhists, but making communion with the omnipotent was an unshakeable obligation which readily invited mechanization. In terms of the purpose for which it was designed, the prayer wheel was an enormously efficient machine.

The foregoing by no means exhausts the possibilities for the application of role-playing theory to technological innovation, nor are they meant to. It is the intent of this writing to delineate the *generalities* of a new approach to development, rather than attempt to supply an exhaustively detailed description of procedures.

Planning Mechanization for the Transitional Type of Society

A. *General Mechanization* This is the first and most basic stage of general planning, and one which should have the dual objectives of propagating mechanization and indoctrinating the society in the principles of power technology. One method, already briefly mentioned, for accomplishing power indoctrination is through the encouragement of a rapid build-up of light, informal modes of transportation. There will be little, if any, social resistance to improved transportation and, with encouragement, motorized bicycles, small motorcycles and automobiles may be made to permeate the society in a relatively short time. As they do so, they will bring local initiative into play in building and maintaining rudimentary road networks that will contribute, later, to providing a transportation base for general industry and agriculture. The movement, by bringing in numerous small engines, will also help to create a corps of mechanics as well as casual overhaul and repair skills in the general using population.

A build-up in transportation may be encouraged in a number of ways. The government may help to extend credit for the purchase of small, motorized vehicles; it may repeal all duties on their import, and assure that they reach the public directly and with minimum added cost after import; and it may stir up an interest in vehicle ownership through active propaganda. The government can extend its development role by applying the foregoing principles to the dissemination of *all* types of machinery. Most of the transitional societies presently have high import duties on road vehicles and machinery, and they impose a high tax on gasoline. Both of these sources of revenue probably have socially debilitating effects greatly outweighing the benefits they bring.

Transportation growth will stimulate other broad, related areas. Transportation, communications, and power generation proceed as parts of a broad development wave, with transportation at the leading edge. The unfolding of an area road network is a significant breakthrough for other types of development. Wire communication lines tend to follow alongside roads and railways, for reasons that are both technical and social. Roads and rail lines clear away the underbrush, and they further make installation and maintenance easier by providing for on-site transportation in the servicing of these utilities. Beyond this, a communication line is a logical social supplement to a transportation system, allowing it to be used with greatly increased efficiency. Communications will seldom be found, and would be of little utility, without some transportation medium allowing for physical response to communicative interchange. It is futile to communicate with urban centers of other neighboring points unless the contact can be 'followed up' by some physical step such as a buying trip, a marketing junket, etc. Communications also enhance the efficiency of the transportation system by substitutively conserving on the use of the facilities of that system and on human time. A telephone call placed in advance may save a personal trip, or make one trip serve simultaneously for several.

Electricity shows the same dependence upon transportation networks as do communications. Without access for the farm area to the goods of the urban market, and without urban outlets for its own produce there would be little progress made toward rural electrification. It is when the rural community, through regular contact with urban centers, begins taking on urban folkways (staying up at night until later hours, taking entertainment by radio media, consciously reducing household and outdoor labor through mechanization), that electrification begins attracting rural interest and making an impact upon the rural community. The foregoing was meant to point out the basic importance of transportation to development, and to point out that considerable contribution to the creation of transportation facilities may be obtained indirectly and through informal channels.

A second means for encouraging the development of power technology is through the creation of facilities for hydroelectric power generation. Power is derived from three main sources: liquid fuel, coal, and electricity, and, quantitatively, in that order. Because it is easier to transport, and because its known reserves have greatly increased during the last few years, there has been a shift away from coal to liquid fuel so that the latter now dominates the power field. Electricity comprises only about fifteen per cent of the total amount of energy consumed in the transitional society. However, electricity assumes an importance far beyond what might be inferred from its consumption figures, and when produced by hydro-generation is a major factor in development programming, and for several reasons. While the sources of other power are waning, the prospects for electricity brighten with each passing year. Not only is the world's water-fall potential virtually untapped, but looming on the near-horizon are such possibilities as electricity generation by atomic fission, by the conversion of solar energy, by tidal flow, etc. Additionally, the hydro-generation of electricity may be made synonymous with irrigation and various other forms of land reclamation which also may be significant aspects of development. And finally, electricity is important to development because of its amenability to a wide variety of uses. It provides services over a much broader spectrum than do the other types of power. It not only reorganizes the social milieu by providing illumination, and news and entertainment contact with the outside world, but it powers a great variety of labor-saving devices, from heavy belt-driving power units down to tiny, less than fist-size fractional horsepower motors.

To date, the great hydro-electric producers have been North Central and Northern Europe, highly industrialized areas which have compensated for a lack of fossil fuels with electricity. Even in these countries, the potential for further hydro-electric power is vastly greater than what is being presently realized. As for the world in general, over two-thirds of the nations presently utilize no more than three per cent of their total, potentially available hydro-electric energy.

While they greatly contribute to the development of a power technology, the creation of hydro-electric power facilities must be approached with caution. This type of project is typically time-consuming and its construction may come at a staggering cost, especially when the project is carried on through to include the development of an accompanying irrigation complex. Ordinarily, care must be taken to hold the scope of dam construction within reasonable limits, and the irrigation adjunct probably should be deferred, in most cases, until there is sufficient base of agricultural mechanization to make it profitable.

Although the creation of a power technology is a cardinal factor in development, a society cannot live by power alone. The society must temper this prerequisite by also planning its technological expansion along avenues that will bring fairly prompt material returns. One prospect in this connection is the application of stimuli to the *mechanization* of select, existing, private industries. Various types of government and 'foreign aid' assistance can be utilized to expedite mechanization within these industries, once principles have been derived for establishing logical development priorities. An industry's candidacy for development may be considered from the standpoints of its past performance; its potential for increased performance; its relatedness to other sectors which are under accelerated development programming; and its potential for utilizing resources with which the society happens to be well endowed. While it is difficult to set up hard-and-fast rules governing selection, the following criteria are generally applicable. Development priorities should be assigned, in this order, to:

1. Established industries which have shown unusually rapid growth rates. Preferably, these concerns should be producing finished export goods. Industries already competing effectively on an international market probably have the strongest potential for maturation to great size, and it is this quality that is most needed for success in development. In some of the smaller emerging countries, a few large industries could provide the vital additive putting the society on a footing of genuine prosperity. Even better, if this class of industry could be made to grow larger on its own, with a minimum of government aid, these funds could be channeled instead, to other projects so as to broaden the entire development front.

2. Industries which directly back-link to agricultural *inputs* and which show every evidence of eventually being able to produce a

finished item ***at less than the cost at which it can be imported.*** If the cost of domestic production exceeds the import cost, the difference will have to be subsidized at public expense. If it exactly meets import competition, the only internal gains are in its local convenience or the fact that it is under home control, for whatever these may be worth, plus the revenues originating from labor wages. Labor wage is not a sound source of income nor does it have, in a rapidly automating world, a stable future. After allowing for the foregoing, it is usually still possible to find a number of back-linked industrial areas whose exploitation would be genuinely advantageous to the society. The types of industries generally fitting this category are the manufacture of chemical fertilizers, insecticides, animal feeds (such as the bulk residues of the oil-bearing seeds), light agricultural machinery, farm tools, etc.

3. Industries which are forward-linked to agricultural *output.* This relationship is especially profitable when the output is an established, specialized, agricultural primary export commodity for which the present market is firm, and for which there is a strong foreign market. When the market for the refined product is healthy, the developing society, if it can muster the industrial facilities necessary for domestic processing, may be in the advantageous position of being able to divert all, or a large part of its primary export from the foreign market to home-based plants. If the diversion is appreciable, the reduction in export supply should aid in further raising the price of that fraction which remains on the export market. Food processing plants, especially when the food is of a type known throughout the world and the stock can be grown only in limited geographical areas, may be an attractive candidate for development, and may be one which, at the very beginning, can direct its finished product into the world market. It is almost axiomatic that a developing country's specialized export commodities be rechanneled, in part at least, into home-based processing systems. The market already is established for the finished good, the prospects for meeting foreign competition are in large degree assured, and the country's affairs are placed more squarely under its own management and control.

The mechanization of agriculture will be a more difficult proposition, and one that should not be undertaken on any large scale at the beginning of a development program, unless it has been proven that there is *no* potential within the society, for industrial growth. This latter is an improbable situation. Meantime, in the typical development program, it may be feasible to encourage agriculture to take some limited steps toward mechanization while a technological base is being laid in other sectors. Factors militating against any extensive future progress in this area are the present clogging of the land with an excess of labor, and the formidable task of attempting to surplant straight techniques with machinery as opposed to, in improving industry, the easier proposition of substituting improved machines for existing ones. Full-scale agricultural mechanization probably will not occur until there is an industrial center from which it can radiate. This center will produce the machinery for agriculture, some of which may have to be specially designed for the particular needs of the developing country, and it will provide a base for the diffusion of technical skills. The mechanization of agriculture will be extremely difficult so long as the present overpopulation of the rural sector persists, and it is not likely that a significant part of this excess can drawn be off, as presently envisioned, by attempting to create opportunity for nonrural employment. Industries that are given intelligent guidance in their growth, that are mechanized along the most advanced lines, will not consume, in their operation, a substantial quantity of manpower. Excess farm labor, eventually, may have to be removed from the land through outright social subsidy.

Because there is, in most of the developing societies, an overweening interest in agricultural development and a standing corps of farm extension agents, or their equivalent, to aid in agricultural programming, it is inevitable that at least a light accent will be placed upon the promotion of agriculture. And it is far better that this promotion be focused upon the introduction of new tools and machines than upon changing straight techniques.

Tools and machines are correlative, not compensatory of one another. If a farm is outfitted with machinery, it also likely will have a full spectrum of hand-tools. There is no operation requiring a greater variety of tools than does farming, and existing skills in the use of tools will have a strong bearing upon the subsequent rate of mechanization. Tools on a modern farm include hand and sledge hammers, log chains, post-hole augers, several classes of ground-spading and grass-handling forks, several grades of shovels ranging from the narrow-bit spade to the scoop shovel, painting equipment, chain and rope tackle, fence stretchers, a full span of mechanic's tools, carpentry equipment, and perhaps a small machine shop with a forge, drill-set, etc., etc. The modern farmer must know how to maintain, and, sometimes, how to mechanically overhaul, power units and relatively complex power-driven machine systems. He often learns how to employ explosives in clearing ground, how to weld, and how to construct his own farm buildings. In contrast, in many parts of the world, farm operations are carried out with a team of bullocks and with a machete which is used for everything from mowing grass to felling small trees. Although the underdeveloped farmer achieves a surprising skill and versatility with the few tools at his disposal, they cannot begin to substitute for the broader inventory needed for efficient farm operations.

The underdeveloped area is generally in need of a heavy build-up in hand-tools, and the acquisition of these items can serve as an intermediate step toward mechanization. Although the full stock of tools used on the Western farm would be prohibitively expensive and not fully appropriate for the agricultures of the retarded areas, certain items of the inventory have proven useful and inexpensive, and their use should be further propagated. For areas with peculiar tool requirements, it might be profitable to put design engineers to the task of developing special, improved tools, and then attempting to interest local manufacturers in producing them.

Machinery might be classified, upon the basis of its motive force, as being of two general classes: human or animal powered; and engine powered. Planning for farm mechanization leads to the conclusion that while light grain shellers, seed cleaners, and the like, would be useful in the emerging area, it is preferable to postpone heavier mechanization until members of the farm community become organized on a scale where they are able to afford and operate these complex, engine-powered equipments. The cost of modern mechanization is beyond the reach of all but the large land holders, and of these, it is not the old, land-owning families that may be expected to attempt mechanization, but the recent, large-scale land investors of modern outlook. Meantime, the peasant usually has little concept of machine maintenance or its relationship to the longevity of the machine, and he lacks operator skills. Modern agricultural machinery is expensive even by Western standards (a large tractor may easily cost six thousand dollars), but by the standards of the peasantry of backward society its cost is truly astronomical.

About the only ways in which agricultural mechanization can be introduced early in programming, assuming that the land holdings are large enough to warrant it and are laid out so that it can be employed, is through the domestic manufacture of specially designed, light, and inexpensive farm power-units and machines, and through governmentally or privately owned machine pools. Most of the developing societies are located in the tropical zone, which has a type of agriculture sharply differentiated from that of the temperate zone and one ill-suited to much of the agricultural machinery that has been developed for temperate areas. The heavier garden-type tractors and their attachments would be highly appropriate to some types of underdeveloped agriculture, and the local manufacture of these units could provide one focal point for industrial development.

Machine pools conventionally furnish machine and operator, and work on a custom basis (charging a set sum for unit of land serviced). For a custom plowing service to be economically feasible, the rural area serviced should be large enough to absorb the services of at least ten tractor-plow sets. Since they probably will operate at a loss for the first two or three years until the service builds up patronage, machine pools, in all likelihood, will have to be governmentally supported if they are attempted. Where the pool is workable, it is an excellent way in which to bring the backward farmer into first-hand contact with the modern machine and allow him to experience its advantages. Associated with the machine pool, there should be an educational program which trains the farmer in machine operation, maintenance, and simple repair.

Animal-powered equipment is applicable in most of the developing areas, but there are numerous problems involved in its production. The manufacture of these items is virtually obsolete in the advanced nations, and the animal-drawn equipments which were formerly manufactured in the advanced countries were designed for horses. Many of the developing societies do not have horses, and these Western-made implements are too heavy for lesser draft animals. There is the further difficulty of interesting manufacturers, in either the West or the developing societies, in the resumption of the production of a class of machinery now obsolete and abandoned in the technically advanced parts of the world and which, because of its inferiority to engine-powered equipment, has a very dim future even in the emerging countries. Dragging a society through the intermediate stage of animal-powered equipments, beyond what they may presently have in use, seems pointless. As an interim measure, however, the types of animal-powered implements now in use in the emerging areas could be profitably improved. There are designs for oxen harness which greatly enhance draft efficiency over that obtainable by the shoulder yoke or the head saddle. In some areas, experimentation is underway in the testing of a simple, flexible, all-wooden, animal-towed drawbar to which a number of implements can be attached interchangeably. But after all is said and done, the power source of these devices is still the plodding, underpower, ox-team. It seems that the development of agriculture must content itself, temporarily, with improving upon the efficiency and range of farm tools, and in supplementing these, when possible, with specially designed, light machines or with pool-managed farm machinery. The society will be able to make the full step to modern agricultural equipment only after it has acquired an industrial base and a reasonable advancement in power technology. Agricultural development was one of the last stages to advance in the movement of Western technology, but when it finally did appear it advanced at a dramatic clip.

B. *Development of Heavy Industry* It is a quite casual matter to talk about physically disseminating light mechanization throughout a society, but quite another proposition to determine how, and from what sources, this machine stock can be secured. And since mechanization is to be made the basic tenent of development programming, provisions for obtaining the quantity of machine stock needed will have to be made an incorporate part of programming at its very outset. Light machine goods can be acquired in two ways: by building up domestic facilities for the manufacture of engines and general machines (heavy industry); or by importing them from the advanced manufacturing countries. For the present, most of the emerging societies are pinning their hopes on the latter course, but for a number of reasons they have not been successful in securing adequate capital from foreign suppliers. This difficulty has been caused, in large part, by the poor financial circumstances of the developing countries, but another set of constraints on the international flow of capital arises from the internal mechanics of technological growth and the way in which the growth process seems to dampen international trade, in general. Although this set of inhibitory factors may be playing a secondary role now, they will become increasingly felt by those having trade dependencies upon the technologically advanced nations. And, beyond this, they have a high relevence to the question of whether a small society should attempt to develop its own production system independently, or fit itself in as a segmentally reciprocating member of a *community* of producing nations.

In the well ordered, hyper-rational world of the economist, each inhabitant takes those resources at his disposal and produces what he is most skilled at making. He exchanges that part of his production which he does not consume, for the other things he desires. The more specialized he becomes as a producer, the greater is the part of his production that will be traded. If we were to take the hypothetical case of an isolated community of one hundred familyless individuals, each of whom was a production specialist and able to draw freely in his production upon community-held raw materials, if the system were in perfect balance, each, logically, would be expected to retain one per cent of his output and to trade the other ninety-nine per cent in equal parts. This sort of reciprocal interaction leads to an ideal system of interchange. By a fluid distribution system, goods can be freely exchanged throughout a broad area, with everyone, because of the increased productivity growing out of specialization, standing to benefit. If nations could only be persuaded not to erect trade barriers or to remove those presently in effect, so the reasoning goes, whole blocs of nations, and perhaps the entire world, could be brought into a single, reciprocating trade network. In addition to creating a material superabundance, this ecumenical trade union would set up interdependencies which would help preserve the peace and would lead to a world-wide political superstructure.

This is a comforting picture but, unfortunately, it is not the direction in which the system seems to be moving. International trade, much less than showing a tendency to approximate this situation is, if anything, drifting in the opposite direction to an extent to make it evident that if there is ever to be a world supergovernment, it will grow, not out of trade interdependencies but out of the more compelling need for international political stability.

Unless they become members of international trade blocs, the production systems of nations, as they progress technologically, show a tendency toward involution. Even when nations *form* trade blocs, involution still occurs, but within the bloc, with a rapid diminuation of trade outside this enclave. This trend, since it relates to the relative stage of technological advancement of the society, is most apparent in the West, for example in the dynamic and internally coherent technologies of the United States and England. Both of these nations were heavy exporters in the early nineteenth century and both still are, relatively speaking. The United States and England, together with Canada, Japan, and six other European nations accounted, in 1954, for eighty-three per cent of the world's total export of manufactures.[1] The United States has been, far and away, the heaviest exporter, sending abroad, in 1964, approximately twenty-five billion dollars worth of commodities, nine billion of which consisted of machinery and transport equipment. And yet, for both countries, the United States and England, although their total production has risen steadily over the years, the proportion of that increase which goes into exports has steadily declined. This trend toward relative decline has held steady on through the intro-

[1] A. K. Cairncross, 'World Trade in Manufacturing Since 1900,' *Economic Internazionale*, VIII, no. 4, 10.

duction and growth of mass manufacturing methods, and probably has been accented further by the maturation of the agricultural sectors in both countries. There is every reason to believe that mass manufacture and a burgeoning agriculture should have reversed the trend, but they did not. It has held equally for imports and exports.

TABLE I

Ratio of Merchandize Trade to Gross National Product at Current Market Prices for the United States and the United Kingdom

	1913	1929	1938	1950	1960
United States Exports	6·1	4·9	3·6	3·5	4·0
Imports	5·1	4·5	2·5	3·4	3·1
United Kingdom Exports	19·8	14·9	8·2	16·3	14·1
Imports	24·9	22·7	18·7	18·9	17·5

Source: A. Maddison, 'Growth and Fluctuation in the World Economy, 1870–1960,' *Banca Nazionale del Lavoro Quarterly Review*, June, 1962.

The United States now exports only four per cent of its prodigious annual output, and imports even less. While it is difficult to construct a meaningful analogy for this situation, it might be said that a subsistence farmer, a member of that most self-sufficient of all occupational groups, who managed to live so totally within his own resources that he sold only four per cent of what he grew, and bought in similar quantity, would be considered independent indeed. If, as a society increases its productivity, it tends to consume an ever-increasing portion of that production internally, this leads to the hypothesis that as technological development proceeds it helps to integrate the resources of a society and, in doing so, gives it a greater self-sufficiency and tends to further internalize its production activities. Thus, the economic ideal of free international trade may collide head-on with the stubborn concept of an ecology, in which, what is already a relatively closed system is bounded with increasing rigidity by its own internal processes.

There are several classes of evidence, in addition to import-export statistics, that suggest that there is a technological inturning of production. There is a high rate of production *redundancy* that is evident both on the international and intranational markets. On the international markets, one sees an outpouring of goods of similar types. There is none of the technologically advanced nations that does not produce some type of automobile, television sec, radio, camera, typewriter, commercial calculating or computing machine, wearing apparel, etc. There is no nation that is an exclusive producer of a given class of consumer good.

Within the technologically advanced nations, production redundancy exists on a broad, *regional* basis. Although certain geographical areas may exercise a limited type of production hegemony, this is, mainly an eye-catching dominance that tends to obscure the far greater number of ways in which internal production systems are duplicative of one another. In the United States, Detroit is known for automobile production, Chicago for meats, New York City for wearing apparel, etc., but an examination of the broader technologies of these areas shows that they share with one another (as well as with London, Paris and Tokyo) the production of a great flow of universal goods such as electric motors, rubber tires, pencils, home appliances, bedding, clothing and a sea of articles defying enumeration. The giant urban center may dominate its immediate hinterland but it is extremely improbable that this influence will carry over to create much dependency in surrounding socio-technological regions.

Another type of evidence of a growing trend toward production involution, or localism, is the disproportionate acceleration in the rate of local consumption as the technology grows. A poor community has little in way of machinery. A technologically advanced community acquires a machine for almost every job, sometimes carrying this to an extreme where the machine is able to show little superiority over erstwhile manual methods. The well-equipped U.S. household may own one or more electric toothbrushes, electric razors, rotisseries, hedge shears, lawn-mowers, a dishwasher, coffee-makers, mangles, food-grinders and food-mixers, etc., etc. As the number of these items grows, the quantity that is produced in the local area also increases. The goods that are imported become fewer and more exotic in nature.

Production redundancy quite patently reflects a redundancy of technologies. Why do nations, and even broad regions, tend to develop roughly similar types of technologies? There are several reasons that may serve to explain this. Regional and international social inequalities create barriers to the free flow of trade. The low rate of return which their manual labor brings, in exchange for finished goods brought in from outside, helps to drive home the point to backward peoples that if they are to have these things they will have to devise means of producing them at home, using advanced technological facilities and substituting their own cheaper labor.

Moreover, there seems to be inherent in every human community a desire for self-sufficiency. The desire for local control and for autonomy in government seems to be prompted by more than the ethnocentrism accompanying militarism or nationalism alone. On the technical side, as a society's technology grows and as its rate of internal consumption and wealth increase, it becomes increasingly possible to realize large-scale production economies on a local basis. The swelling local market encourages more sophisticated types of manufacture, and these enterprises establish a growing number of cross-links between basic types of industry and spawn still other local basic industries.

Coupled with the foregoing is a tendency, on the part of the technologically growing society, to make more intensive use of local resources. Whereas manual methods, or crude technology, will pass over certain natural resources out of an inability to process them, an advanced technology will frequently return to these same resources and bring them under a highly profitable exploitation. A technology begins by utilizing its more easily processed resources and then broadens its base as its wealth and abilities grow. Early oil operations began with shallow wells exploited primarily for kerosene and lubricants. Within a few decades the oil industry, under the stimulus of the automobile, had progressed to deep-well drilling techniques, to off-shore drilling operations, and now to a search for methods of extracting petroleum from oil-bearing shales. Somewhat at variance with the foregoing is one school of economic thought which holds that the most effective units of a given natural factor are the first to be used, so that alternative methods are always less effective, and because of this, more expensive. For example, the richest agricultural lands are always exploited first, thus creating a situation in which the output of these lands can be duplicated on the less productive remaining land only by cultivating relatively greater areas and at much higher costs in labor, fertilizers, etc. This idea is based entirely on short-term, theoretically rational use, and does not take into account the broader aspects of technological advancement.

And finally, also standing in the way of free-flowing trade are the difficulties mentioned earlier. Strained balances of payment, inequalities in the terms of exchange, and the sheer magnitude of capital needed, as opposed to what can be imported, virtually dictate that a society prepare, at the beginning of development, to establish its own heavy industry, to produce as much as possible of its own machine goods, and to produce, eventually, practically all of this class of goods internally.

Just as a growing technology ecologically integrates the physical resources of a region, so does it organize the region's human population. It integrates people into a tightly knit production system and, in ever-shifting patterns, redistributes them spatially. So long as a society is in the growth stage, that is, short of automation, an individual is limited in his relationship to the technology to, principally, one of three different *stati*. He may be assimilated productively into the technological system as an integrated, active contributor to its processes; he may live in a condition of pluralism as a member of a special sub-society within the broader one; or he may be thrown, by coercion or choice, into the category of 'Displaced Persons.'

The disemployed poor and the unemployed rich both fall within the classification of displaced persons. Both groups are unneeded by the society and must work out special techniques for survival. The rich have a *modus operandi* by which, through stored wealth or absentee ownership, they continue to share in the fruits of the system although they may sometimes reside in distant foreign lands or live as 'world wanderers.' The disemployed poor, lacking any better accommodation must survive on whatever subsistence they are able to entreat or pilfer from the larger society, and they will continue to live so, and in increasing number, until some solution works through. Their plight is without precedence. The Afro-American, under slavery, was a needed member of the production system, his value being reflected in the high prices usually associated with slave sales. Slavery productively distributed people over a broad geographical area. After emancipation the Afro-American, along with the poor, unskilled whites, was absorbed into the unskilled and semi-skilled labor ranks where both groups have largely remained. Now, caught in a situation of limited educational opportunity and rising automation, both are being increasingly constrained to the ghetto or slum, and in the process both are becoming more vulnerable. As in South Africa, sharpened segregation makes the disenfranchised group more easily controlled and increasingly subject to the will of the dominant society. Thus, both groups are slipping into an even more precarious position than that occupied by the slave. Much less than having a price tag on their bodies these peoples are, as automation increases, unwanted; their very presence is an irritant and cause of embarrassment to the remainder of the society.

Pluralism is a way of living vividly illustrated in American Indian society subsequent to the establishment of the reservation period. Pluralism may proceed for an indefinitely long time interval, with a given ethnic group living as an enclave within the territory of the larger society. But to do so it must fulfill certain conditions. The lands which it occupies must be relatively valueless, so that they are not perceived as a necessary resource to the growth of the surrounding technology, and it must have some sort of production subsystem of its own in order to reduce its dependency upon the larger society to token aid. In its inclusiveness a growing technology either absorbs the human or, having no demand for his services, rejects him unless new arrangements are made for the distribution of goods and services.

The foregoing is not meant to imply that the ecological areas which technology creates and the so-called 'natural' region of the biologists are one and the same. They are, in fact, far from coincidental. A technological complex is nourished by its total root system which, in its transportation media of rail and ship, may reach out to bond *several adjacent regions* or, for the more exotic items, it may temporarily hurdle oceans. Iron ore may be excavated in one region and transported several hundred miles to be refined in another region. Tungsten, teak and olive oil are regularly transported to points thousands of miles distant. Thus, the socio-technologically created ecology is man-machine made. In its massive transregional remarshalling of resources it often creates rigid patterns which run directly *counter* to the generalized arrangement of the biological ecology. The socio-technology tends to restructure natural, adjacent regions along more efficient, *specialized* lines, rearranging the growing of flora and fauna so as to best achieve balance within its own broader framework. One region may emphasize the grazing of cattle, another the growing of cotton, and another the cultivation of tea, etc. However abhorant this trend toward assigned specialization may be to those concerned with preserving a 'natural balance in nature,' it will undoubtedly continue so long as the technology finds advantage in bending the resources of the region to serve its own overvaulting needs.

It is peculiarly noteworthy that the world's great technological complexes are located in the temperate zones, and that most of those showing late, but rapid growth are also located in these zones. Climatically and in their general biologies these areas are similar to one another, one more factor encouraging technological redundancy. Although the imports of these technologies are sizeable in absolute terms, relative to those resources drawn upon from within they are quantitatively minute. Hence, Temperate Zone innovation, its sciences and engineering research, have tended, of course, to evolve about Temperate Zone resources. And the result has been a technology which is undoubtedly peculiar to the Temperate Zone. Temperate Zone societies, having an abundance of coal and iron have developed road vehicles made almost entirely of steel, and they find it necessary to venture outside the society only for such minor items as the latex used in tire manufacture. Similarities in resources and general environment tend to contain and propagate technology within the Temperate Zone, making it easier for the Temperate Zone nations to plagiarize the technologies of their advanced neighbors and allowing them to underpin these technologies with their own, similar natural resources.

On the other hand, the technologically lagging nations, which are located primarily in the tropical zones, in attempting to mimic the only technological model at hand, that developed in the temperate area, encounter all manner of difficulty. If they adopt Temperate Zone technology bodily they also must import a disproportionately great quantity of resources from the Temperate Zone. And they will be forced to secure them on grossly inequitable terms of exchange and for a technology which must be made to operate in an environment with which it is, in many ways, incompatible. The tropics have yet to develop systems of technology for industry, and especially for agriculture, which are optimum for those two areas. Until they do so, and desist in the wholesale borrowing of alien systems, they will labor under a handicap.

In the light of area ecological integration, the society probably could best proceed in development by a program designed to seed each potential socio-technical area individually with mechanization. In the large multiregional nations this would mean, contrary to present practice, encouraging rather than discouraging, production redundancies between geographic areas. The technologically advanced nations seem to have followed this pattern of development historically, and they grew without significant help from outside.

It is in the development of heavy industry that an emerging society can use foreign aid where it counts most, and it is here that it can borrow from the aid-giving countries the type of service in which they are most expert. The establishment of engine repair and manufacture shops as well as factories for the manufacture of electric motors; the development of a substructure of tool and dye-making industries along with the training of general machinists, trade specialists, and machine operators, is a much more concise and less expensive approach to development than is usually employed; and it is one in which outside aid can be of more value than is presently being realized from it. It is not likely that this type of aid will be given to the emerging countries, the present suppliers of much of the world's raw materials, ungrudgingly. The emerging society, when it is offered aid, will have to decide what it needs and insist upon these things rather than accepting the usual shipments of outmoded rifles, pickmattocks, 'Care' packages, and odds-and-ends that it is presently being given. It makes no more sense for a developing country to accept blindly whatever form of aid is offered to it, than it does for the borrower of a bank loan to accept the loan in whatever form the bank fancies it should be given. This latter type of business is best described as a 'sharecropper transaction.'

C. *The Large Scale Industrial Project* This represents the next higher order of difficulty in development programming and, barring certain exceptions, it is an area into which the developing society will not wish to enter until it has succeeded in starting the establishment of a technological base. The most likely exception to the foregoing rule would be the creation of large-scale, heavy industries for the production of engines and machines. These industries should be as heavily automated as possible so as to avoid reliance upon what will be, in most cases, a badly underskilled domestic population. They should be operable by a handful of imported managerial and maintenance personnel, and their function should be that of helping lay the physical base for the society's technology.

Large-scale integrated industry is, thus far, fairly much the monopoly of the technologically advanced countries. The emerging societies do not have the technological experience or physical facilities for establishing enterprise on this scale. The larger technologically advanced nations are quite capable of establishing industrial complexes under the most difficult of conditions, but they are reluctant, in the face of growing nationalism, to commit their finances to the establishment of entirely self-sufficient, integrated industrial systems on the soil of the developing nation. This reticence is deepened by the shortage of skilled labor in the developing society and by the absence of general facilities and complementary types of supporting enterprises. A large steel mill may be constructed only to find that its production is throttled by poor transportation or by a coal industry which is too underdeveloped to give it proper support. Assuming that a private foreign concern can be found which is agreeable to the proposition of developing industrial facilities on foreign soil, for the emerging country to allow it to do so on the usual terms will invite the usual trouble. Foreign ownership profits will syphon a substantial amount of finance out of the country, the foreign concern will attempt, understandably, to keep production costs such as labor and raw materials as low as possible, and there will be the inevitable local resentment against foreign management.

If, and when, the developing society decides that it is ready to undertake the establishment of large-scale industry, there are a number of factors that must be taken into account. If it makes this attempt early in development programming, its market will be too weak to absorb the volume of output coming from the industry and, consequently, the industry will have to be girded for competition on international markets. A project for the development of large-scale industry should be initiated only after a detailed survey of natural resources, a study of the international market and, when possible, preliminary entry into a foreign trade agreement. The project should consist of one, or a few, select industries, each of which has internal complementary characteristics permitting the industry to be integrated into a single complex for all phases of its operation, from the processing of raw materials to the manufacture of a finished product. At the outset, all physical facilities should be designed for production in massive quantity and with the maximum of automation. The foregoing strategy rests upon the rather easily demonstrated thesis that volume production with high standards of quality control is obtainable only by maximum mechanization, and that human labor, however underpaid, cannot hope to compete, ultimately, with machine production. For it to attempt to do so will, eventually, further depress the society's standard of living. Wage income cannot, therefore, be counted upon as a reliable source of societal wealth. Rather, the flow of income must come from the net profits inherent in the final product, plus the additional marginal revenues indirectly realized by the government through holding labor wages in this sector at the level prevailing generally in the society.

If the large-scale industrial project is attempted early in the programming, its costliness, and a need to guarantee equity in the distribution of its earnings would necessitate its being owned and controlled as a public corporation, with profits being channelled back directly into the society's institutions and into the continued expansion of the industry itself. If it follows the large-scale industrial development tack to any extent, the emerging society will not forge ahead unless it successfully captures a fair share of the international market, and to do this it must use the industrial techniques of the materially advanced societies. By commandeering a part of the market, it will be able to draw upon the superior buying powers of the wealthier nations. By early and thoroughgoing automation, coupled with the direct management of profits through government channels, the emerging society may act to avoid a dilemma which, increasingly, is facing its more conventionally oriented, industrially advanced neighbors – how to distribute income and maintain domestic purchasing power in the face of increasing automation and an accompanying unemployment. The developing society, when it ventures into this area must plan beyond merely catching up with the world's more materially advanced areas. It must lay plans which are calculated to move it to the forefront of productivity. The whole object of integrated industrial development should be to propel the society's industries directly into the mainstream of 20th century technology without undergoing a re-enactment of the painful preliminary growth stages earlier experienced by today's technologically advanced societies. It should be added in closing, however, that for most of the transitional societies it will be some time before they are able to develop large-scale industries to any appreciable extent. Meantime, there is much to be done in carrying out the preceding two stages of mechanization.

Indoctrination and Skills Development

Educating a society for technology will entail a widespread social programming that must be initiated and managed concurrently with the very first stage of physical facilities programming. By no means does every member of a technologically advanced society have a detailed knowledge of technology or a specialized skill, but virtually all must have a *general* familiarity with, and orientation toward the system. The professional man, the housewife in the course of carrying out her duties, and even the small child, must have a knowledge of how to use the tools and machines surrounding them and the circumstances under which each is appropriately used. While a developing society will not require that every one of its individuals be made a skilled specialist, its training procedures will have to be made unusually intensive to help compensate for the fact that the learner is not everywhere surrounded by tools and machines, and does not have the opportunity to learn by doing, as do members of the technologically advanced society. It is not the purpose of this writing to lay out a detailed description of methods of education for technology. This is the task of educators who should be associated with the planning group. It is suggested here that educators might design their programming to give both, formal and informal coverage, in three broad areas – preschool orientation, public school orientation, and adult training.

If a major objective of education is to cultivate technology within the society, then it should begin by indoctrinating the individual, early in childhood, with the ethos and skills of the industrial society. The pictures a child looks at, the books he learns to read, the toys with which he plays, and the types of movies to which he is exposed will be powerful determinants of his early attitudes, aptitudes and ambitions. Such toys are erector sets, miniature steam engines, battery powered devices, and the simpler and less expensive toy machines which are designed for disassembly and reassembly can be potent learning media, and with proper arrangements they can be disseminated to the individual family, or at least to organized community preschool play groups, without undue expense. The lifeway of the technologically advanced society should be made to take on a familiar ring to the child in even the most isolated community, and the folkways and functionings of the advanced society should be reiterated with the same constancy, but perhaps less sycophancy, that the old McGuffey readers employed in reaffirming the reigning virtues of turn-of-the-century American society.

Within the public school system, particularly in its upper levels, excellent opportunity is offered to expose the child to specific manual arts and crafts training courses and to other more generalized types of technical training. If the machinery and the power necessary to operate it are available, students may master, rather quickly, the techniques for wood and metal working. The technologically advanced societies have developed a wealth of training methods and materials relevant to this area of instruction. Its primary aim, however, should not be one of necessarily preparing the student for a trade, but rather to give him an exposure to the general techniques of machine operation and maintenance. Special instructional emphasis, considerably more than is found in Western society, should be placed upon the operations of electric motors and liquid fueled engines; on methods of gearing and obtaining power transmission from these units; and upon their repair, overhaul, and maintenance. Once a society acquires an understanding of how power units operate and how they can be employed, it is on the road to mechanization. Technical training should be made to saturate the entire school system and, to the extent that the culture permits, it should be extended to both sexes. The training of female students in the use and operation of a full range of household appliances, and instruction in automobile driving, would make their contribution to technological growth. In all, within the developing society technical training should be made a sizeable proportion of the overall curriculum. It is here, in the school system, that special educational effort should be concentrated. It is this group, whose habits and attitudes are not yet fully structured and who are most easily reoriented, that will be eventually most influential in reshaping the society.

At the adult level there are two areas of education – skills training, and technical training at the professional level – both of which are important. There are three major avenues for organizing for training skilled workmen, and this training may take place within several different settings. There are the possibilities of: training abroad, that is, dispatching persons to technologically advanced societies for training in residence; the importation of technicians who act in a direct advisory capacity and may spend part time giving 'on-the-job' training; and the importation of technical teachers whose primary function is to develop skilled personnel within the society.

There is no reason why schooling abroad should be confined to college students and professors. It could be applied from the training of the technical categories, to acquiring on-the-job training for skilled and semi-skilled workers. The program should have the dual orientation of providing job training for the individual in a realistic work environment and exposing him to the broader attributes of a technologically advanced culture. Because of the importance of this second, or acculturational feature of the program it should, if possible, be extended beyond the individual worker to include his entire family. The acquisition of new attitudes and experiences in consumption and new living standards will have a much greater carry-over effect to the developing society if the entire family, rather than just the husband, is exposed to the foreign environment. The shopping predilections of the mother are quite positive determinants of the family's style of living, and, once established, they tend to persist. Although a family international program may be without precedent, the dispatch of the individual skilled worker for training abroad has been tried recently on a modest scale and with apparent success. From 1954 through 1957, some 6,500 Chinese students were sent to the Soviet Union for higher education, and 7,100 Chinese workers were dispatched to acquire job experience in Soviet factories.[1]

Because of the great number of people involved and the cost of their transportation and housing, the training abroad of skilled workers probably will remain more of an aspiration than a realizable ambition. On the other hand, for the engineer, training in a technologically advanced society is imperative. This discipline is particularly difficult to teach within the backward area. Even the best equipped laboratory is an impoverished representation of an authentic and well-integrated socio-industrial constellation. The flow and stocking of materials, major problems of human and machine organization, and the whole gamut of management problems are undepictable outside their natural setting. The technical college which attempts to locate in a traditional folk society must face the fact that

[1] Pepelasis, Mears and Adelman, *Economic Development*, Harper and Brothers, 1961, p. 371.

it will have to operate in a partial technical vacuum. There will be an absence of machines; and lying beyond the regime of machines is a whole socio-technical realm of behaviors which cannot be simulated in the engineering laboratory or in the underdeveloped society, and a knowledge of which is extremely important to engineers in their future capacity as industrial managers. The wearing of safety goggles, the use of steel-toed shoes which are not only of safety value but which allow the worker to make effective use of his feet as well as his hands, the wearing and laundering of fabrics which are especially suited to the industrial environment, punctual arrival and departure, wage and salary standards and the methods for negotiating them, the ability to operate not just one, but a range of related machines, the methods for maintaining a balanced flow of material and labor, the supporting role of the research laboratory and the place of the comptroller's activities in the organization – all are matters of high relevance to the engineer's training and are to be found only in the technologically advanced society.

Because of the importance of his role to development, the engineering student must be accorded *special* educational treatment. The socio-technical vacuum at home, occasional resistance to engineering types of training on the part of the local elders, and the traditional stigma often attached to work by the elite, jointly indicate that not only should engineering training be conducted abroad, but that the educators of those societies should develop a special curriculum for the engineer from the underdeveloped area. This student's later role in home development will be critically important because he must organize home enterprise from its very foundations. The training he is to receive should be broadened so as to enable him to manage all the functions connected with this broad responsibility.

The graduate engineer who returns to an undeveloped area faces quite a different situation than does his counterpart in the technically advanced society. The former likely will have to create his own employment, while the member of the advanced society will have his work cut out for him and waiting. The highly specialized engineering training that would help his advanced counterpart find a job would, to a degree, penalize the engineer from the underdeveloped society when he returns home and begins work. He needs course work which is generously rounded out with other disciplines which are, in some respects, more important to development than are the straightaway application of engineering techniques. Since, in most cases the engineer will have to found, or assist in founding, the enterprise that is to employ him, he must know how to assess the natural resources within the area, determine what types of production are most feasible, appraise the supply of human skills available, and then be able to test the final efficacy of the proposed enterprise through an expert analysis of the market. He must know how to go about raising finance, how to procure plant capital and raw materials, how to recruit, train and manage personnel, and how to negotiate the sale of a product on a national or, frequently, on an international scale. A description of the work which the engineer from the undeveloped area will be required to do, makes the curriculum necessary for his training fairly evident. He must be taught, in addition to general engineering, the basics of corporate and business finance, marketing, personnel management, and some of the further-ranging subjects such as physical geography and statistical methods.

The great bulk of skills training administered within the underdeveloped country undoubtedly will be carried out under the tutelage of technicians, both informally (on-the-job) and in formal classroom training. It is in the supply of these technical personnel and the machinery about which their teaching efforts will revolve, that the technologically advanced nations can play their most crucial role in assistance. The fact that the United States' experience in sending technicians abroad has produced rather disappointing results, comments more upon the way in which these individuals were employed than upon the effectiveness of technical aid. This point will be discussed further under the next subject heading.

ASSISTANCE FROM FOREIGN COUNTRIES

A realistic examination of world-wide aid is further evincive of the simple aphorism that, 'Those who are best helped are those who help themselves.' Foreign aid is reviewed in some detail here, not because of its potential for assistance but because, with so many of the developing societies placing a heavy reliance upon this type of assistance, it is appropriate that it be reappraised in a soberer light.

Foreign assistance may come in the indirect form of private investment, or more directly as monetary loans, the extension of credits, or as outright donations or 'grants.' It may be extended to the developing country as money; capital equipment; food stock; technical assistance; or military offerings along the lines of armaments, aircraft detection networks, and military advisors. Although 'military assistance' may appear to be incongruent with the concept of *aid*, it is often preferred as a part of a total package, and, to date, has comprised approximately one-third of the total assistance granted by the United States.

The developing society can draw upon three general outside sources for assistance: 1. the ecumenical agencies, principally the United Nations; 2. the Western bloc; and 3. the Communist bloc.

Ecumenical Aid

The United Nations, as the only sizeable organization with a world overview, has evidenced an interest in taking two types of international action, both of which could be helpful in development in the materially lacking nations, if they could be carried to fruition. It has attempted to prop up and stabilize the sagging market for the primary export commodities produced by the underdeveloped nations; and it has sought to gather grand-scale development finance for the establishment of a fund from which non-discriminatory, international loans could be made. It has been unsuccessful in both endeavours, and largely, because of opposition from the affluent industrial powers. Meantime, for the past fifteen years the export market for primary products, which declined by three billion dollars in 1958 alone, has been erratic and, in general, declining. The drop in some exports has been staggering. For example, Indonesian rubber production fell by forty-three per cent during the single year of 1959. During the sixteen years following 1950, the losses in primary export revenues of the underdeveloped countries has greatly exceeded the economic aid which they have received, most of which has come from these same nations to whom they sustained the losses, their trade partners.

The United Nations has made a number of attempts to smooth out the prices of individual primary products, usually through the combined measures of setting quotas and manipulating buffer stocks. Under the buffer arrangement a circle of sellers and buyers are brought together into a council which tries to balance supply and demand by agreeing in advance upon the quantities which should be produced and bought. Next, the council establishes a buffer fund which is large enough so that it can, by its own buying or selling actions, dampen market upswings or downturns. It buys or sells, as the case may require, to maintain the commodity price between agreed upon maximum and minimum points. As prices rise toward the established ceiling, the buffer fund must intensify its selling activities, and as prices decline from a mean to the established floor, it must increase its buying. The buffer fund has had a long and wavering history since its inception in 1946. By 1962, international agreement had been reached on only four commodities – tin, wheat, olive oil, and sugar – and even in these four cases the agreement covered only a *part* of the total international trade transacted in these commodities. The crux of the matter is that in buffer agreements all parties, buyers and sellers, must contribute to the fund; but deviation above the mean price level inflicts increased penalty upon the sellers, and conversely, when prices fall, the load shouldered by the buyers increases. If price declines continue to follow the trend of the past ten years, the industrial buying nations would have to foot at least two-thirds of the buffering outlay, a situation tantamount to their subsidizing the developing countries' export crops. These large nations view themselves as being on a free market and dealing with trade partners, not trade beneficiaries. Almost any price stabilization measure conceivable would necessitate intergovernmental regulations which would tend to regulate the market, and would, therefore, be found objectionable by these same nations. For these reasons, the advanced nations have been unwilling to enter into international price agreements on a serious basis.

The United Nations has likewise made several attempts to set up an effective system of development funding. The first step in this direction was the establishment of the International Bank for Reconstruction and Development which, popularly known as the *World Bank*, became operative in 1946, and had as its prime mission the lending of assistance for the rehabilitation of the war-torn nations. This bank has been followed by other financial institutions such as the International Finance Corporation, and the International Development Association. They share common defects which, try as it might, the United Nations has not been able to remedy. Judged by the severity of world need they are vastly undercapitalized, and that capital available to them they loan with all the circumspection of experienced banking institutions. By 1962, the World Bank had loaned a total of 6·4 billion dollars of which, by rough estimate, about ninety per cent had gone into development programming. All these banks are nominally public organizations but they, in fact, depend upon private financing support; and since voting control depends upon the amount of capital owned, the banks' policies are shaped predominantly by a few powerful Western nations. Membership of the World Bank is comprised of sixty-eight nations, with the United States holding about thirty per cent of the total stock, and England, the next most influential member, holding about thirteen per cent. Insofar as finance is concerned, the United Nations has, thus far, not been able to contribute appreciably to international development or, in reality, to exercise control over the financial institutions which are nominally listed in its name.[1]

Western Bloc Aid

The individual Western nations lend assistance through private investment and several types of publicly contributed aid. Private investment from the Western European countries has been rising with the national fortunes of these countries. Europe supplies about forty per cent of the gross assistance from the Western bloc, the United States furnishing the remainder. In addition, the Western European nations have extended a great deal of export credit which, indirectly, boosts their investments abroad much above that showing on the cash ledger. The total inflow of Western private investment as long-term capital into the underdeveloped areas, as published by the International Monetary Fund in 1960, had reached an annual rate of over two billion dollars, but with more than half of this going to Latin America.

Direct, publicly contributed aid has generally followed the pattern of private investment. In the Western bloc, the United States government is inequivocally the chief lender of direct aid and, in addition, through its disproportionately heavy financial investment it controls the boards and policies of the few international banks big enough to support large-scale development projects. Although the American government began lending abroad as early as 1934 (through the establishment of the Export-Import Bank set up to promote U.S. export trade), it did not employ aid funds in pursuit of state policy until 1942, with the establishment of the Institute of Inter-American Affairs. The Institute was designated as a weapon against the influence of Nazism in Latin America. The use of foreign aid against communism became an acknowledged philosophy in 1951, when an attempt was made to combine a welter of uncoordinated economic and military assistance plans under the Mutual Security Act Program. This was a kind of holding company that was succeeded by a much larger one, the Agency for International Development (AID), which was consolidated in 1961.

[1] For detailed information on various aspects of the United Nations' and other international aid programs refer to the most recent of the series of publications emanating from the United Nations Department of Economic and Social Affairs:

'The Promotion of the International Flow of Private Capital,'
'Yearbook of International Trade Statistics,'
'Commodity Trade and Economic Development,'
'International Assistance to the Less Developed Countries,'
'International Flow of Long-Term Capital and Official Donations,'
'Economic Survey of Agriculture in the Far East.'

This latter direct assistance program, the largest single loan source in the Western world, was appropriated 3·36 billion dollars for the fiscal year 1966. This sum amounted to about seven per cent of the expenditure that the United States considered to be of minimum necessity for its military defense, or about one-half of one per cent of the nation's Gross National Product. Given outright in a single chunk to India, it would have raised the average per capita wealth of that country by about seven and one-half dollars for a period of one year. As the appropriation originally stood, of the seventy-two countries scheduled to receive U.S. aid during 1966, seventy-four per cent of the total 3·36 billion dollars was to go to only seven countries (Brazil, Chile, Nigeria, Tunisia, India, Pakistan and Turkey), leaving less than one billion collars to be prorated among the other sixty-five nations. *In toto,* during the period 1954–1960, the combined Western bloc gave bilateral economic assistance to the extent of approximately 9·5 billion dollars (about 1·5 billion per year). Of this, the United States gave a little more than half, with the French supplying the surprisingly large proportion of almost a quarter of the entire.

Another form of aid given by the Western bloc, but not exclusively by this group, is technical assistance. Technical assistance alone, in the manner in which it has been applied by the Western nations, particularly by the United States, has not proven to be the development catholicon expected of it at the time of its inception in the early 1950's. Consulting services, the advice of specialists in the field and the like, almost always, it was found, must be followed up by steps requiring capital. In most instances where it has been used solitarily, the service of the specialist has been proven to be wasted, and hopes have been stirred in the recipient nations which have ended in frustration. Western trial and error has led to a revision where technical assistance now supplements economic aid programs, rather than venturing forth on its own. Technical assistance now concentrates its efforts by sending experts out to work on special projects where they make intensive study, render advice, and then return to a regular working base, rather than remaining in a particular area and rendering more generalized services as they once did. The Peace Corps comprises a limited type of exception to this policy. Technical assistants also have found ways in which to attenuate their services by giving intensive training to understudies who may relieve them at an early date, and by organizing local training institutions. Technical assistance has been granted on the most concentrated scale by the U.S.S.R. which, by 1961, had about nine thousand technical assistants working in twenty-eight countries and engaged in such spectacular projects as the Aswan Dam and the Bhilal Steel Mill in India.

The United States must alter its technical aid program if the country is to provide viable assistance. It must concern itself less with showing the developing nations how to utilize established capital facilities (if they only had them!), and concentrate more upon showing them how to *create* production capital. Technical education is essential to this endeavor and technical assistance can go far in helping to supply this vitally needed educational service.

One of the more active assistance programs has been the dispensation of U.S. agricultural products under the Agricultural Trade and Assistance Act of 1954, more familiarly known as Public Law 480. Public Law 480 allows for the distribution of U.S. surpluses under three different provisions: free distribution to cope with famine or disaster; distribution abroad by voluntary, non-profit, and inter-governmental organizations; and overseas sales of U.S. surpluses in the currency of the buying country. In this latter case, the funds derived from the sale are banked in the recipient country and can be used in part, or in whole, to finance further development programming. This placing of proceeds from the sale of food stock in an account which is referred to as 'counter-funds,' makes the program, in effect, a government grant, loan, or gift, depending upon the final disposition mutually agreed upon for these funds. Under this program, exports from the United States have been running at about 1·5 billion dollars annually (at regular export market values). This type of aid shows every promise of continued growth, inasmuch as the European Common Market nations and some other advanced agricultural countries have the avowed production goal of achieving agricultural surpluses and expending them as foreign aid.

U.S. agricultural aid has proven reasonably effective as a stop-gap measure, and has future potential because it dovetails as a partial solution to agricultural overproduction in the United States, and thereby caters, to a degree, to the donor's self-interests. It is now openly acknowledged as a marriage of convenience between the excess food producers and the food needy. It is not without its critics. It is charged that the program inhibits agricultural growth in the recipient nation, creates unfair competition with the recipient nation's other food suppliers, and simply leads the farmers of the advanced nations on to still further excesses (in food production). On the positive side, surplus food imports allow the developing nation to increase its importation of needed production capital, sparing a cash outlay which can now be spent for these latter goods.

Even more importantly, surplus imports permit the developing nation to increase the purchase of foreign equipment with less chance of distortion of its foreign exchange balance, a handicap that has severely limited capital acquisition in most of the developing areas.

Communist Bloc Aid

Building on a program that began in 1954, the U.S.S.R. and other centrally planned economies have granted aid on a rapidly increasing scale. It is the usual rule that Soviet aid is provided through credits supplemented by technical assistance, with the loan program carrying for a period of twelve years at a rate of interest of 2·5 per cent. The principal usually is repaid in the borrowing country's export commodities at prices which are fixed at the outset of the transaction. The prices for development materials and supplies to be furnished by the creditor nation are also agreed upon in advance. This method of price fixing has had the effects of stabilizing the borrowing nation's commodity prices, allowing it a rapid means of repayment, and stimulating the rate of its development by opening added outlets for its production. It was because it followed similar policy that Great Britain was so helpful in the pre-World War I development of the United States and Canada. The British needed, and welcomed, the primary commodities coming from these developing countries, and provided them with a ready market by which to pay off their obligations to British investors.

The Communist bloc concentrates the bulk of its economic assistance in *industrial* development, with about one-quarter of the total being prorated over transportation and hydroelectric development. By early 1962, the Communist bloc had disbursed a total, in aid, equivalent to 6·5 billion dollars, and was continuing to grant aid at the rate of about 1 billion dollars per year. The Soviet Union donated about seventy per cent of the total, Eastern Europe twenty per cent, and China the remaining ten per cent. Only a limited amount of the whole was given in grants, and most of this came from the Soviet Union.

Low interest rates and concessions to take repayment in kind have given the Communist aid program strong appeal to the emerging nations, and have brought the Western program under increasing competitive harassment. But in spite of the facts that the Communist program is well conceived and shows regularly increasing potential, it has, thus far, been gravely deficient in quantity. The aid coming from this bloc shows promise of high effectiveness in a few isolated cases, such as in Egypt and Cuba where it has been allocated to specific and highly important projects, but in general, it has been scarcely enough to create a ripple. Furthermore, on occasions the aid-giving Communist nations have become overcommitted in their acceptance of commodity repayments and, having bargained for more than they could consume, they have dumped the excess on the international market, thereby depressing open-market prices for the exports of the nations to which they were granting aid.

Evaluation of Aid

It is difficult to make a precise evaluation of the world's various aid programs. The majority of Western writers on the subject are convinced, however, that aid is having worthwhile effects. U.S. aid programmers and politicians exhort the other materially well-off nations, 'to share a greater part of the foreign aid burden'; they freely employ such euphemisms as, 'The great nations of the world are showing increasing realization of their responsibilities to their less fortunate neighbors'; and they passively accept the world-wrenching, debilitating, partisan conflict between international aid programs, and between the incompatible ends of military assistance and development aid as, 'facts of life which could hardly have been otherwise.' Most aid-granting authorities have been preoccupied with 'bit and piece' improvement in existing programs and have shown little inclination to question the wisdom of their basic policies. They seem unaware that most aid programs are failing to attain their objectives, and that the depression which enshrouds over half the world's population will continue to deepen day-by-day until there is a radical turn of events. This dilemma cannot be laid as is so often tried, exclusively at the door of uncontrolled population expansion.

Considering the ways in which aid has been used and abused by both donors and recipients, the ways in which it has been enlisted to the economic and military ambitions of the world's leading powers, the capriciousness with which it has been alternately dangled before the would-be recipient and then snatched away at his first 'political misstep,' and its high susceptibility to ever-threatening and severe reduction by donor legislative bodies, it is difficult to take the current aid programs seriously. If the world's nations can be said to be sincere in their desires to promote development, then it must be conceded that their military intentions are, by statistical comparison, approximately twenty times more sincere. The present annual flow of world-wide aid is approximately five billion dollars, which compares, by conservative estimate, with a world-wide annual military expenditure of one hundred billion dollars, and amounts to less than one half of one per cent of the seven hundred billion dollar gross national income of the donating countries. If the world's total annual aid assets were distributed evenly in cash among the one-third of the world's population which is suffering from hunger and deep need, it would increase their per capita prosperity by about five dollars per year, a rather meager sum. It is arithmetically evident that if the underdeveloped countries had been given a choice, back in 1950, between export commodity price floors at then prevailing prices, and foreign aid, they would have fared much better by choosing the first and forfeiting foreign aid altogether. This is to say that the advanced nations could do much more for the backward areas by cleaning up their business relationships with the latter than they are presently contributing through foreign aid. Unilateral economic aid is not a pretty thing; it corrupts both the giver and the recipient. It is seldom given without an expectancy of something in return. It is usually offered on political grounds which, at their mildest, imply a definite political and economic commitment by the recipient country; and at a graver level it is proferred as an entire package of which military armaments, training, troop stationing rights, and intelligence gathering concessions are a part. In consequence, adjacent nations which already may be experiencing tension in their relationships with one another are armed (sometimes by the same 'benefactor') against a 'common enemy' only to experience mounting fears of one another. And the groundwork is thus laid for major warfare between societies whose main concern should be in learning how to feed themselves.

A major offender in the mis-issuance of aid has been the United States. Not only are funds regularly issued for questionable purposes, but the philosophical framework within which aid is administered is so anachronistic that it will in time inevitably bring about its own demise. The governing policy of U.S. aid is one of concentrating mainly on agricultural programs, leaving industrial development to follow later and explicitly under private, rather than governmental control. This would seem to be, at least as development programming is viewed by this writer, a badly oriented policy. Their personal attitudes towards private and public management have led some U.S. congressmen to take the stand, as they did on the construction of an aid-financed steel mill in India, that U.S. aid funds (*funds publicly donated by U.S. citizens* through taxes) must be taken from under the foreign government's administration and placed in the hands of private businessmen or, it was threatened, project funds would be withdrawn altogether. In other cases, development fund managers and bankers lending money for foreign development will give such assistance only to privately owned and privately managed projects, but they insist that a guarantee of the loan's repayment be posted by the borrowing government (in this case the foreign tax payer). This is a strange hybridization of 'socialistically backed free enterprise' calculated to warm the heart of any astute 'entrepreneur.' In most of the emerging countries private enterprise does not have the experience or the access to resources necessary for carrying out large-scale development projects. Moreover, to prostrate foreign aid entirely to the type of reasoning displayed above is to pervert it to the status of a business deal rather than treating it as the matter of deep public concern which it is.

A good part of Western aid is given in cash and without adequate supervision over its use. Since the greater part of this class of aid is now given as loaned funds rather than as grants, repayment will invariably upset the borrower's balance of trade, thus placing limitation upon his importation of capital from outside. Cash loans have had two other negative effects. A sudden infusion of wealth into the society has, on several occasions, set off a spiralling inflation; and a lack of accountability for fund expenditures has touched off wholesale graft and embezzlement within the recipient countries. The extent of this miscreance no one has dared estimate. Further, Western import restrictions on the developing nation's commodities have denied the borrowing nation an opportunity to repay in the only way it can, and have failed to broaden its marketing prospects.

The prospects for appreciable foreign aid being dim as they are, the developing nation must look to its own interior resources. The outlook here is brighter, but the country's internal means probably still will be gravely short of what will be required to carry it through to the crest of development. Even if they were efficiently husbanded, internal resources, by general estimate, could supply only about one-third of the investment needed for development. Within these countries private investment funds are scarce, and those funds that accrue are either invested in land, loaned on a short-term basis at exorbitant interest rates, or invested abroad. In the public sector there are many obstacles to raising finances through taxes. Income taxes are non-existent in some of the emerging areas and in others the rates are so low, and evasion so universal, as to make them an illusory source of help. When other types of tax levies are enacted, they, too, will encounter resistance and evasion. High import tariffs will lead to lively smuggling enterprise, and high taxes on consumer goods will be circumvented to a great extent through illegal trade channels.

If, after sorting through its own resources, the society finds that it is still unable to support a conventional development program, what then, are the alternatives? Obviously, the society will have to turn to a different type of programming. It will have to make maximum use of those resources it has by striking directly at the heart of the problem, by concentrating upon the formation of a domestic technology, by inducing a general mechanization and a capability for creating its own production facilities. Significantly, but hardly surprisingly in light of every-day experience, the nations which have developed most rapidly have been those whose peoples tightened their belts and their resolve and struck out on their own initiative and capabilities. All the technologically advanced nations had to go through this process at one time, and more recently both Russia and China, as well as war-shattered Japan and West Germany, have enjoyed remarkably rapid success in achieving self-propelled growth. And it also goes without saying that, for the society that is just now beginning to concern itself with development, it greatly helps to have a guiding program based upon sound principle.

Part Four

ON THE HORIZON

9

SOCIO-TECHNICS AND PRODUCTION CONTROL

Production control is used here in the broad sense of ownership and management of a society's production facilities, rather than in its narrower meaning of local production supervision. Thus far, discussion has been limited to describing the effects of man-machine interaction within the work environment. But the changes occurring at this level will communicate themselves upward, and outward, so that the broader aspects of the growing technology – its modes of production control, media of exchange, systems of distribution, etc. – will come increasingly under the dominance of the production system. The succession is one in which new mechanical configurations will increasingly replace traditional social controls. The *broad* framework within which production mechanization is occurring is social. Our present modes of ownership and labor usage are social hold-overs from a pre-industrial, feudal period, which will be either amalgamated into mechanical extensions of our production activity or, if not amenable to mechanization, will be rejected from the system altogether. The criterion for the survival of these factors will be their compatibility with a growing mechanization, and those not tractable to this process will be forced into discard, not by bloody revolution but by the system, itself, in its natural course of growth.

All of the world's technologically advanced societies are in a state of flux, but they face a future of far more momentous change than the transition described by Marx, from feudalism to capitalism, or than the movement described by Marx, toward communism. Even if the free enterprise societies were able to utterly vanquish the communist states, driving them back into the feudal fold from which most of them only recently have emerged, the victory would be a hollow one, because inherent in the technologies of all advancing societies are forces which inexorably will propel them into new systems so radically different as to tame communism by comparison. Communism prescribes old and familiar tonics. The shape of things to come can be only vaguely inferred from the rumble of still distant, subterranean forces. One has only to examine models to see how far we have come, and to appreciate the distance we may have yet to go.

DEFINING EFFICIENCY

An Economic Model of Efficiency

Considerable economic study has been given to the relative efficiencies with which societies make use of the economic factors at their disposal. A frequently cited example of economic efficiency comes out of a study of the economic folkways of the Indians of Panajachel, Guatemala, published in a 1953 report by anthropologist Sol Tax. Entitled *Penny Capitalism*, it has made popular reading because of the exemplar set by the group 'in economic efficiency,' in the competitive attainment of a maximum of self-efficiency within a locality of extremely limited resources. Panajachel is described as a microcosmic capitalistic society, working without machinery or corporations, with every man his own boss, and, in the intense competition with others, making the most of what he has. The factors of production are allocated with 'maximum efficiency.' The Indian is described 'above all else as an entrepreneur, a businessman . . .' who lives in 'a money economy organized in single households as both consumption and production units, with a strongly developed market which tends to be perfectly competitive.'[1]

The present author, in visiting Panajachel some ten years later, and viewing the community from a sociological perspective, came away with a radically different impression than that created by Professor Tax's article. Located less than 100 miles from a modern capital city, Panajachel's Cakchiqueles Indians carry out all soil tilling and crop cultivation with one implement – a giant-size hoe. Although the village is set in a natural beauty making it a favorite watering place among Central American tourists, and although its truck garden plots stand impressively neat, row upon orderly row, this overall impression is blurred when one looks beyond to the living conditions of those who tend the gardens. They are one of the world's poorest peoples. The grinding daily demands of work leave the children practically no time for school or for other social 'frivolity.' The Indians live in dirt-floored, windowless huts, without medical attention or adequate diet. While they may provide a model

[1] Sol Tax, *Penny Capitalism*, University of Chicago Press, 1963. (Originally published by the Smithsonian Institute, Institute of Social Anthropology, Publication No. 16, Washington, U.S. Government Printing Office, 1953).

of a narrow type of economic efficiency, the inner reaction of a visiting Western statesman would be to declare the community an emergency area. A technologist's first thought would be that here are a people who are desperately in need of aid in development. A social scientist, noting the almost universal excesses of alcoholism in both sexes would classify Panajachel as a socio-pathological society. He would further see in it an enclave that was culturally involuted and failing to assimilate from the surrounding society the technics necessary to achieve humane living standards. Panajachel, as a model of allocative efficiency is analogous to the drowning man clutching at a straw. As a non-swimmer, the victim is allocating his energies in the most efficient way open to him. He is drowning in a remarkably efficient manner.

A common failing in the economic model is its tendency to treat labor as a purely rational, non-human part of the model. The way in which this thinking spills over into the general body of economics is illustrated in the following counsel. 'Where human effort (labor) is cheap relative to the price of other agricultural factors, a one-man (or family) farm may be *efficient* (italics mine) with a small garden type tractor; on the other hand, where human effort is relatively dear, a one-man farm may be efficient with a combination of two or even three tractors that differ in size and type.'[1] This tenet neglects the higher values inherent in human time (liberty); it bends human labor to meet local definitions of efficiency at the expense of obtaining a broader *social* type of efficiency, and it overlooks the fact that as production methods narrow down to a competition between manual labor and mechanization the former will be reduced to working for an increasingly miserable pittance. Human advancement, after all, should be the basic objective of any national development program.

A Technological Model of Efficiency

Although considerable effort has gone into the development of economic models, relatively little attention has been given to the *social* impact of technology. No particular effort is being made to decipher its trends or their possible consequences. How poorly formulated public thinking is on this subject can be nicely illustrated by the course of an imaginary discussion between a lecturer and a college classroom audience.

[1] Theodore W. Schultz, *Transforming Traditional Agriculture*, Yale University Press: New Haven, Connecticut, 1964, p. 122.

On the Horizon

Members of the class are asked by the lecturer to project themselves into the following situation:

Imagine that the time is five decades in the future and that you hold the title of 'National Secretary of Production Planning and Control.' The interior of your office is equipped with a large console which controls a computer and select input-output devices. These computing and communication devices are parts of a huge, fully automated production complex, and through them you can obtain or transmit almost any type of production information that you desire. The console enables you to issue instructions in connection with the processes of production, and the output equipment enables you to interrogate the system for any information that you may need in decision making.

Let us further imagine that the computing system has just reported to you that the inventory of warehoused passenger-motor-vehicles is rapidly dropping to the pre-established critical level, and it asks your concurrence in reinstating the manufacturing process. However, on this particular occasion, rather than perfunctorily endorse an automatic action you decide, for once, to reassert your authority and essential humanity by studying the matter a bit and making your decision known in a somewhat more personal manner. The computing system has already made, and is holding for your inspection, an analysis of the next quarter's national requirements for passenger cars. It has summed up the number of automobiles consumed during the last quarter, tempered this figure with a projection for seasonality based upon trends for the past five years, subtracted the increment of quarterly population decrease for those of driving age, and taken into account diverse social fads such as a recently awakened interest in hiking into the city but insistence upon making the return trip home by automobile. Thus, when you interrogate the information output system in your office it informs you as to exactly what types and quantities of passenger vehicles should be produced for the next quarter, and, in a confidential aside especially tailored to your ego, it reassures you of your authority and essential humanity. To help in keeping automobile styling fresh, the design preferences expressed in the most recent of the regularly conducted public surveys already has been fed automatically into the production control computing system. All you need do now is to set into the console instructions regarding the particular types and numbers of automobiles you have decided should be produced, and press the initiatory button.

This last act alerts a vast concatenation of automata extending from the iron ore ranges to the most remote railheads, and initiates a wave of mechanical activity that proceeds without a single act of human intervention at any point. Heavy mining equipment begins excavating ore which is then automatically conveyed to water transports, loaded, and carried to smelting mills where furnaces have been pre-heated and are waiting. The ore is refined, rolled into sheets or processed into intermediary billets, passed on to fabricating plants where the required automobile parts are stamped, milled, cast, etc. These parts are then fed into a huge assembly plant where they are subjected to the most rigorous quality tests and where they are finally flowed together, in assembly, into complete, finished, finally tested, and warehoused motor vehicles. As they are needed by the public this same system will automatically load and transport them to the appropriate geographic points.

'Now,' you add in addressing the class, 'in your capacity as National Secretary of Production Planning and Control, how do you think your production system should be integrated into the broader economic system and into the social system, in general?'

The first reaction will be one of bemused silence. Then the question will be countered by a series of other questions.

'How about the natural resources? Who owns them?'

You reply, 'This is for you to decide. This is a part of the problem I am asking *you* to work out.'

The latter enjoins the comment, 'Well, in order to make the system work, I suppose you'd have to arrange to have both the raw materials and the production equipment owned by the state. But that would be socialism.'

And still another question that is bound to crop up, 'How would you arrange it so that people could buy these automobiles?'

You reply again,

> That is also a part of the problem that I am asking you to work out. However, we might give the problem more intelligible structure by assuming the following. If the natural resources were publicly owned, if the production machinery was also publicly owned, if production expendibles such as fuel were automatically processed and supplied, and if machine maintenance and parts replacement were taken care of automatically, in short, if all production facilities were publicly owned and all production activity was carried out automatically, what should be the cost of the finished product?

Since the answer to this question is not forthcoming, you supply it yourself. 'Since there are no human services involved and no direct outlay for materials, why not give the item *gratis* to whomever needs it?'

Now the answers are quick in coming and range all the way from 'That kind of system would never work at all because no one would be able to make a profit,' to 'This would lead to a complete breakdown of our economic system because everyone would be unemployed.'

The type of situation just depicted always gives rise to deep-seated public ambivalence, and yet, viewed in its simplest terms it represents a near ideal point. It is the ultimate material goal of the production engineer, the inventor, the manager and for all others concerned with attaining maximum efficiency in production. Encouraged by these forces, we are moving rapidly in the direction of full automation. Its attainment should be considered an even more desirable goal from the *social* standpoint. In universal proportions it would mean that all mankind could now have what it wants merely for the taking. Being amply provided for, man could now divorce himself from the work-pit and spend his lifetime, that most precious of all 'commodities,' as he chose. Super-abundance, the most desirable of goals and one that society is obviously and unconsciously driving toward is, indeed, a difficult one for it to *accept*.

It is not easy, but it is possible, to visualize a production system that is sterile of labor because we have industries that are nearing an extreme in this respect. It is somewhat more difficult to reconcile one's self to a system devoid of human management, but then there is a generally recognized movement in this direction, too. But it is virtually impossible for most Westerners to accept the possibility of a system's being able to operate without ownership or profits (if only by the state), despite the facts that while labor and management are, at least prior to automation, functional facets of production, ownership has never had any strong, direct functional relationship to production. Thus, the conventionally oriented student-observer is left dangling with the enigma of a technically achievable future production system that has no workers, no managers, no owners. And he rejects the system, on social grounds, as 'impractical.'

SOCIETAL VIEWPOINTS

Peoples in technologically advanced societies are acutely aware of the general meaning of the word 'production.' Time and motion men make minute study of the dimensions of the hundreds of tasks found in industrial society, labor unions regularly express their fears of the displacement that will result from a climbing efficiency in production, and the owners of capital hunger for its more productive employment and the profits thus realized. Maximum productivity is a major goal of the modern industrial system. However, this concept is never publicly qualified, nor are the final ends to which our production capabilities should be directed ever found woven into a coherent social philosophy. This might be viewed by some as a cardinal sin of omission, for the way in which we conceive of our production facilities would appear to be helpful in determining the effectiveness with which they are used, and the ultimate goals toward which they should be directed. Another, and perhaps more rational explanation might be that lack of public sensitivity to the problem merely reflects that the process of technological change is still in an inchoate stage, and that as the socio-technical processes governing change grow and become more articulate they will, themselves, bend the technology towards new goals, and mold appropriate public attitudes.

Societal outlooks on production may be described, as a matter of convenience, under three production philosophies, which differ from one another, mainly, in degree. We might refer to these three as the philosophies of 'scarcity,' 'plenty,' and 'super-abundance.'

Our social thinking is basically oriented around the concept 'scarcity.' The processes of selling personal time for income, of exchanging this income for goods and services, of electing from among the goods and services offered on the basis of 'rational choice,' of continuously arbitrating between competing desires, and the occasional yielding to impulse in satisfying some of the subtler cravings, all these behaviors are operative only within the condition of *scarcity*. The idea of using paper money as a means of controlling productive activity, and the custom of guaranteeing this fiat by certificates redeemable in a precious metal are scarcity concepts that set the tone of the entire resources management system. Scarcity is considered by most authorities as a natural state of affairs, and by many as an essential natural selection mechanism by which the mettle of men and nations is tested and improved in an unending struggle to acquire and to hold.

At a second level of thinking is the later, and more fashionable, dialectic of 'plenty.' Although the achievement of plenty is periodically restated as a goal of the national economy, the objective is a hazy one and is seldom specified beyond its being the attainment of 'an adequate standard of living for all members of society.' The goal of plenty is a cheery and undefined future cornucopia. The *minimum* standard of living necessary to meet the definition of 'adequacy,' the production which will be required to support it, and the means by which these particular goods and services are to be distributed are never publicly specified. The philosophy of plenty is more of a social tonic than a call to action. It is a warming re-affirmation of the goodness of the system, and it serves notice to all that government is aware of its responsibilities; but it makes no commitments.

At a third philosophical level is the concept of 'super-abundance.' Because his thinking and his institutions have been built around the concept of scarcity, Western man is not at all at home with the notion of super-abundance. In fact, because of the momentous social changes implied in its production potentiality, it is generally looked upon as a *threat* to the better interests of mankind, rather than a blessing. A few decades ago the prospects for super-abundance or disemployment were considered so remote as to hardly deserve discussion. 'The more we mechanize, the more jobs we create,' became the public byword. This contention, coming in pre-automated days, seemed a reasonable one and its longer-range validity was seldom questioned. The old social vision of a vast, labor-consuming production system is quite at odds with one which recasts the human in the primary role of a consumer and emancipates him altogether from the production process.

Present day attitudes toward super-abundance are akin to those held toward full automation. This is understandable because the two are linked so interdependently as to be practically synonymous. The degree of automation employed will determine the quantity of production attainable, and automation, thereby, becomes the social pacemaker. Lip service is paid to the desirability of production in abundance, but it is considered practically unattainable. 'There will always be limitations set by a scarcity of natural resources.' 'Or,' the argument runs, 'true super-abundance cannot exist because it will always be necessary for the consumer to obtain goods through some sort of purchasing arrangement,' and, 'Finished goods will always carry an inherent cost of materials plus labor.' Even at the full bloom of automation, 'It will still be necessary to procure the raw materials from their owners' and, 'There will still have to be human employees who design, build and maintain the machines of production,' and in addition, of course, 'There are those who own the machines and must be compensated for their use.' The argument continues that, 'Even if full automation were attainable it would be undesirable. Everyone would be thrown out of work. Hoodlumism and crime, fed by idleness, would greatly increase and the now functionless citizen would waste his day drinking beer and watching television.' And finally, it is felt that, 'In a society where people get "everything for nothing," this only breeds resentment and leads to a crippling dependency.' The recipients of public welfare funds are pointed out as examples of this last 'truth.' But hardly ever does anyone think of another, equally good, example – the very rich. Although some of the rich show evidence of demoralization, just as do some of the members of every social class, in the aggregate their independence greatly enriches their lives and allows them the time and freedom to carry on works, in the arts, sciences and in government, which are often of a highly important nature.

The easiest way in which to demolish argument favouring the possibilities of an eventual super-abundance is to show patronizing agreement with the idea in principle, but to dismiss it in the 'practical' grounds that it is 'utopianistic.' This is favoured ploy within the academic community and one showing oblivion to the facts that every thinking human is to a degree an idealist, and that every social movement of the past has owed its origins to an idealism. However, the utopianists are of the extreme pursuasion that meaningful change is attainable only through a thorough-going overhaul of the social structure. Utopianism further implies a radical, rapid, and *deliberately planned* type of change, such as that found in the several historical attempts to establish utopian communities. Quite the contrary to these schemes, the movement toward automation seems to be an evolutionary process. It is an outworking of inexorable forces and is not to be lightly wished away as 'a nice, but impractical, utopianistic *philosophy*.' It is on the way and it is not likely to be deterred by anything short of a physical cataclysm. And, in its movement, it is upsetting all the traditional economic precepts of competition, ownership, management, and fiscal policy.

COMPETITION AND PRODUCTIVITY

It is claimed that for viability, flexibility and maximum efficiency within the productive system, producers must have their competitors. According to this viewpoint, the greater the demand, the more attractive are the prospects for profits and the greater are the number of competitors who are enjoined to the contest. Each competitor will attempt to make maximum profits through maximizing sales. In his competition for a share of the market, each producer is portrayed as an antagonist who attempts to lower his price just below those of his opponents. The result is said to be a system which flexes quickly in response to changes in supply and demand and one which is stimulated to a high efficiency in production by unceasing effort to pare production costs. The public is claimed to be the ultimate beneficiary.

Under closer scrutiny, the system is lacking in most of the competitive qualities commonly ascribed to it. First, there is general semantic confusion surrounding the term 'competition.' Social scientists have long pointed out that the concepts of competition and cooperation are inextricably intertwined. Under the most rivalrous forms of behavior, such as athletic contests, there is a profusion of mixed competitive and cooperative behaviors. Opposing ball teams vie conspicuously for possession of the ball, but the prior training, scheduling of the event, bringing the rivals together and having them compete in observance of numerous and well-defined playing rules, are all evidences of cooperative behaviors that are generally overlooked. And so it is in most human activities. Competition and cooperation in pure form are pure abstractions and in everyday pursuits it is impossible to set or maintain a regulatory ratio between them.

Given the freedom to do so, a competitor will try to eliminate his rivals completely from the game. In illustration of this last point is the tendency of successful Western enterprises to grow and, in the process, either absorb or banish the competition. There is great competitive advantage associated with 'bigness.' The high specialization of labor and the resulting efficiency enjoyed by the large organizations will, in time, drive their lessers to the wall. The advantages of this type of organization to the general society are also quite obvious. Consequently, there is less and less preoccupation, in materially advanced countries, with devising controls against monopoly or with the prolonged breast-feeding of small business. If attempts to curb big business were successful, and small business were cultivated in its stead, this would only result in waste and increased cost to the public. The more highly mechanized an industry becomes, the more efficiently it can organize its production factors, and the lower become its production costs. Hence, automation is greatly expediting the trend toward large industry.

Big business achieves unusual stability because, through its growth, it has been enabled to acquire generally stabilizing social traits. It is a multifaceted endeavor bearing more resemblence to a tiny society or nation than to conventional small business. It acquires a strong voice in political and social affairs. Its broad base is not seriously threatened by change in ownership; and its assets are so great and diversified as to make their use of general social concern.

It is a gigantic consumer of goods and services as well as a seller; and, in addition, it has grown into a grounds for the training and employment of myriad skills. Like societies and nations, large enterprises may merge with other groups but they almost never simply disappear

Big business is stable and it imparts stability to the society around it. In big industry, the decision to enter into the production race is influenced by factors far removed from the immediate market and the prospective competition. The cost of tooling for new enterprise, the palatability of a new candidate-product to established or potential manufacturers and its consonance with their present or planned product lines, all will bear upon the reception that it will receive. The motives that prompt large industry to enter a given production field may be described as 'rational' rather than as opportunistically competitive.

On the other hand, the 'free' or unregulated entry of small enterprise into the production race results in many abuses and social penalties. There is always a lag between the time of apparent demand and supply. When a new, and particularly strong market for a given item becomes manifest, it attracts the interests of great numbers of speculative producers, each of whom is faced by two prospects. If he enters the field early and vigorously, he may enjoy strong temporary competitive advantage (if the market holds firm). However, if the market should meantime fail, he stands to lose all. The speculative nature of unregulated enterprise is mirrored in its failure rate. Approximately half of the small enterprises founded during an average year will fail within twenty-four months of their date of founding. The fruitless expenditures of money, and the resulting employment dislocations are wasteful and unjustifiable. Not only does this system fail to accommodate the public interest, but the shifting unemployment it causes, enfeebles the public. Many of the larger of these small enterprises will have been founded on funds raised by public subscription, that is, through the stock market, and in these cases employees and investors alike will pay the tariff of failure, with the cost, in the last analysis, falling upon the public.

Whether he be large or small, and despite the alleged ubiquity of competition, the highly successful entrepreneur may enjoy disproportionately great reward. This reward takes the form of undue profiteering. And since, within this speculative system there can be no set standards for profit, the public is again the loser. Profits, set without regard to the basic worth of the article or service offered, but instead, based solely upon what 'the market will bear' are considered legitimate booty and may be raked in under any one of three different fortuities. First, the few who take an early risk and find themselves far out in the lead of the competition are, at least for a time, in a position to levy excessive charges. Secondly, those few who have enjoyed the supreme success of growth, and have consolidated into enterprises of Gargantuan size are enabled to control prices through sheer monopoly. Finally, there is the similar case, where a few powerful entrepreneurs are able, by formal or informal agreement, to 'fix' prices. Price fixing is a normal outcome of entrepreneural growth and consolidation and, contrary to the impression created by the press, it is a widespread practice. Price fixing, despite common allegation, need not take place in whispered conference or behind closed door. Price trends are so slow-changing, and the intelligence of allied types of operations is so widely shared that prices may be fixed by a projection of trends and maintained by tacit agreement without a single, covert act of collusion. Against this type of action, the public may have grievance, but no legal recourse.

In any event, competition is not the tidy regulator of human affairs that it is often made out to be. The very large companies, those who champion it loudest, are its deadliest enemies. And if it were, in actuality, as freely flowing as it is popularly claimed to be, it would be socially costly. The trend away from competition undoubtedly will continue so long as production specialization and centralized control continue to offer a potential for increased productivity. And even beyond this point, competition will continue to decline as the fruits of production are awarded on more direct, non-monetary bases.

OWNERSHIP AND PRODUCTIVITY

General Characteristics

How did ownership originate, and what are its relationships to the factors of production and to a changing technology? In order to get at an answer to these questions one would have to examine the relationships of ownership to control, responsibility, and accountability – the attributes which are believed to be supplied by ownership, and to be essential to production.

It is fruitless to try to pinpoint the exact origins of ownership. It may be speculated, however, that its early appearance might have rested upon quasi-functional grounds. For example, a regularly recurring relationship between a tool and its individual user could have led, in time, to an established technique for its use. To minimize disruption of the technique it is further logical that the individual's relationship to the tool would be increasingly specified by the individual and society. Tools and other items of property, if left unmolested in the immediated vicinity of the user would take on added functionality because they would always be conveniently close at hand. Further, the technique would not have to be modified and readapted to the individual peculiarities of a strange, substitute tool, as would be necessary in a culture where property is freely rotating. Thus, the technique could be made stabler and more predictable if agreement were reached between individuals to accord certain items of property exclusive 'usership.' Since the artifacts associated with early technology were undoubtedly crude in their mechanics, there was a high ratio of technique (human input) to mechanical operation. As technology progresses, technique is absorbed increasingly by mechanical operations and as the ratio shifts increasingly toward the latter, there will come about corresponding changes in ownership.

Ownership, for its existence, requires two attributes in the physical item with which it is associated – propinquity and scarcity. Although its crust may contain rare resources and a totality of resources outstripping those of earth many times over, if an ingenious scientist were to burn Jupiter to a cinder with a lazer beam, this would occasion little public objection beyond that concerned with the astronomical effects of the act upon this planet. Objects that are universally commonplace or beyond the range of social interest will not likely be subject to monopolization.

Is ownership essential for control? Control is a social property, and as evidenced in government bureaus, the military system, and corporate management, it can occur on planes quite apart from ownership. Personality dominance, unique gifts of talent, age, etc., not to mention completely delegated authority, function within all the aforementioned groups to produce social structures of clear-cut leadership and followership. These groups are obviously self-controlling. Yet, it is steadfastly insisted by economists and others interested in rationalizing ownership that ownership is essential for *satisfactory* control. While this may be true for very small, personally owned and directed enterprises, the relationship between ownership and control becomes more dilute as the organization grows in size; and the two become effectively severed when the organization is legally incorporated and brought under management by proxy.

How does ownership relate to responsibility and accountability? And to what degree do the three form a matrix in which property is inseparably embedded? These questions can be examined best by turning to the military system which, since one of its two main functions is the destruction of property, will scarecly be found to have conventional property responsibilities, and which, despite its sometimes vast holdings, in actuality, 'owns' nothing. The military share this lack of ownership with governments and bureaucratic institutions in general. They all *control* property, which is variously marked 'property of,' 'possession of,' 'held by,' but which is almost never referred to in the personalistic term, 'owned by.' These agencies may seize property through 'expropriation,' but they are never said to 'steal' it. In brief, the concept of property in the collective sense differs significantly from its private usage.

The military, in trying to conform to the property responsibilities expected of it by the larger society, makes a great show of standing up to this responsibility. Although it cannot make restitution, because it is merely a body of personnel possessing no property in their own right, the military, nonetheless, makes a fetish of keeping accounts and making and maintaining precise distinction between 'accountability' and 'responsibility.' The particular officer using an item of property is 'accountable' for it and his commanding officer is 'responsible' for it, which is to say that if the item is lost because of carelessness or disobedience on the part of the user, the commanding officer is 'responsible' for seeing that he is charged (held accountable) with its cost. This meticulous pinpointing of financial accountability to the individuals accords with the philosophy of the greater society, allows for evasion of organizational responsibility, and provides an escape route for both, the individual and the group. The mechanics of the system is well illustrated in a story that has long circulated in military circles of how a blundering naval officer, convicted of causing the loss of a battleship, was brought to personal account for this multi-million dollar disaster by regular deductions from his monthly pay check. However, through annually recurring 'errors' in the navy's accounting entries this vessel was successively redefined as a 'cruiser,' a 'destroyer,' a 'gunboat,' a 'rowboat,' and, finally, a 'gravy-boat,' which was paid for with dispatch and the whole incident closed.

Ownership, after it is severed from work operations and their personal guidance, becomes a social ritual having no more importance to the functions of production than do the religious or political settings within which production takes place. As techniques become absorbed by the machine, ownership becomes more obviously functionless. This does not mean that we cannot have a situation in which there are a handful of huge industrial complexes that have eliminated all laborers but still retain their owners, but to point out an interdependency of ownership and labor, and an ultimate dependency of both upon carrying out some function contributing to production. Both were originally contributors to technique. As labor's functions are transferred to the machine, ownership, the sole survivor, is left stranded in an increasingly forlorn and difficult-to-rationalize position.

Managerial Ownership

Managerial ownership is a direct form of proprietorship in which the individual may act in the three capacities of owner, manager, and operator. This is ownership in its strictest private meaning, and it is characteristically associated with infant capitalism and small enterprise. It is invested in a single person or, at most, in a few partners (who may be members of the same family), and it is usually transmittible by heritage. It is commonly subject to certain laws established to prevent its infringement upon public interests, but, with the exception of these curbs, the owner is formally free to dispose his property as he wishes. He may sell or trade it; he may employ it to whatever extent of its full capacity he desires; or he may direct it to new types of activity. The property and the behavior of its other supervisory personnel are fully subject to decisions made by the owner.

Private ownership coupled with personal management was carried over from the medieval guild to the small business and the small industry; and as new lands were settled and old estates were broken up it brought agricultural lands under a new and highly personalized type of control. Perhaps the feature most favoring it is the unstinting personal interest that it can bring to focus upon new enterprises. However, managerial ownership becomes an increasingly cumbersome form of control as enterprise expands in size, so that, eventually, it will be replaced during the growth process with ownership by proxy, which leads to new forms of organizational control that are much more compatible with large-scale organization.

Ownership by Proxy

Ownership by proxy is a share-held equity which can range all the way from short-term speculation holdings in commodities to longer-term interests in production facilities. Its basic vehicle is the negotiable certificate and its general medium is the stock market.

Buying securities is, in many respects, comparable to buying a sweepstakes ticket, except that the stock gamble will bring more modest returns and is much more secure. The securities investor, rather than just buying a chance to share in the winnings of the 'horse' actually acquires part-ownership of the 'animal' and a right to share in its prize earnings. His money is physically secured and at least some degree of reward will be forthcoming, although he exerts no more positive influence upon the outcome than the gambler does upon the performance of the horse. The stock market operates, in many respects, with all the abandon of a Latin American lottery. At its extreme, it is a means for making money, not through a demonstration or personal worth but through the gambling philosophy of either losing or 'striking it rich.' At its stabler, and more responsible 'blue chip' level it takes on more of the air of banking enterprise; the returns are modest, but the monies invested are relatively secure. But in all cases, it makes for a peculiarly egocentric orientation of enterprise. In the broader social spheres of assisting the society to obtain maximum productivity or in giving the individual worker personal security, the stock market does not even pretend an interest. It is an impersonal means of making money for its subscribers. Any positive social by-products that it may create, such as heightened employment, are purely fortuitous. A society that has learned to live with an anomaly as bizarre as the stock market, probably can learn to tolerate almost any type of system.

The stocks by which corporate industry are owned, are bought and sold in complete divorcement from the reality of the work situation. The concern of the stock buyer is not with the social merit or quality of the product which the industry makes, but with the ability of the industry to make money. Information regarding the product is seldom obtained through first-hand observation by the prospective stock owner, but through formal announcement, rumor, or the 'growth charting' activities of stock brokerage houses. The seller of stock, however long he may have held it, during his period of owner relationship to the company probably made no personal acquaintance with his workers or even with his paid managers. He will sell just as he bought, on a purely speculative basis.

Within this owning group, equity and control are sharply hierarchical. Although it is often vaunted in the United States, the capital site of capitalism, that the majority of people are 'capitalists,' the fact is that fewer than seven per cent of U.S. stockholders hold a monopoly on well over ninety per cent of the outstanding stock. This tiny minority exercises almost complete control over matters of broad corporate policy and management.

The big dealers, the masters of finance who live and make their way in this jungle of abstraction can, by deliberately heavy buying or selling, drive prices up or down almost at will. This behavior is not illegal, and its ethic seldom so much as comes up for discussion.

Even the more openly fraudulent behaviors are seldom publicized. An example of a common type of malfeasance is the geologist who, in conducting exploratory drilling for an oil company makes an exceptional strike, swears the crew to secrecy, and then enters into conspiracy with a select group of the oil company's officials in the heavy buying of stock which is surrendered by holders who have no idea of its true potential worth. When made public knowledge, such practices cause an uneasy stirring, but they cannot be wholeheartedly condemned or effectively combatted for the reason that they are no less ethical than the system which gives them rise. They are regrettable but logically predictable outcomes. At the final extreme of abuse, corporations which are weak and in trouble are sometimes bought in wholesale lots for the sole purpose of milching their remaining assets dry and then throwing them into final discard.

Share-held, absentee ownership of the facilities of production have almost completely rearranged the relationship between the worker and his job. The effects of divorcing the worker from the earlier trade guild practice of carrying out labor in the home, of separating him from possession of the tools with which he labors, of substituting a highly segmented task for his former overall production responsibility, of estranging him from the final process of personally marketing the finished good, have been noted by many but seldom taken seriously except by psychologists and others concerned with problems of mental well-being. The isolation and 'compartmentalization' of the individual, although doubtlessly exaggerated is, nonetheless, a lamentable and apparently unavoidable part of the industrial revolution. This movement has shrunken the individual's psychological dimensions and fitted him, as a functional part, into the larger mechanical system. The loss of identification with his work has been accented by an inability on the part of the individual to understand, or in any way control, this amorphous system of which he is a minute part. It has been only recently, and well along on its development cycle, that the industrial revolution has given evidence of materially benefiting mankind in general, rather than just a privileged few. Many of its effects are still heavily suspect to modern scholars and to the elders of traditional society.

And yet, with all its faults, for the technologically growing society, ownership by proxy is a great improvement over a managerial type of ownership. It releases production from influences which would certainly stifle its growth, as would be the case if it were to remain under managerial ownership. While ownership by proxy is still restricted to relatively few people, it allows for a somewhat broader and more socially satisfying distribution of assets. A society of large-scale enterprise under managerial ownership would be an archetype of autocracy. Ownership by proxy gives the organization a continuity and a lifetime separate from that of mortal owners. The organization is not indirectly afflicted by the effects of mental disorganization, physical illness, or the death of some, one person. It becomes less subject to being treated as a transferable asset. Large corporations seldom go broke or out of business. Although they occasionally merge (an action that usually improves production), because of the magnitude of their assets and the great sums that would be involved in such transactions they are seldom sold in the conventional sense. Some have become known as 'family corporations,' employing members of the same families over the generations.

The foregoing described a few of the benefits realizable through ownership by proxy. There are many more, the more important of these having come from making a clean-cut separation between ownership and management. The further virtues of this historically new type of management will be discussed later in this chapter under *Administrative Management.*

What is to be the ultimate fate of ownership by proxy? As tested by its susceptibility to mechanization, it fails, completely, to show any authentic functional relationship to production. It cannot be merged with the production system, and if this were attempted it would appear as a nonsensical intruder. Moreover, when managerial ownership abdicated in favor of management by proxy, although this improved the system, it, at the same time, meant a surrender of whatever moral claim ownership might formerly have had to a direct sharing in the fruits of the system. However hoarsely its advocates try to maintain the fiction of its legitimacy, its rights have been lost, and this collapse of its moral base is making it easier for the society to tolerate further diminuation of ownership's status. Labor, in its growing estrangement from the production system is beginning to show this same vulnerability. As they are forced out of participation in production, both ownership and labor lose entitlement to financial reward from the production system; and because no logical ratio can be set governing their respective compensations they will be increasingly at one another's throats until both are ejected from the system to take place alongside other members of the society as participants in a revised reward system.

In the interim, the owner of production facilities will continue to enjoy two advantages. Through the profits he reaps he will be enabled to buy more goods, and to exert more social power. The first of these two rewards will lose meaning as people obtain direct (non-purchased) access to consumer goods; and the second probably will be at least partially diluted by new, non-material types of power emblems. Ownership by proxy probably will be tolerated just as long as it does not penalize production unduly; eventually it will atrophy, with ownership securities declining in value as they are surplanted by broader forms of social security and new types of social controls. Ownership will finally disappear entirely because it will have lost its meaning in a changed social context.

The preceding is not, of course, new or original speculation, nor is it without its critics or apparent counter strains in the real world. In the Soviet Union, because legislative and administrative measures have not proven, by themselves, effective in eliminating waste in the use of natural resources, there is a growing tendency to combat this problem by thrusting ownership accountability directly upon the corporation, by forcing it to pay for the natural resources that it consumes in production. This procedure is viewed as being in keeping with the broader features of Marxian value theory in that distinction can be drawn between the individual expenses and the socially necessary expenditures for the replacement of each unit of natural resource consumed in production, if indeed it is even replaceable. These latter expenditures are made the basis for an economic evaluation of natural resources and for their fiscal management. It is felt by some Soviet planners that this strategy would curb waste also by forcing the enterprise to develop longer-range and better integrated plans for the use of resources.[1] It is difficult to conceive of how corporate ownership, in view of the prodigal wastefulness and despoilation occurring at the hands of virtually *all* past forms of ownership, could much improve the situation. Moreover, for the using industry, within a collectivized society, to pay for its own resources smacks of the same logic as the banker who attempts to do business exclusively with himself, on his own capital.

MANAGEMENT AND PRODUCTIVITY

Administrative Management

Despite its random, unpatterned financial support, industry ordinarily manages to stay on a fairly even keel. This stability is, in large part, due to an historically new group, 'the managers.' This enclave has been described aptly as 'the new power elite.' Because of the stature and potency of the organizations they represent, they yield power all out of proportion to their personal income, wealth, or

[1] Exchange of Opinions: 'Evaluation of Natural Resources'. (By Yu. Sukhotin. *Voprosy ekonomiki*, No. 12, December, 1967).

other private power attributes. This executive corps, acting more as an independent entity than as spokesmen for the absent and never-seen owners, makes the organization's basic plans; and it is to this group that the work force responds and that the stockholders defer in matters of decision-making. Ask almost any shareholder what his corporation's plans are for the next five years and, in all probability, one will discover that he has given the matter no thought beyond anticipating dividends. Ask this same question of an executive manager and he will answer, except for that gray area subject to purturbation by the vagaries of the market, in detail and with clarity. It is rather obvious that this dyad, management and work force, could have managed from the beginning, quite well in complete divorcement from the owning stockholders if, initially, they had been given other means of finance.

As the managing arm of an invisible ownership, administrative managers bring to the organization a number of stabilizing traits. In lieu of the one-man type of decision-making found in managerial ownership, there is now a multiple sharing in decision-making by individuals of high professional competence who are welded together into a group of manifold and well-balanced specialties. Not only is planning under this corps more precisely detailed and better organized, but it is stripped of the inconstancy of one-man rule where, like the nineteenth-century robber barons, the owner is sometimes tempted into extremes in outdoing his rivals, or into yielding to the impulse to 'go for broke.' A corps of skilled managers brings the organization under rational control. The organization is removed from extreme dependency upon the judgment of one or a few men who usually work under conditions rendering them somewhat prone to error, and who, as they age, decline in competence and willingness to act imaginatively. The professional management group is purposively subjected to a variety of career experiences in their personal development, and to this group new blood and enriching new specialties are added continuously from the outside.

What is the future for a group having so much to offer? It is not rosy! As decision-makers they are, at best, too slow and uncertain. Their functions can be mechanically amalgamated, and to great advantage, with production activity. The forces that will cause them to melt away and perhaps, in time, disappear altogether, are already at work. The mechanization that began the displacement of the blue-collar group will continue to etch its way – through the 'computerization' of record keeping, management coordination, and decision-making – into the ranks of white-collar workers. It will first displace the lesser record keepers, and finally, through its access to, and ability to rapidly manipulate massive, overall systems' data, it will be able to improve upon the most fundamental of management decisions, ultimately even overriding the need for 'management by exception.' This latter is a special management action covering irregularities that crop up in the system that cannot be routinely processed and, therefore, must be ruled upon as individual cases. They occur because of still existing mechanical rigidities in the data processing system, and because it is known by the contributors of data that exceptions will be tolerated.

Engineering Management

We have already discussed the engineer as a change agent in his relationship to the *machines* of production. Less noticeable, but quite important, are the ways in which he elaborates upon the innovative role in his relationships to the *product* – in the product's design and in the technical management of its manufacture. A virile production system, once initiated, will spread its influence throughout the society. It will gather round itself a new set of folkways that will be communicated to the surrounding society by way of its employees, its philosophical advocates, news media, paid propaganda, etc. The materially advanced societies of the West are standing monuments to this truth. The architect of production is the engineer. He is especially trained in change-making and, with the exception of those of the group concerned with maintenance, he will be found, occupationally, only where change is actively pursued.

The engineer entrains technical and social innovations in both production and distribution; and an increase in distribution pressures greatly accelerates the rate of a product's diffusion. This combine of effective production and distribution has repeatedly proven its abilities to broaden a market to an extent that is outright irrational, to a point where a given commodity may be so 'overbought' as to seriously depreciate competing 'standard of living items,' which are less tangible but more important. The large automobile manufacturing corporations and the producers of cosmetics are cases in point. The increasing penetration of Western producers into the world's remote markets is an example of another type of massive production expansionism. Engineering innovation will change old markets and create new ones almost overnight. The advent of a significant product improvement, like the extremely durable stainless steel razor blade, will cause almost immediate shrinkage in the item's overall sales but, nowadays, seldom with long-range negative effects upon the producers. They quickly compensate by the development of new products and new markets, and in the process they usually become bigger than ever.

An engineer is concerned with the niceties of prices, costs, economies, etc., only insofar as they affect his prospects for staying employed and for continuing to ply his skills. If the costs of capital equipment or operating procedures are too high, he will attempt to engineer new, cost-cutting production methods, but by-and-large, costs are not the dominant governors of his behavior. Even when there is a radical decrease in production costs, the price of the product is usually allowed to drop only gradually and over a long period of time. No doubt, this is, in part, a profit-making strategy, but it is supported by the preference of engineers or technical managers for giving the product greater functional value, for making it more attractive to the buyer, instead of simply lowering the price. Thus, on the mass-producing market, prices within given product classes tend to be monotonously uniform and, usually, well above a legitimately justifiable level.

The engineer is production oriented. Although he may be regarded by some as the slave of the businessman, it would seem more appropriate to think of him as the businessman's genie. The detachment of these professionals from purely economic considerations, and the uniformities of their professional behaviors have been long overlooked by students of the socio-technical system. Engineers attempt to create superior products, not just from the narrow view of trying to best the competition, but because they have been taught to search for design excellence. Without the engineer, a universe aswim with businessmen will not make much change in the physical world, nor will they, ordinarily, attempt to. Tradesmen of the undeveloped areas are in intense competition, but this has not lead to changes in production methods or in the design of the product. This same static condition historically characterized Western society until the engineer happened upon the scene. And when he began exercising his skills, it was not that the businessman exhorted him to greater heights of ingenuity but rather, it was that the engineer dragged along the businessman and the banker as somewhat reluctant and timourous partners. Whenever they are dependent upon the funds of businessmen for their support, laboratories and research facilities will be obtainable only if it is relatively certain that they will be repaid out of increased profits; and the selling of the business world on the potential value of these facilities has been, and still is, a painfully slow educational process.

The role of the engineer has not been appreciated by classically inclined economists. Economists try to compare systems in terms of their 'economic structure,' in disregard of the fact that in their more important aspects these systems appear to be essentially the same. They are, above all, uniformly operating *production* systems of standard engineering design. Whether the setting within which the system operates is a gigantic, family-owned, private industry in West Germany, a Russian, socialistically-directed industry located in the Urals, or the peculiarly private, welfare-oriented mixture found in Japanese industry, the system seems to operate uniformly well. And it does do because in each of these cases it is essentially the *same* system. The economic factors which create inflation or depression may grind the engineering system to a halt, but these are social anomalies besetting the engineering system from outside. Spared from these irregularities, the system moves normally through the inertial forces of its engineering and broader socio-technical factors, and those who try to ascribe its basic governance to some other factor, such as price, run into a succession of conundrums.

EXCHANGE MEDIA AND PRODUCTIVITY

Money and the Market

While the production system of Western society may lumber on under the most cumbersome of ownership schemes, there is one of its trappings that can bring it to a quick and agonizing standstill – its media of exchange. When its money 'goes bad,' or its market sags, the entire system falters and fails, and the road to recovery is long and arduous.

Money is an investiture of confidence in the society's willingness, and ability, to stand behind its obligations. Underlying it is a further mutual entrustment that the agreed upon value of the fiat will remain stable and reasonably unchanging relative to the overall market. When this confidence is shaken, as it is under progressively severe inflation, faith in the longer-range economic trend also wavers.

Public confidence in the free enterprise system is easily undermined, inasmuch as the entire structure rests on little more than market speculation. There are no commonly held production goals upon which society can pin its hopes. Recognizing this weakness, some industrial leaders will attempt to forestall approaching panic by enunciating company goals, but these are usually misty in character, and they come too late. The causes of depression are bred in the marketplace, but their effects are soon felt in the places of production. Depression of this type is unknown in the preliterate and 'less sophisticated' societies. Therefore, one is led to the conclusion that the trouble must lie, not in the mechanisms of production or distribution, but in the media the society has devised for the exchange of its goods and services. These media, mere ancillaries of the system they were originally intended to serve, occasionally become its master. With private ownership unwilling, and unable, to assume further responsibility for the system's proper functioning, supporting finance is withdrawn and, because of this, public pessimism further deepens. This spreading panic, emergent from a psychological condition within the stock market, rapidly radiates throughout the society and communicates itself internationally. During the interval, 1796–1923, the United States experienced thirty-two business cycles, these cycles having an average duration of five and three-quarters years. Other of the Western industrial countries have had closely parallel experiences.

Many weighty tomes have been written on the cause of economic depression. Some are rooted in psychological theory, some are based upon the operation of physical factors within the production system, and still others are based upon some type of monetary theory. Most of the latter (and they comprise the great bulk of business cycle theories) share a common tendency to prescribe, as a remedy for depression, some further type of manipulation of the society's money. In the framework within which it must operate, the logic is irrefutable – if production was blocked by some negative change in public attitude toward the fiat, the fiat must be manipulated until it is restored to public favor. Meantime, the catastrophy is made all the more ludicrous by the fact that in most past depressions there has been no perceptible diminuation of need, despite the atrophy of that most infallible of all economic bellweathers, 'demand.' A further search for causation usually will reveal no decrease in the worker's willingness to produce, no flagging of interest on the part of management, and no radical change in ownership or in management policy. In the absence of any discernible relationship between the economic factors, the unpredictability of the market is explained by economists, in the last analysis, by the cliché that 'no system is perfect'; and the reason given for the system's imperfection is that 'human nature is imperfect.'

Economic depression sometimes comes with surprising suddenness, and always with a force that rends the entire society into helplessness. Unable to gauge the probable duration or the final severity of the trough, small and large enterprises alike, prudently close their doors early in order to preserve their surpluses so that, if necessary, they may be used in a last-ditch defense of their basic capital assets. Various public works programs and other 'pump primers' are finally brought into play, but the road to recovery is never a short or easy one. When asked his opinion of the causes of depression, the man on the street will usually profess ignorance, while the academician likely will make the erudite observation that depression is the result of a complex interplay of numerous variables. A somewhat more plausible explanation, and one that is psychological rather than economic, is 'loss of public confidence.' But the crux of the matter is that *depression is basically unexplainable*, and therefore unpredictable, because it is an outcropping of unarticulated, non-rational processes. Ironically, man, who unhesitatingly applies controls to the technical spheres of his activities, stands by helplessly while the social system in which these well-regulated activities are embedded is allowed to rush pell-mell like a driverless locomotive.

If there is one economic control that is claimed to be effective during an emergency, that control is central coordination through government. The present 'pump priming' programs which many of the Western countries keep poised in emergency reserve are fragmentary, centrally controlled measures. In accordance with its responsibilities, the government presumably will formulate production plans, set goals, and allocate the necessary physical and human resources. And it is supposed to do these things with little regard to the depreciated status of its currency. There are, however, two serious handicaps to any far-reaching effort to steady a faltering production system through central planning. Applied early enough to be truly effective, these controls will likely be opposed as unwarranted governmental meddling in private affairs or as a premature and needless expenditure of government funds. Applied semi-posthumously to forestall further dip, the central program must be so massive as to be, indeed, tantamount to a thoroughgoing socialism. For these two reasons, there cannot be effective controls against economic disaster in most of the Western countries. With this in mind, the more highly socialized societies, such as Russia, in the belief (and hope) that serious periodic economic malfunction is unavoidable in free enterprise society, openly maintain a policy of holding trade relations with the Western free enterprise countries to a minimum so as to escape the backlash from the depression they are sure is to come. So long as production control remains so strongly subject to the influence of the stock market, and nothing more, there is a strong possibility that Russian conjecture will prove correct.

Credit

Within the larger institution of finance there is an interesting manifestation, and one of relatively recent vintage – the massive extension of credit. The practice of acquiring present possession on a pledge to pay in the future is a widespread one, and probably as ancient as mankind. However, the proportions to which the custom has become inflated during the present century, despite its basic disconsonance with the broader financial system within which it is lodged, make it an historically unique occurrence.

Credit is a means for fattening currency. Just as currency is a pledge to abide by agreed upon values, credit is usually a pledge to repay out of potential but, as yet, unacquired resources. One might speculate that credit may serve as a barometer indicating any one of three situations. First, it may indicate the degree of adjustment between production and consumption. If the desire for a given product is less than the supply, it may be necessary for the seller to extend credit as an added inducement in getting the excess stock off his hands. This is a condition of short duration, and may be expected to disappear with time and appropriate cut-backs in production. Secondly, when the desire to purchase a certain good or service is widespread and intense but the individual lacks the ability to pay, this condition may encourage the extension of credit. In this way the seller stands, in the long run, to maximize profits. Thirdly, and importantly, the extension of credit is an excellent gauge of the rate of growth of production capability. In the absence of any better technique, it serves the production system, and society, in disposing of goods rather than permitting them to pile up in surplus. It is an interim measure for relieving the pressures that have built up in the production system because of a lagging and inefficacious system of distribution. Credit is a means for hurdling the obstructions that conservative finance sets up in the channels of distribution. It may, also, have high utility as an index, or flow gauge, for the indirect measurement of the trend toward automation. Credit is no stranger to the houses of finance and strict propriety, but it is an interloper which, as it battens, becomes ever more of a menace to the final integrity of both of these orthodoxies.

As recently as a bare half century ago, credit was looked askance as the improvident's dilemma, and in retail circles it was usually associated with the profiteering 'company store.' Children were taught the virtue of thrift, and responsible adults followed the dictum of 'pay as you go' rather than suffer the social mortification of indebtedness, and the accompanying interest penalties. Since that time society not only has moved into an era of easy credit, but *an era which credit has made possible.*

Credit has become a growth engine which is indispensable to the continued economic well-being of Western society. It has steadily increased in volume at all societal levels and within both, the public and the private domains. A year of successful financial management in public administration is hailed as one in which there has been little or no increase in public indebtedness. However, before the books are finally closed it invariably turns out that there were certain 'slippages,' and there was invariably an increase in the public debt. The United States' national debt increased from 1·26 billion dollars to 290 billion between the years 1900 to 1960, inclusively, an average rate of increase of almost five billion dollars per year. Indebtedness among the governments of Western European nations followed a closely parallel course.

The growth rate of government indebtedness, however, when compared with those of industrial producers and the consuming public appears almost stationary. Indebtedness in the private domain is literally running amuck. In the United States, during the ten-year period, 1950–1959, while federal indebtedness inched upward ten per cent, corporate indebtedness increased by the staggering amount of 200 per cent, and consumer indebtedness rocketed above this latter figure to an increase of 250 per cent.

Each year, there is less public concern expressed, within the Western nations, about bringing the public and private ledgers back into balance. Government, industry, and the consumer proceed to steadily expand upon credit. The reason for this is simply an ever-expanding ability to produce. One might conjecture that in following this trend for a few more decades, credit will have ballooned beyond any realistic accountability, and will shade off into a system of distribution which operates free of finance altogether. This point will have been reached when production is in such volume and carried out with so little input of human labor as to have no significant cost factor. The sages of business programming are already speculating that the ubiquitous credit-card system can be replaced, eventually, by a general, integrated, computerized, accounting network that can maintain personal accounts without the necessity of having any cash, whatever, pass through the individual's hands. By the time this procedure becomes technically feasible, it is quite probable that it will not be needed. When goods become available to an extent that will warrant this method of income-expenditure accounting for the individual, the opportunity for making commercial profits will have been stripped of motive, and finance will have lost meaning.

Suffice it to say that credit, perhaps more than any other factor, serves as a gauge of our steadily expanding ability to produce.

Credit will continue to expand until it passes any realistic prospect for, or genuine expectation of repayment by either, debtor or creditor. Indeed, it may have reached that point already and is acting as a bridge to a new and radically differing socio-technical system. To appreciate its present magnitude, all one need do is imagine the social effects if broadspread depression were to ensue, and foreclosure was made on all indebtedness. The result would be indescribable chaos.

MEASURING THE TREND TOWARD AUTOMATION

Inasmuch as the movement toward automation is an inevitable concomitant of socio-technical development, it is appropriate that ways for better defining and describing this movement be discussed. The movement toward automation seems to have been occurring in two broad, successive waves. The first phase of the movement was a groping one of relatively long history, wherein machine components were aggregated into larger, more fully integrated, and more efficient mechanical systems. We might refer to this process as 'mechanization.' The second phase of development involves making the machine system self-regulatory. The machine becomes equipped eventually, with highly discriminatory sensors and a flexible feedback loop which almost completely, or entirely, disengages man from the system. We might label this second phase of development as 'automation.' However, the foregoing are more in the way of crude, surface descriptions of processes than definitions. It is important that we develop methods for describing the internal *workings* of the process. We must quantitatively identify the point on the development cycle of automation where we now stand; we must isolate its more important side-effects; and we must devise means by which to give the movement whatever guidance is possible.

It is noteworthy that a phenomenon as portentious as the movement toward automation has not been brought under systematic study, while its more particularized social and psychological side-effects have been studied rather exhaustively. The reasons for this neglect range from apathy to outright opposition. The subject is a formidably broad one with which to grapple, and there is sensitivity in high places to the possibility that the findings may be given negative interpretation. In instances where limited studies of automation *have* been carried out, it is claimed by industrial management that the data were later used against them in their negotiations with the unions. Workers view progressive automation with apprehension, while managers treat it as proprietary information that can be rightfully withheld from labor as well as from competing industrial concerns. Meantime, the whole issue is given added heat by the steady upswing in unemployment. These difficulties notwithstanding, it is extremely important to its planning that the society determine, as accurately as possible and with celerity, the current state and future trends of automation.

There is probably no one, single, measurement criterion which will give perspective to the present or future status of automation. Rather, what will be required is a composite of indexes which have been derived from careful analyses and tests, and have been found to be useful in certain combinations as descriptors, or predictors. The sources of information from which such indices might be extracted are both social (e.g., labor statistics) and technical (machine performance data). This is to say that in obtaining productivity information it will be necessary to deal with both man and machine sub-systems, and with combinations and permutations of the two. The study necessary to derive these indices may take place at three levels: it may center upon given types of man-machine systems; it may be applied to given classes of industry; or it may be applied to production or consumption traits permeating the overall society.

Analyses of the performance of man-machine systems could be made through conventional time and motion study combined with performance data from the manufacturers of production machines and tools. A great deal of random information in these two categories has already been compiled. Of special importance, is the present labor slack or, put another way, the production-lag in a given system. To get at this factor the man-machine constellation would have to be measured in its performance as a totality, with the performance information sought being the difference between the manifest and the latent production capabilities of the system.

Manifest production might be defined as the *present* production norm, the observable rate of production for a given system or complex of systems. Latent production would be the *maximum* production volume that system is capable of attaining under optimum conditions of man-machine organization and management. The discrepancy between the two can lead to either, or both, of two effects – human displacement or production increases. Occasionally the two effects become apparent simultaneously. During time of national emergency, for example, there are occasional cases in which production rates may be increased markedly with an accompanying reduction in manpower, and with no addition in equipment. The same end-effect may become apparent, in a somewhat different way, during, or following periods of economic recession. At these times a relatively heavy cut-back may have been made in the work force without causing any appreciable slow-down in the rate of production. Thus, indices with a capability for discriminating between manifest and latent production rates could have broad social usefulness. They could be used to test for the degree of potential disemployment danger inherent in a given production situation or in the society as a whole; and they could be applied to determine the society's maximum production potential, in the event that it should become badly needed.

When study centers upon given classes of industry, it will involve comprisons of overall input and output characteristics. Quantitative determination would have to be made of the total amounts of fuel, raw materials, and other input units consumed in production, and this quantity would be compared with the total number of finished items produced. This would provide gross standards and measurements of production efficiency and trends. Study of overall industrial performance could also derive its data from broad social statistics, such as annual Gross National Product, output per capita, and, more definitively, the total output of finished items by class. Trends in machine design, in those industries which have already achieved a breakthrough into automation, should be given special attention. It might be possible to identify common points in the evolution of these industries at which breakthrough has occurred. If so, these findings might be applied in predicting trends in kindred industries, or in industries using similar production systems.

At the point of applying broad production measures to the overall society, one finds a number of highly useful indices which are already established and for which there are a great deal of available data. Examples of two of these are: the changes in ratio that have been steadily occurring between the utilization of human labor, draft-animal power, and machine power; and changes in the amount of available horsepower per capita of population. The power commanded by the average citizen is an excellent index of the society's standard of living. It is estimated that the physical output capability of the average adult male is about one-twentieth of a horsepower. This figure, divided into the total horsepower existing within the entire society, might be interpreted as a mechanical equivalent of the number of tireless, blindly obedient (and narrowly specialized) slaves over which the society holds sway.

And finally, in way of broad indices there are the massive, easily studied, and important trends in unemployment. Overall displacement occurring within the work force, while not necessarily a good index of productivity, presently has heavy and direct bearing on purchasing power, and hence on the consumption capability of the society.

The approachs suggested above have the limitations of all empirical approaches, but they might assist in the formulation of theory. There has been little theoretical speculation on the causative factors lying behind, and driving the movement toward automation, and most of the hypotheses advanced have been economic ones. One of the better known economic schools holds that mechanization has been encouraged steadily by increased wages and a desire on the part of industrialists to circumvent this cost as much as possible. The most convenient means for reducing the cost of labor is by eliminating it through mechanization. One might just as easily argue on the other side of the fence, that increasing mechanization is causing increases in wages. This chapter concludes with a different hypothesis, namely, that ownership, labor, and all their economic linkages are purely a social skin, and as such, all are subject to perturbations originating in the deeper-lying socio-technical processes. They will be gradually changed by a growing technology.

10

SOCIO-TECHNICS AND COMMODITY MANAGEMENT

DISTRIBUTION

Distribution is the vital link between production and consumption. It is a set of machine functions and techniques by which a given item of production is managed from the time it leaves the site of production until it reaches the hands of the consumer. Ideally, its attentions should be allowed to center almost exclusively upon the mechanics of transporting goods and providing for their intermediate storage.

The methods by which a country distributes the fruits of its production will have strong relationship to its development progress. Antiquated distribution techniques are an obstacle to development in most of the emerging societies, and they are impediments to a faster rate of development in most of the materially advanced societies. In the retarded nations, the systems for distribution are unmechanized and clogged with needless numbers of functionaries; and their plight is not helped by the Western nations who advise them on matters of development programming and who are, themselves, only beginning to emerge from a *Middle Age* commerce. The criteria for a good distribution system are twofold – it must be essentially equitable in its services and it must be efficient. The more it foreshortens the distance between production and consumption the more simply it will operate, and the lower will be the final cost to the ultimate user. In other words, that distribution method serves best which causes least clutter in the system.

The level of a society's standard of living will be a compound product of the vitality of its production system, the tastes of its consuming public, and the ability of the distribution link, between the two, to broadly channel the flow of goods and services throughout the society. Production volume is heavily dependent upon methods of distribution and physical facilities for distribution, but, however high the production rate may be, it will not meaningfully relate to the society's standard of living unless there is an *equitable* distribution of goods, namely, that they flow evenly to all members of society as they are needed. A society may be highly productive, but if it contains exaggerated differentials in purchasing power it will not enjoy a high standard of living. Few societies have ever been fortunate enough to have a democratic sharing of wealth; most have been disadvantaged by low productivity. Today, however, for the first time in history nations are breaking through production barriers, but, usually, only to discover that they are still hobbled by anachronistic methods of distribution. Maldistribution is universal. It is apparent in the pinched international flow of goods from the wealthy industrial nations to the poor ones, and it is visible in the skewed channeling of goods and services inside almost all these societies, rich and poor, alike.

Inequalities in Distribution

Very little of the abundance produced in Western society finds its way to the world's impoverished masses. The most immediate need of the poorer nations is for food, and it is here that the West has the greatest production surpluses. Continuing surveys by the United Nations reveal that 2/3 of the world's peoples are under-nourished. Half of this group, or 1/3 of the world's population (slightly over 1 billion people), live dangerously near the border of starvation. Yet, in the face of this need the world's greatest food producer, the United States, wrestles with the peculiar problem of contriving ways to constrain its agricultural production. Food stocks, the most vital of all commodities, are discouraged from production by government subsidies which monetarily recompense the U.S. farmer for leaving land lie fallow. Before this type of control became effective, and before the advent of large-scale government storage facilities, there were instances of the wholesale destruction of 'unmanageable surpluses' in order to prevent them from glutting the domestic market. Such extravagant and irresponsible behaviour certainly will not be remembered kindly by historians of the future. It is possible that United States agricultural policy is stirring more hostility abroad than is the much publicized race issue inside the U.S.; and it is a safe assumption that very few of the world's hungry are overwhelmed with sympathy for the United States in its plight in dealing with 'the agricultural surplus problem.' This is not in exclusive censure of the United States, for it takes a general concert of will and action to break down the traditional international barriers to distribution. U.S. agricultural exports will, invariably, collide with the interests of the farmer of the recipient country as well as with the interests of the country's other external food suppliers, and they will thereby arouse strong opposition. It has been a case of the interests of the few, overriding the needs of the many. An encouraging note, however, is the gradual annual increases in the export of U.S. agricultural surpluses under the auspices of U.S. Public Law 480.

Inside many of the underdeveloped societies there is a tendency, which has long historical antecedents, to view the economic system as a closed one. These folk have no clear-cut concept of production and very little interest in its processes. Preoccupation with the commercial activities of buying and selling has either blunted, or preempted, inventive ingenuity and the concept of creativity. As many individuals as can be possibly accommodated will squeeze into the sales cycle, and the result is a finely fragmented, overly cumbersome commerce which yields little profit to anyone. Commerce on a small scale, easily entered and painlessly fled, can harbor a disguised unemployment as high as that found in underdeveloped agriculture. This same phenomenon of 'commercial crowding,' with qualifications, also characterizes Western society, and to a far greater extent than its members realize. The West, too, has been long ensnarled by the ancient 'trader philosophy,' a quagmire from which it is just now showing a tendency to emerge.

The Sales Function

As the mounting tide of production that entrained the industrial revolution continued rising, the practitioners of the ancient art of mercantilism stepped into a different role, one more consonant with the new production dynamic. The trader of antiquity gave way to the 'merchant prince.' The spawn of the new commercial revolution were merchandizers and specialists in persuasion. None among the group travelled to buy at distant marts, nor did they personally supervise the transport of what they bought, returning with it over remote land routes or sea lanes, as had their predecessors of antiquity. Transportation was now handled by still other intermediaries who delivered the merchandize at the retailer's door. The merchant's purpose was now to preside over an 'establishment,' an advertised meeting ground for goods, and a buying clientele. The merchant became the 'dealer,' the coordinator of volume who no longer bought by bits and pieces from tiny artisans' shops, but acted as a highly paid mediator between an indefatigable production juggernaut and an apparently insatiable public. The question of present day pertinency is, 'What services does the merchant carry out and what are their socio-technical values?'

The most cursory of examinations of the relationships between the dealer and manufacturer of the late nineteenth and early twentieth centuries convinces one that the dealer had much to offer the manufacturer of that day. This period marked the beginnings of high-volume production, a condition which began to create special pressures for mass outlet. The sales proprietor offered to the public several types of specialized services which the production-oriented manufacturer, physically and socially remote from the ultimate buyer, was unable to extend. The sales proprietor additionally accommodated the needs of the manufacturer by giving him a quantity of outlets, making it possible for the latter to quickly exploit a large geographical area by laying it off into subdivisions and servicing each of these through a large regional distributorship. This added distributory power enabled the producer to concentrate his attentions, even more exclusively, on production specialization and the attainment of higher quality. The dealer, as his representative, made it possible for the manufacturer to establish an indirect but nonetheless 'personalized' relationship with the buyer. This had the effect of encouraging 'repeat buying,' and it quickly echoed customer complaints concerning the product to the manufacturer and expedited needed change in product design. Additionally, the dealer could offer finance services, either his own or, more generally, those of supporting agencies specializing in finance. This service indulged the customer by enabling him to acquire early possession of goods, and in so doing it gave still further leash to production.

In his role as intermediary between producer and consumer, the sales proprietor supported the manufacturer's warranty throughout its lifetime, and, in case of a major defect, he usually replaced the item out of his own stock, returning the defective one to the manufacturer. Finally, the proprietor carried out what was purported to be an educational program – he explained the use of the commodity to the prospective buyer, demonstrated its operation, and helped the customer to reach a decision to purchase it.

However, the sales pattern was not then, nor is it now, as clear-cut a function as the foregoing might imply. There is usually not just one, but a hierarchy of sales *strata*. The number of sales levels through which an item passes, depends upon the character of the item and whatever special provisioning may have been arranged by the manufacturer's sales liaison staff. A basic commodity such as an automobile may go directly to the retailer dealer, while many of the smaller classes of merchandise may pass through a succession of two or more distributors and wholesalers before reaching their final outlet. Each of the agencies, through whose hands a commodity passes, exacts the cost of transportation and administration, makes its own charge for handling, and adds a net profit charge.

The Sales Function Re-examined

In the era of specialization and high-volume production it is justifiable, and desirable, to make a separation between production and distribution services; but the inner structure of each should be governed primarily by technical considerations rather than special, individual interests. Retail outlets should be efficiently organized and conveniently located with respect to the customer. They should accord with the general principles of bringing to a single selling point a great variety of merchandise and allowing the shopper to choose freely that particular item which best satisfies his needs. As for the offering of credit, this can be a genuine service only to those who desire credit. To have the cost of this service indirectly prorated over the entire customer population is unjust. In fact, during the earlier part of this century the cash buyer frequently was able to buy directly from the wholesaler, at wholesale prices. The so-called 'fair trade ethic,' a term used to justify the collusion of retailers, wholesalers, and manufacturers to stifle the free market by maintaining set price levels, works counter to several other 'business ethics' such as 'giving the customer the most for his money.'

Another service offered by the dealer, a short-term warranty guaranteeing the serviceability of the commodity, is also of questionable value. Because of the high standards of quality control and thorough factory testing maintained by most manufacturers, defective merchandise seldom gets through to the market. When minor defects do get past these filters it is cheaper, in the long run, for the customer to pay for this repair directly through a service agency, than it is to subsidize the dealer to care for this eventuality. If the defect is a major one the manufacturer will usually accept, and replace, a returned item a great deal more cheerfully than will the dealer. In fact, the dealer is only carrying out the terms of the manufacturer's warranty, and on matters not covered by the warranty he usually abides by the manufacturer's decision. It is understandable that the dealer cannot extend free repair or replacement services if the cumulative cost of these become so great as to cut seriously into his profits. Since the requirements for services are, in general, fairly modest, the manufacturer should, and sometimes does establish field service facilities to care for them.

Finally, the 'educational service' that sales people claim to offer with the item probably constitutes more of a negative, than a positive contribution. Salesmen, in general, are technically ill-informed about the products they sell, and usually are not particularly inspired to acquire a more expert knowledge. After all, the basic philosophy of the school of salesmanship is that one plays on the emotions, not the intellect, and very often this must be done by subduing the customer's better judgment. When this practice is adhered to, a salesman's knowledge of the product is of little value, anyhow. Countless books on the subject point out that a salesman can successfully influence almost any prospective buyer if he employs the proper set of psychological tactics. Legitimate differences between competing products are passed over by sales personnel because the dealer for whom they work is usually constrained by the supplying manufacturer to carrying his line, exclusively. In those cases where there are two or more competing lines on the floor, a 'good' salesman will concentrate on the one showing the greatest margin of profit, or on those, because they are less attractive to the public, that have been lingering overly long in inventory. Aware of these facts, the shopper usually welcomes the opportunity to avoid harrassment at the hands of sales people. When, in lieu of their 'guidance,' he is given freedom to examine the merchandise at will, compare, and arrive at his own decisions (asking for information if he wants it), he will take much greater satisfaction in what he buys. In essence, the traditional sales function is a service that the consuming public probably would do better without.

There is a recent strain for the simplification of distribution in Western free enterprise society, particularly in the United States, but traditional methods provide the means by which a large part of all merchandise is still handled. These methods cause needless bottlenecks in distribution, and greatly inflate the price of the commodity. For example, a mass produced kitchen range requires, in its total creation, the efforts of literally thousands of people. The extracting of raw ores, their loading and transport over long distances to smelting centers, their milling and refinement into components of various sizes and shapes, the assembly of these parts by scores of persons, the quality control, finishing, and testing of the item, altogether constitute an almost uncountable variety of mechanical and human work activities each of which contributes to the stove's creation. This multiplicity of highly specialized tasks is merged into such an efficient production flow that it may be possible to produce a reasonably good kitchen stove for approximately sixty dollars. However, by the time this same stove reaches the home of the buyer, its cost will have been multiplied about four times over, or to approximately 240 dollars. Something logically inexplicable has happened to this commodity in the short course of its journey from the factory's loading dock to the user's kitchen. It has probably passed through at least two business establishments, a wholesaler and a retailer, and at each of these points functionaries have added service charges and heavy mark-ups.

Those of the persuasion that this redundancy contributes to the well-being of society because it 'makes more work and money' have little understanding of the social meaning of either. There is a vast difference between an activity of genuine social usefulness and an idle shuffling of merchandise and money. A commodity can have value only to the extent that it is of utility to the user. If the production process is well organized, an item in manufacture takes on steadily added value as it moves along the production line. The end product will be a physical entity of a certain value and utility. Further unnecessary human handling, and this can be infinite, will add only to its cost, not to its utility. Thus, there must be a minimum of manipulation in the distribution process so that money can be recycled back, as directly as possible, into the vital production process, rather than being allowed to reverberate, at the public's expense, within the distribution chain.

There are recently awakened movements which promise, in time, to eliminate many of the obstacles in the present distribution system and to overhaul its *modus operandi*. Foremost among these is the discount house. The discount store collates an unprecedented variety of merchandize at outlying physical locations which can be conveniently reached by the public. The larger of these have grown from such origins as the mail order business, and are so gargantuan as to be able to buy in train-load, as opposed to car-load lots, and to demand a control of quality which is frequently more rigid than that maintained by the manufacturers, whom they subsidize, for their own best brands. Their great purchasing power also holds manufacturer's profits to a minimum, in that they can, within reason, stipulate the prices they will pay. They buy in great quantities, and present these goods to the consuming public with maximum efficiency and minimum mark-up. Despite earlier forecasts by their assailants that they would be unable to stand behind the merchandise with warranties, that they lacked the 'personal touch,' and that they would have scant appeal because of their frequent inability to make credit arrangements, discount outlets have flourished steadily, and with strong patronage from the lower class which, formerly,was believed to have an unseverable and almost total, dependency on store credit.

Other short-cuts in distribution are making an appearance through such selling techniques as the 'technical representative.' Technical representation may be carried out by an individual or by a small firm acting as a local representative for one or more large producers. The foremost personal characteristic demanded in a technical representative is technical competence in the area in which he makes representation. A technical representative is more of a consultant than a salesman. In fact, these professionals are sometimes as conspicuously lacking in the quality of personal suasion as they are outstanding in technical competence. To a degree, the idea of the technical advisor is being extended to the floor of some of the larger retail outlets.

Advertising

Traditionally, advertising has been considered as a necessary augmentation to the sales function, and, indeed, it is claimed by its advocates that advertising is the first estate of mercantilism. Its practioneers claim that it, like salesmanship, is basically educational, that it informs the public of the advent of new products and briefly describes them and how they function. It is purported to be a tonic for the entire production system. Under advertising's impetus, the public is stimulated to increase its purchasing and this improves the health of the entire economy. It is not, say its advocates, a nullifying collision of forces where one advertiser simply takes business away from another, but a wedge through which the entire market is broadened. It is often pointed out that cigarette advertising has greatly increased the cigarette market in general, rather than working deprivation upon the weaker competitors. Everyone, including the public, has benefitted. This myopic logic, besides showing little regard for anything other than self-interest, overlooks the more basic fact that, thus far, the consumer still is of limited means and, if induced to increase spending for tobacco, will have to curtail expenditures in other realms such as education or medicine. Thus, while, in a limited sense, advertising may widen the market rather than deepen the competition, in a broader context it merely intensifies competition between larger segments of the overall market. Advertising, in itself, has no ability to increase purchasing power.

Few activities have attracted more attention than advertising; and few labor with greater reward, with less tangible evidence of accomplishment, or with a service of more dubious value to society. Dozens of popular tracts have described the deliberate waste-making created through planned obsolescence or through the design of components that are intended to fail after a certain amount of use. Forcing the discard of an item by a public that is deliberately made style conscious by frequent restyling, or calculatedly building defects into an article so as to necessitate its replacement, are commonplace, publicly recognized, and reprehensible behaviours. Although unprosecutable in act, in spirit these tactics are as criminal as any other type of fraud, and a great deal more costly to society. Stylists and manufacturers' engineers collude in the creation of an unsatisfactory product. The advertiser supplements their work by attempting to create psychological dissatisfaction with the product almost as soon as it has been bought. It is pointed out that the 'very latest' products have greatly improved features, and the styling is changed in an attempt to demonstrate this contention. Each is urged to keep up with his neighbor in the prestige race which advertisers have learned to exploit unendingly. The only saving grace of these ploys to create aesthetic dissatisfaction with an item is that they, at least, make the item's physical defects more bearable when they shortly do become apparent. The entire corps – designers, advertisers and their allies – defend these practices as in the interest of the public and the economy. 'After all, the more frequently the individual replaces his automobile the more work he creates for others, and the better it is for the whole society.' Strangely, this aphorism is widely believed, although brief reflection will disclose that nothing is further from the truth. The two groups which have been prominent in peddling this cliché are the sales people and the advertisers, whose business it is to sell, and who attempt to keep sales rolling by any strategy imaginable and without particular regard for such trifles as the truth.

Frequent replacement, whether it is foisted by the manufacturer or unintentional on his part, has a negative or inhibitory effect upon the standard of living. If an item is constructed by maximum utility in the first place, society becomes the beneficiary. Let us imagine that in the construction of an automobile, the manufacturer made every effort to attain maximum mechanical reliability, advanced functional design, and low cost. Let us further suppose that he was so successful in these respects that one automobile would now last the buyer for a lifetime, without repair or parts replacement. Unlike the present high cost of automobile purchase and regular replacement, which consumes a significant part of the family's funds, the new costs could be more easily afforded and the utility of the vehicle would remain high year after year. The lowered outlay would release funds for other types of commodities, for increased expenditures on education, roads, libraries, medicine, recreation, travel, etc. The acquisition of these new goods and services, which hitherto could not be afforded, would elevate significantly the family's standard of living.

A materialization of the type of situation just described could also be a social boon in other ways. Because automobile production would be radically decreased, workers could be released from the automobile industry where they had been maintained by a hidden type of social subsidization, for other types of work for which there was a genuine need. Some workers could be shifted to the building of schools, highways, etc., while others could be released to acquire further education. This reallocation of manpower would benefit the standard of the entire society.

When employment and production are maintained synthetically, the burden falls upon everybody. As labor input decreases and utility of the consumer increases, everyone benefits. The ultimate in social accomplishment would be such ingenuity in social and production planning that the individual would be able to obtain everything he needed at no cost, thus freeing his attentions and energies for more important matters than that of eking out a living. For those who prefer the other alternative of work for work's sake, there are such examples as the early Egyptian dynasties. With the majority of their population living under slavery, these empires were eminently industrious, but most of their effort went into the construction of burial monuments. These edifices, once completed, were economically inert, devoid of utility, and of no real social value. The *society literally buried its production output along with its deceased* monarchs, and although it sustained an employment level of close to 100 per cent, it marched on to socio-economic insolvency. The difference between building pyramids and expending great sums in the excessive or *needless* manufacture of automobiles is only a matter of degree. In both cases, effort is expended without achieving significant utility. The society that attempts to center its activities around the production and trading of automobiles is operating on the same plane as the fabled Arab society whose members all made a living by trading camels with one another. At an extreme, the rationales are one and the same.

Aside from the question of deliberate waste-making, is that of the ethic of an advertising which unrelentingly attempts to manipulate public opinion for its own ends. Much has been written describing the awesome attempts made by advertisers to influence public behaviour. Occasionally, advertisers discover an 'ultimate weapon' such as subliminal stimulation, which, in the belief of some congressmen, beginning psychology students, and advertising 'experts,' has demoniacal potential for the complete enslavement of the public psyche. This nonsense aside, the hard fact remains that the advertiser makes life for the average person a great deal more nettlesome proposition than it need be. The advertiser's point is driven home by a deadening repetition of jingles, slogans, photographs, etc., and as one advertising pioneer pointed out: in a medium whose life-blood is sheer emphasis, bad taste may sometimes succeed admirably where good taste fails altogether. Thus, appeal to the emotion is substituted for appeal to reason as advertisers happily go their ways in dissuading the public from the exercise of better judgment. Once an effective opening wedge is discovered, the public is bombarded with this shilalegh until it somehow eventually disappears, but only to be replaced by another.

The enticement offered to the buyer of this service, that advertising's cost can be deducted from income as a business expense is, unfortunately, all too true. What otherwise would be public revenues are siphoned off, and must be compensated for by other tax taken from the consumer's pocket. It is further maintained that advertising outlay is an innocuous expenditure, because it comes out of the profits of the seller. There is no way in which this claim can be logically validated. If funds were not spent on advertising, and if the law of supply and demand operated as effectively as is claimed, then, obviously, the conserved funds could be subtracted directly from the cost of the commodity. Of course, this will bring the counter-argument that without advertising and the increased volume of business it creates, the margin of profit would narrow and the commercialists would have to charge more than ordinarily. This, too, is a questionable proposition. As it stands, the seller is able to maintain a set margin of profit by loading advertising, just as he does all his other costs, directly onto the public. The public is the all-being of the market. It is the only entity from which profits can be made, or to which expenses can be charged. It bears all costs.

As for the assertion that advertising educates, anyone who has had much exposure to its copyright soon discovers that it is clothed in almost every device except the simple expedient of imparting pertinent information. It is, throughout, an appeal to the emotions. Although advertising is effective in alerting the public of the advent of a new product or brand, this same information could be disseminated just as effectively, and more tastefully, through carefully prepared announcements. Significant events occurring within the market show a surprising propensity for propagation by word-of-mouth. It has been the recent dilemma of several producers to have made highly significant improvements in their products, only to discover that they had exhausted every advertising superlative on their other stocks and were now playing upon the ear of a deafened public. While they were pondering means to 'really put this message across,' it was discovered that news of the product's merits had already spread through informal channels.

Countless sums are spent on advertising; and the buying public, in purchasing the advertised commodity, pays the bill in full. It was estimated that in the United States, during the year 1964, 14·0 billion dollars were spent on advertising. This amounted to approximately 78 dollars per capita, or more than the entire annual per capita incomes of the world's thirteen poorest nations. A part of this expenditure was for sales announcements, but what was far-and-away the greater part went solely for product promotion. In return for this latter outlay, the public received a service that was bereft of fact and often downright misleading, intent upon persuasion without regard for the public's real needs, unsolicited, and intrusive upon the public's purse and privacy.

To reiterate, what is needed in lieu of the costly and uncertain services of commercial advertising is a direct, simple, and straightforward medium for broadcasting news of product changes, new products, and other changes in the market. If the financial journals can apply this principle so successfully in describing the stock market and related aspects of the financial world, it would appear to be also applicable to describing the consumer's market. It is noteworthy that the breed of men who buy bonds and stocks *in quantity* do not do so at the behest of popular advertising. They insist upon a sounder source of information.

Distribution is the technological interlink between production and consumption. In a progressive system, it cannot be said to have a separate identity of its own, it is an appendage to the production system. Its antiquated and dying *factoti*, the merchants who distribute goods, are immaterial to technological development in some respects, and downright inimical to it in others. Normally, as the production system increases in potency the relative number of people located in the distribution chain will tend to lessen. The production system creates pressures which demand increasingly streamlined distribution, a distribution expedited by easier credits and untrammelled with salesmen and other middlemen. The discount house and a spate of credit granting agencies have been making a radical change in distribution in Western society, and they are only a first step toward a whole new system of mechanized distribution.

It would expedite technological development greatly if the public had a clearer understanding of the place of distribution in the development process. Effort expended to expedite distribution, especially at the beginning stages of a development program, with the exception of those steps that must be taken by the public sector to complement development in agriculture and industry (e.g. the provision of transportation and storage facilities), will be largely wasted. There is little point in quibbling about the niceties of distribution at an early stage of development, because there is little to distribute. Distribution is merely a functional appendage to production, and as production becomes progressively stronger, its folkways, its methods, and its outward-surging pressures will force rapid change in the distribution system. Meantime, the individual can best help the whole process to change by acquiring a better understanding of it.

CONSUMPTION

The total welter of activity involved in production and distribution comes about, in the last analysis, in response to consumption, and it is in the process of consumption that the efficiency of the first two is tested. It is here that a society's true standard of living becomes manifest. Although consumption behavior usually is treated as a major part of the economic process, it is a non-economic behavior. It is compounded of psychologically conditioned appetites sustained by social convention. Therefore, in the light of our present knowledge of these two fields, to treat the market as a highly predictable phenomenon is to lay claim to an expertness that we do not yet have. The best possible estimates of market behavior still will be only estimates, and they will have to be based on projections of past consumption trends with due allowance for the intrusion of new habits, styles, attitudes, oscillations in the public's purchasing power, changes in production capabilities, changes in the price of the product, etc., etc.

Like the standard of living which it constitutes, consumption is qualitatively and quantitatively relative to the culture in which it is examined. Questions are forever cropping up, in such matters as designing new tax laws, as to how distinction can be made between luxury items and essential goods. As smoking becomes universal among adults, it is predictable that tobacco will be transferred from the luxury category and reclassified as an 'essential commodity.' Because of its capability for integrating home life, social case workers are coming to look upon a television set as a necessity and will approve the expenditure of welfare funds to secure one. It is coming to pass in the wealthier societies that each adult individual feels that he must have his own motor vehicle, and most average-income U.S. families are already supporting two or more vehicles.

The qualitative aspect of consumption is also subject to wide variation. The general type and quantity of goods that the individual will demand depends upon his social class standing and upon what the society is accustomed to consuming. Within the broad framework of social class, more particularized choices will depend upon the way in which the individual's personal tastes have been conditioned. That there are no absolute standards for all societies and all times is a point that cannot be overemphasized. When we speak of the under-developed society and what concrete goals it should set for material advancement, above the level of obviating basic physical wants no absolute standards can be validly set. This indeterminancy, in itself, provides direct stimulus, in the West, to material mobility because there is no socially defined resting place in the individual race for possession, no generally agreed upon plateau which is accepted as sufficient for income, material possession, or power. The individual's desires are insatiable because there are no *criteria* for satisfaction, and he continues through life in much the manner of a squirrel running in a treadwheel. Indeterminancy of accomplishment is, evidently, a major motive force within many of the technologically advancing societies.

The driven quest for the unattainable has led many to renounce the material goal altogether. The more theatrical forms of self-denial are more comfortably carried off in the richer societies where fringe benefits can be easily stripped from the bough, and where a modest, formalized philanthropy refuses the individual an opportunity to experience really desperate need. Even the most fervent 'egg-head' will be found to have a certain aversion to extreme hunger, and few, however relativistic their outlook, will live with equanimity in a social setting rife with cholera, glaucoma, venereal disease, and mass starvation. The foregoing is in way of saying that while it is difficult to establish any logical upper limit for a general standard of living, there are quite evident lower-limit criteria below which the individual, and the society, cannot survive.

Development planners should keep in mind that there *are* absolute standards for the measurement of public health and for programming for its improvement, and that there are concrete standards of nutrition by which it is possible to prescribe proper dietary balance and the requirements for caloric intake. There are less tangible but, nonetheless, concrete minimum standards that can be prescribed for shelter and clothing. A failure on the part of the society to meet minimum standards in any one of the three – food, shelter, or clothing – will entail a suffering which will make interventive remedial action by outsiders necessary and morally defensible, despite the climate of opinion prevailing inside the afflicted society. Beyond this point of meeting its basic needs, the society should be left free to choose its own standards.

Measures intended to insure their survival will be resisted by very few societies, and this insurance is a minimum obligation owed by the more prosperous spheres of the world to the less fortunate. That basic aid is not always given with alacrity may be due, not only to opposition from the conservatives within the wealthier societies, but to dissention from experts. The latter group sometimes voices alarm at the possibility of creating a lasting dependency in the group being aided or, more often, it expresses apprehension that an abrupt outside action might 'upset' the aided nation's economy. In actuality, when a society is so badly afflicted that the survival of its members is in question, its economic system is dysfunctional anyhow, and could hardly be made worse. As for the right of outsiders to intervene, within the materially well-off nations it is considered justifiable, and even essential, to sometimes force help upon members of a given family *against* the family's will. Parents in these societies are not permitted to starve their children or to allow them to go unclothed, unschooled, in extreme deprivation of medical care, etc.

Waste, Repair and Salvage

As a part of the shifting pattern of consumption in Western society, there are also shifting attitudes and behaviors in connection with the utilization and discard of commodities. Accented in the United States by a rapid movement toward superabundance, these attitudes appear strange to the poverty-pinched outsider. Most societies have well defined attitudes regarding the care that a given artifact should receive, the esteem with which it should be held, expectations as to its useful lifetime, and when and how it should be discarded. These attitudes will relate more to the sheer plentitude of the artifact than to any other one factor. Abundance will depend upon, among other things, the quantity, cost and accessibility of natural resources out of which the object is fabricated, and the quantity of human labor necessary to convert the raw resource into the finished article. It, therefore, follows that when a technology progresses to a point where resources are almost illimitedly exploitable, and where methods for production processing are entirely automatic, for all practical purposes the resulting commodity will have no value aside from its utility to the user. If all resources are commonly owned by the society, if they can be technically attenuated to a degree where they are beyond the threat of depletion, and if they can be automatically processed into a finished product, this product can be secured and consumed, given away, destroyed, or abandoned, and then replaced at will without entailing cost or genuine waste. The foregoing condition is not yet fully realizable in any society. In no country, will all three of the following conditions be found to prevail: publicly owned resources; publicly owned capital; and a system of processing that is automatic to a point of being able to perform self-maintenance and create its own machine replacement stock. Even when production costs are pared down by automation to a degree where they are almost purely nominal, the usual conventions will still sanction some charge under the caption of 'legitimate profits.' But the fact that the more industrially advanced of the Western nations are approximating a 'normlessness' in the market is revealed in two ways – by the increasing amount of goods and services enjoyed by the average family, and by the increasing nonchalance with which the family treats these assets. Viewed on a broader social scale, it is quite apparent that Western technology is in a transitory stage of making 'trade-offs' between human time (labor) and material. A comparison between the building construction methods typically used in the under-developed, and in the technologically advanced society illustrates this point more vividly.

Building construction in the under-developed society proceeds very slowly. Scaffolding is jury-rigged; cement is manually mixed on the site, raised aloft in small buckets and manually delivered in the rising structure's interior. Materials are cut with great care so as to avoid unnecessary waste; and, everywhere, human labor is utilized to the fullest possible extent. Careful supervision assures that at the completion of construction there will be practically no left-over scrap.

In the technologically advanced society a quite different situation prevails. Scaffolding is made of factory built modules which are repeatedly reusable and which can be restructured to accommodate whatever type of job is at hand. Cement is delivered to the site 'ready-mixed,' and in the construction of some multi-floored buildings the entire series of floors is precast in stacked fashion – one floor being poured upon the other on the ground – and they are successively elevated and locked in position at the proper levels. There are great quantities of machinery and relatively few workmen on the site. Materials are cut and emplaced in the most expedient manner, and without undue concern for waste. At the termination of construction there is a conspicuous amount of waste on hand but there is seldom any effort made to sort through and salvage any part of it. Instead, it is usually burned, or buried by bulldozer in a deep trench.

The individual who witnesses the two different construction modes just described might be inclined, at first blush, to commend the frugality of the first and to criticize the prodigality of the second. However, this overlooks the fact that economizing in the use of materials, beyond a certain point, carries with it certain penalties on human time; and within any society, as labor costs increase there will be correspondingly less concern shown for materials. While the contractor of the underdeveloped country contrives to find ways in which to conserve on the use of a particular item, the contractor operating on the basis of rational expediency, may, meantime, complete a component having a net value twenty times over what the first contractor managed to save. In most technologically advanced societies, materials savings at the expense of an ongoing operation costs money. The ratio between full materials utilization and scrap probably is a product of conscious and unconscious appraisals of costs by the builder; and one might speculate that, in general, the less concern shown for scrap the richer is the society, the higher are its labor costs, and the more productive are its enterprises. Waste, like standard of living, is a relative matter.

Repair, until fairly recently and in the industrially advanced societies of the West, was a universal practice that extended to the mending or replacement of the smallest, and often most inconsequential parts of a mechanism. The unit's manufacturer ordinarily produced a spare parts inventory and the retail outlet maintained a stock of spare parts and the necessary repairmen. So long as labor costs remained relatively low, if the part to be replaced was replaceable no one quarreled with the procedure's feasibility. However, the unit's 'down-time' (the length of time the unit and the parent component are out of commission for want of repair) could constitute a fairly high indirect cost. Improved manufacturing techniques, the trend toward assembling related parts by subunits, or modules, a changing ratio of labor to materials cost, and increasing mechanization have been responsible for radical change in the concept of repair.

The practice of replacement by module dates back several decades. Its growth is a predictable aspect of the broader process of mass production. The module was first referred to as the 'replacement kit,' and it came into use because the parts of a component were often in such finely balanced mechanical relationship to one another that the replacement of one made mandatory the replacement of the entire unit. A later, and more potent rationale for the module was that since the parts deteriorated at approximately equal rates it was not economically feasible to place a new part among old ones which were probably verging on malfunction.

Modular units first made their appearance in the manufacturing plant, in the invasion of manufacturing processes. Soon afterward engineers began thinking in terms of applying modular replacement to the units they manufactured. This thinking was encouraged by decreasing costs of materials and parts manufacture, and by changing methods of assembly. Very often, the most expedient manufacturing technique for fixing the unit into its final configuration was by pressing or spot welding a case around it. When this type of assembly was used, there was no choice, when it broke down, except to replace the entire unit. As modular assembly became more sophisticated, the module moved into use in highly complex and expensive mechanisms and, in time, became a part of the system's overall engineering. At this stage it became known as 'black-box replacement.'

In black-box replacement, modules are quickly and easily detachable from the parent system. Replacement is effected rapidly. Since pin-pointing the malfunction may require highly specialized testing equipment, and because on-the-spot repair may be intricate, it is usually more expedient, technically and economically, to return the black-box to the manufacturer who usually rebuilds it under highly controlled conditions and reissues it as a 'rebuilt' unit. Meantime, the user may keep a supply of replacement units in stock, or he is assured by the manufacturer of easy access to them at local points of distribution. The advantages of this repair technique are quite obvious with regard to such complex devices as missiles, but it is noteworthy that repair through sub-unit replacement is being steadily expanded in the servicing of the simpler, everyday devices.

One of the more recent technological developments is micro-miniaturization. The meaning and breadth of this movement are not yet generally appreciated but its effects are rapidly becoming apparent in the more popular electronic devices such as radios and tape recorders. Micro-miniaturization is a joint product of scientific discovery, and new engineering techniques for the assembly of ultra-fine components. Science develops new and 'miniaturizable' materials, or it develops novel methods for reducing older types of components to significantly smaller sizes. Engineers then work out new methods for assembling these units into single modules. There is growing use, in electronics, of a technique whereby a large number of functionally related miniature components are embedded in a single, tiny block of plastic. The devices constructed of these types of units are sometimes mistaken by the public for playthings or cheapened copies, but they are usually much superior to their large-size predecessors. The functional quality of their component parts is at least the equal, and usually the superior of conventional parts and systems. The reliability of a micro-miniaturized unit is almost always well above the conventional norm because of its simplified circuitry and parts, and because of the greater physical stability between its parts. Components and circuitry embedded in plastic are far less subject to vibration damage and other disjointing effects.

Repair, waste, salvage, and micro-miniaturization are related concepts and, together, they lead to certain inferences. As the social value placed on human labor increases there will be increased emphasis placed upon modular construction. As progress is made in the techniques of micro-miniaturization, modules will grow in complexity of function and in general capability. As all these factors, plus the mechanization of production, advance technologically, not only will construction and repair be made in increasingly large subunits, but eventually the discard and replacement of entire systems, when desired, will become socially permissible. The foregoing trends might serve as indices of both, a society's rate of technological progress and its state of material wealth.

Changing Patterns

Increased productivity is both a cause and an effect of upward shifting patterns of consumption. Heretofore, the acquisition of material items, the style in which they are displayed, and the manner in which they are discarded have been determined to a great extent by their inherent prestige values. The economist, Thorstein Veblen referred to the preening aspect of this behavior as 'conspicuous consumption,' and illustrated it by pointing out how the wives of wealthy men were adorned with furs and jewelry in specific response to a Western male folkway for parading wealth and power. Non-functional and expensive appendages to physical possessions, such as excessive amounts of chromium automobile trim and body appurtenances of exaggerated size, fall in this same prestige category. In fact, it might be added that all material possessions, including those that may seem to be strictly utilitarian are, as visible evidence of wealth, emblematic. Hence, individual and group prestige rests upon the quantity of goods possessed, their relative monetary values, and the ways in which they are consumed and replaced.

Or viewed in a somewhat different way, the prestige conferred by the possession of an item is a joint function of that item's social desirability and its availability. As the item becomes more abundant and more evenly distributed through the population, its social premium diminishes, and the attentions of the social elite shift to other matters. As automobiles have become more plentiful, and as some families have become 'two or three-car families' there has arisen a tendency to treat them more as transportation devices than as prestige items. The outsize automobiles that were once a sure symbol of social power and wealth have declined markedly in prestige. The attentions of the upper middle class are turning, instead, to classes of possessions which, heretofore, have been a monopoly of the very rich, such as sea-going pleasure craft and summer homes. The purchase of a new family automobile no longer causes the old ripple of neighborhood excitement.

As our productivity increases, one-by-one our material prestige items will deflate in social value. At the extreme, where one can obtain any type and class of merchandise that he desires without cost, his choice will be made in terms of the item's usefulness. If offered a house of any size that he wished, and assuming that this same offer is open to all members of the society, it is reasonable to speculate that few individuals would elect a fifty-room mansion. Since there would be no prestige meaning connected with an oversize house, the individual's choice probably would be fairly consonant with his more basic physical needs. If this principle should turn out to be generally valid, it might imply that the rate of *change* in consumption patterns will correspond closely with the rate of increase in productivity. As the society produces more, the articles that it produces will decline, correspondingly, in value.

It goes without saying that prestige values will not disappear; they likely will be transferred, in part at least, from physical possessions to new types of activity and accomplishment. Competition may shift away from the acquisition of property to the attainment of education, or to new types of power positions. Hopefully, such displacements as may occur will not be meaninglessly random displacements, but will be oriented toward healtheir and more socially serviceable goals. The redirection of social energies from ownership conquest to the enhancement of individual talents would hold advantages for both, the individual and the society. The educated individual derives personal benefits from his training and, in turn, he is enabled to contribute more fully to his society. However, as it now stands, the new channels into which prestige values may be diverted are multifold and cannot be prognosticated with the accuracy that we might wish.

Relationship to Production

To what degree do *established* habits of consumption influence production? It is generally felt that a population with keenly honed appetites will somehow, and from somewhere, secure the goods to which it is accustomed and which it considers essential to its well-being. The classical individual example of this apothegm is Daniel Defoe's fictitious account of *The Life and the Strange Surprizing Adventures of Robinson Crusoe*. Coming as it did, during the first quarter of the eighteenth century and at the beginning of the industrial revolution in England, this novel attests to the mettle and philosophical outlook of a people consciously and enthusiastically launching the age of materialism. Mr. Crusoe, by applying homey but ingenious engineering methods, revolutionized the environment about him, bringing to an isolated island a mimicry of a way of life which the British of that day saw as the finest flowering of civilization. The strength of that early belief has not diminished in the West. Regularly updated and studded here and there with new features such as electronic controls, Robinson Crusoe is re-portrayed to willing cinema audiences time and time over.

This same air of subduing the wilderness with little more than the powers of imagination can be seen and felt in certain national movements. The Israelis, originally a generally well educated group but not one especially inclined toward technology, have duplicated Robinson Crusoe's fictitious feat on a real-life basis and on a national scale. Within a short time, they have converted what was once a wasteland into rich agricultural acreage, and have established the most up-to-date plants and mills, and have even built an atomic energy facility.

Instances such as the foregoing make a convincing case for the proposition that national development can be stimulated by changing the population's attitudes toward consumption. If the society can be made to desire a better way of life, this wish will be communicated in various and subtle ways throughout the society, and will result in, among other things, an improved production system. This approach sometimes goes under the rubric of 'motivation programming.' While its basic premise, that a broadened standard of living will encourage production effort, is probably sound, it overlooks the fact that material standards cannot be improved by mere exhortation. If the individual is to understand and appreciate elevated material standards in any meaningful way, they must be made a reality for him. He must live with these goods and services and become accustomed to them. And, of course, the dilemma of the undeveloped society is that it is unable to provide material wealth for its average citizen on anything approaching a standard of living that might be defined as acceptable by the technologically advanced societies. Physical exposure to a substantially enriched environment can become a reality only for the society's few elite, or for those residing abroad in technologically advanced cultures. Had Robinson Crusoe not been a character drawn from a materially advancing society he could not, and would not, have solved his problems as he did. And, had Daniel Defoe not been a Westerner, it is doubtful that he would have been able to create such a character.

Another oversight inherent in the 'motivational' approach is the assumption that desire, alone, axiomatically will produce a higher standard of living. At least a modicum of technical skill is necessary for the beginning step in technological development. Imagine the technological consequences for the remaining female population if all the males of a technologically advanced society were suddenly stricken and perished from the earth. Despite their already firmly implanted material standards and desire to maintain them, it is doubtful that the survivors would be able to sustain the technology at a level even approximating its former one. In all, it is probably much safer and more logical to assume that, for the undeveloped nation, the relationship between production and consumption is a rectilinear rather than a circular one; that there first must be a growing production system and that this system will fire the public's appetites and create the appropriate adjunctive distribution system.

CONCLUSIONS

The technologies of the primitive and the materially advanced societies are cast from the same mold. And this mold will determine, eventually, not only the characteristics of the production system but the mode of distribution as the latter is drawn into such close alignment with production as to be made an incorporate part of it. For distribution, in the last analysis, is a continuation of the act of production.

What is the inner nature of technology, and what are its growth processes? The quest for these answers twines through a labyrinth of economic and social thought, most of it detritus accumulated during the past two hundred years, to lead to a deceptively simple conclusion. Technology is essentially a set of social and physical relationships, or modes of interaction, between man and the mechanisms with which he works. Technology is a socio-technological entelechy containing the seeds of its own growth, which can, fortunately, be implanted independently of the more superficial social and economic stock factors with which it is commonly associated. These latter, the social class system, the pricing system or, indeed, even the enterprise system, all of which are seen to be highly divergent by cultural area, must, in the growth of technology, ultimately give way to common technical methodologies and uniform social practices, facts that make it possible to prescribe planning principles which are applicable to the promotion of technological growth in the undeveloped and the materially advancing countries, alike.

INDEX